BRING IT!

A collection of libertarian essays from

Tim Nerenz, Ph.D.

What Readers Say About Dr. Tim

Mike H: *Few things you read make you want to wake up the neighbors cheering with a fist pump!*

Julie B: *This piece is so good it actually brought a tear to my eye.*

Allison N: *Wow! Perfect.*

Jacob J: *Amazing.....*

Martin W: *WOW!!*

Susan R: *He is so brilliant.*

Dale P: *Amen!*

Lisa D: *SHARE SHARE SHARE!!!*

Denise A: *You write what I think. Thank You!*

David T: *This one was phenomenal!*

Michael M: *When Reagan said "tear down this wall," Gorbie hired Tim Nerenz!*

Griff C: *Great as usual, Tim.*

Rob K: *Are you reading my mind? I think it and then shortly thereafter you write it (more eloquently than I could).*

John F: *Fantastic Piece!*

Denise A: *I really missed Dr. Tim while I was on vacation.*

Lisa M: *Every new "Moment" is my favorite! LOVE IT!*

Acknowledgements

Thank you to my wife Joanne, to my son Erik and daughter-in-law Jenyl, and to my niece Hannah and nephew Caden for giving me a reason to care about the future enough to try and improve it.

And to all of my old classmates, neighbors, friends, teachers, and mentors from Ironwood, Michigan – it doesn't take a village to raise a child, but it takes a whole town of crazy Yoopers to make one into someone you want to hang out with. Wish I was hanging with you guys right now.

To all my new friends, the radio patriots - Vicki McKenna, who put me on the map, Brian Wilson who added the map of Ohio, and Neil Boortz, who introduced the whole nation to my work – I can't thank you enough for the work that you do every day. And to your fans for accepting me.

Thanks to my friend Herman Cain and my idol Ron Paul for taking the arrows and spears and showing us that ideas can still get you to the top of the Presidential polls. And to the mercenary hatchet men and coin-operated power-whores who took them down for cash, thank you for reminding us all who the real enemies of liberty are.

Many libertarians are hesitant about public professions of faith; I'm not one of them. I thank God daily for His many blessings and for the wonders of His creation. I have never spent an ungrateful day in my life.

FOREWORD
By Vicki McKenna

When conservatives in Wisconsin came under siege by the Blue Fist of Tyranny (a.k.a. public sector union organizers) as it delivered its body blows to the Republic, to whom did they turn for an assist?

A libertarian.

That's because it wasn't conservatives who were under siege, it was LIBERTY that was the target of the Blue Fisters. And no one knows liberty or can defend it like Tim Nerenz.

In the process, a wild and inexplicably wonderful thing has happened in Wisconsin; our "conservatives" have moved beyond the traditional establishment Republican definition, and begun to frame their arguments, plan their offensives and defend their turf with the idea of LIBERTY as their model.

Had it not been for Tim Nerenz, it would have been a lot harder to stay on this path. (There's your CHEESEHEAD NATION, America - now stop making fun of our cows.)

After our governor and legislature dropped the A-bomb of right-to-work legislation on public sector unions, and pulled the curtain back on the single biggest taxpayer extortion scam of the last 3 generations, the blowback was frightening. The *easy* thing to do would have been to fold.

Lesser states would have. Lesser conservatives would have. But they didn't have Tim Nerenz demanding our answer to the question "who owns you!?"

We citizens didn't duck the question or pretend it didn't matter. We answered, "We Do!" loudly enough to be heard over the vuvuzelas, the shouts of "Shame! Shame! Shame!", and the bongo drums of the left. "We Do!" was the battle cry that united conservatives and libertarians in defense of LIBERTY.

After that, the Blue Fist could hit us as many times as it wanted to. We had resolved not to go down for the count. And we knew we had Tim Nerenz in our corner.

It's hard to make freedom make sense at the ground level while the bombs are going off and the seething hoards are at the gates. It's hard to convince a people surrounded not to run, but to stand and fight. It's hard to make the complicated Rube Goldberg machinery of government easy to understand. And yet, somehow, Tim Nerenz does just that.

Only a gifted messenger could pen the essay "Own It" so that it could be transformed from a political critique into a call to fight, then again to a call for self-reflection and embrace of personal responsibility. Few truly write words to live by. Tim Nerenz does it every week on his blog.

The call to LIBERTY is paying dividends in our state as we just posted one of the best budget records in the country thanks to the fiscal reforms empowered and embraced by people who look at government through libertarian-colored glasses.

"Eh," but you say, "he's your friend. Of course you're going to write nice things about him - especially since he let you write the Foreword for his book!"

OK, don't take it from me. After posting one of his last blogs on my Facebook page, I asked my "friends" and listeners to come up with a list of "Tim Nerenz Facts" (like those crazy, over-the-top accolades made famous by the guys who love Chuck Norris.) One person posted this: "The Federal Reserve creates fiat currency out of thin air—but Tim Nerenz creates pure gold coins from his MIND."

My listeners would tell you that's only barely hyperbole.

Vicki McKenna is a Wisconsin talk-radio icon who hosts a morning show on WISN Milwaukee, and an afternoon show on WIBA Madison. She has listeners and fans around the world, who follow her on iHeartRadio and her Facebook Fan Page.

AUTHOR'S INTRODUCTION

The best thing about writing opinions is that you are never wrong. Everything I write is my own opinion, and as luck would have it, I am the world's foremost authority on me, so there is no source corroboration needed. It's a lot more efficient that way – and good for writing on planes.

"Bring It" is the third collection of columns that were originally published on my blog site, *Dr. Tim's Moment of Clarity*. I write a couple times a week about politics, economics, current events, Constitutional issues, human potential, and libertarian ideas.

I have often said that libertarian is a better adjective than noun. If you are libertarian-thinking, or perhaps libertarian-leaning, you will find this book to be familiar territory. Conservatives – you will like most of it, but there will be a few places you may have to hold your nose and soldier on.

And liberals – I'm sorry, but whoever bought this book for you is laughing hysterically behind your back. I'm sure you are great mothers and fathers and we still have the Packers, our veterans, our reverence for nature, and our love of dogs to unite us. You don't have to do this to yourselves; put it down now and go in peace, my friends.

It is difficult to say how many people have read or heard at least one of these articles over the year – some low number of millions would be a fair guess, given the subscriber base of the liberty sites that reprint them, the listenership of the radio hosts who have read one or more on the air, the activity on my Facebook Fan Page and my own site statistics.

My purpose in writing is to make libertarian ideas accessible to normal people – i.e. people who don't obsess over politics and ideological purity. I believe that the American majority is economic conservatives and social neutrals. We want to keep what we earn and we don't want someone else telling us what to do.

A full 1/3 of the country now self-identifies as "independent" when asked party affiliation. I write for them. I also write for every disaffected Democrat and Republican that wonders when their party left them and why – Goldwater Republicans and Kennedy Democrats. I write for every Libertarian who couldn't quite find the words to rebut the nutcase label hurled at us for suggesting that liberty be put into practice.

I call my blog "Moment of Clarity" and my goal is exactly that – to bring clarity to issues that are made to seem incomprehensible by those who spin, lie, and self-promote for a living.

The columns I write are not biblical truths; they are not peer-reviewed journal articles to be vetted for citation errors. If there are inconsistencies, I am happy about it; ideological purity is the boast of a closed mind.

Liberty is the absence of government in choice; government is the absence of liberty in choice. Tyranny is the absence of choice in government. It is not very complicated.

This book begins in May of 2011 where my second book, "Capitalista!", left off – with the piece "Own It", my reaction to the Wisconsin Democrats' appalling behavior in response to their losses in the 2010 elections. It ends with the title piece, "Bring It", another commentary on Wisconsin's unionists and their campaign to nullify those 2010 elections through a recall of Governor Scott Walker.

I didn't set out to write a book about Wisconsin politics; it's just that our nation's second civil war – the one between the citizen and the state - was waged right here for much off the year. It is not right versus left, Republican versus Democrat – it the State versus You. I have picked my side, and I hope that you have to – or will by the end of this book.

I don't write for a living, I run a manufacturing company. I've been in the business of making things for nearly 40 years now, and have lived through the post-industrial transition of this nation, for better and for worse. Along the way, I learned a little bit about jobs, trade, competition, human potential, capitalism, economics, government, public policy, foreign affairs, prosperity, and comparative governments.

Not because I studied these things, although I have; but because I live them every single day. What I have learned is that liberty is good policy. Enjoy the book. Let me know if you like it.

Tim

TABLE of CONTENTS

Own It

Although I am not a Democrat or a Republican, I used to understand why other people would choose to be one or the other. While I can still understand how some people can be Republicans, it is beyond my comprehension how anyone could still be a Democrat in Wisconsin in the age of YouTube.

The Democrats' response to losing an election here has been appalling; disgraceful conduct documented with phone cameras for the whole world to see. Democrat rallies and protests have been marked by profanity, intimidation, death threats, vandalism, trespassing on private residences, anti-American rhetoric, boycotts of neutral businesses, extortion, and fraud.

My dear Democrat friends, that is not what democracy looks like; it is what *Democrats* look like. Your Party has become vile, disgraceful, and disgusting, and you have lived long enough in denial of what and who you have become. Own it.

It's not just the mob scenes that disgust. Perhaps the most dishonest political ad in history was run by Democrats in a supposedly non-partisan Supreme Court race, exploiting the victim of child abuse for political gain. Own it, Party of the children.

Your Democrat legislators wore union t-shirts on the floor of the assembly while in session; shouting and throwing things and threatening to kill a female Republican lawmaker. This is how you treat women who think for themselves. Own it, Party of women.

Your public sector unions – firefighters and teachers - organized a campaign to drown out yesterday's taxpayer rally on the steps of the Capitol building. You exist now only to deprive others of their right to be heard; and your idea of civil is dropping F-bombs at a child who came to hear Sarah Palin speak. You have embraced disgrace – so own it, Party of civil rights.

You booed the national anthem. Read that again, friends; take a moment to reflect fully upon the depths to which your Democrat party has sunk, and then OWN IT.

On that same day the office of a recall drive against one of the 14 AWOL Democrat Senators was burglarized with computers and petitions stolen – just like Nixon in 1972. You also threatened to blow up a radio station over content you don't like. You were busy little fascist criminals on Saturday - own it, Nixonites .

If these are just isolated examples of people acting out, then show me where your Party leaders have denounced them. Who have you expelled from your Party for the shame they have brought to it? And who is your Ron Paul, your conscience who calls you out when you have strayed from your core values - Charlie Rangel?

Your Democrat State Senator Lena Taylor recently got herself on TV to rant against some $142 million of tax breaks Governor Walker has given to his cronies, but when asked, she could not name one. Your comprehensive plan to balance the budget and avoid default is to chant "Fox Lies!" This is the depth or your intellectual curiosity and the extent of your economic literacy. Own it.

Yours is the party that extended our military stay in Iraq, increased our commitment in Afghanistan, spread that war into Pakistan and Yemen, and started another in Libya. When it was Bush dropping the bombs, you came to us Libertarians and begged us to join you to stop him; haven't seen you around now that is your guy killing little brown people. He lies to you and you love him for it. Own that.

What does it take for you decent Democrats - and I know there are many of you who will read this - to walk away from a Party that has already abandoned the principles that attracted you to it in the first place? How much of your pride are you still willing to forfeit to a Party that has none? What is your last straw – does blowing an angry horn at a downs-syndrome person for waving a flag not do it for you?

It's your mirror you need to look in every day, not mine. It was a far less obnoxious abandonment of principle that led me to leave the GOP many years ago. It is true that I get along better with them than with Democrats as a rule; that rule is that they don't send me death threats when I write something they don't like.

Nearly a third of the American electorate is now non-affiliated with either of the two major Parties; each Democrat/socialist/union rally drives more of you into our camp. You Democrats do not persuade us with temper tantrums, threats, profane personal attacks, and all manner of judicial chicanery. I don't even know what you stand for anymore; I don't speak drum.

Yours was once the Party of Kennedy; it is now the Party that boos the national anthem. Own that – and then walk away. You will feel better about yourself, and you might just save your Party from the hooligans who have run it into disrepute.

3-3-3

It didn't take long for the establishment GOP to figure out how to dump on Herman Cain – if you can't attack the man, attack the plan.

For the record, I don't like Mr. Cain's 9-9-9 tax plan either; I would much prefer 3-3-3. Because the problem is not just how we tax; as Milton Friedman said, the real rate of taxation is the rate of spending, and we spend about 12-12-12. We can thank both of the establishment parties for that.

And spending is what candidates should be focused on; yet to date only Ron Paul has told us specifically what he would cut - $1 trillion worth in year one. That puts him $1 trillion into the lead in my book. The rest talk in platitudes about economic growth and spending restraint - not unlike then-candidate Obama in 2008 who promised the moon and stars while conveniently leaving out the part about how much the spaceship would cost.

Here's my plan to cut down to my ideal weight: I will only add three pounds per year instead of the five I was planning on for the next decade, and I promise to grow to 7'6" in year 10. Economists would score that as a winner; the CBO would issue a glowing report; Joe Biden would start counting millions of pounds not gained and threatening to rape me if I quit wrapping my donuts in bacon before I deep fry them. Or something.

I know exactly what Herman Cain is thinking with 9-9-9, because business people like us understand that human behavior changes in response to incentives. Prices will come down when costs are lowered because competition will demand it. Leveling the playing field will allow capital to flow to the best investments, not tax-gimmicks like Solyndra, and the jobs will come roaring back. People will buy things based on their intrinsic value, not overpay just to get a deduction.

Markets will begin to function again and the good times will roll; it is a plan of economic liberation based upon an understanding of human action - the kind of thing a business guy would come up with and a politician would stare at dumbfounded for days on end. The attacks on the 9-9-9 tax plan ignore human action, relying on static analysis and arithmetic comparisons to current pay rates to try and discredit it.

But economics is not arithmetic; it is the study of how people get what they want. When the rules change, so does behavior; and in predictable ways, even if the current administration's economic team doesn't understand how to predict them. Business people – the main street kind – develop a pretty good sense of human nature, as we are dependent upon the voluntary decisions of our customers to succeed. It does not surprise me that Cain would be the one to solve a problem; or that the establishment in both political parties would hate him for it.

They like the status quo just fine, and they have orchestrated misleading attacks to thwart any effort to simplify and flatten the tax system. They are betting that all of us have by now been hooked with one rock of tax-crack or another that we cannot imagine living without. Most of us who will howl about losing our home mortgage deduction will never put two and two together and realize that our loophole is one of the causes of the housing bubble and economic crisis it brought about. We all like bad things to be someone else's fault; we just disagree about who else to hang it on.

Fair is when everyone is treated the same. 9-9-9 does that, as would 3-3-3 or 29-29-29. The most ridiculous standard to hold up a tax reform plan against is what some people pay now. If the deal-breaker is anyone paying a penny more than they did this year, then let's just leave the most corrupted and corrupting tax scheme in the history of mankind in place and wait for the collapse to come. And quit making fun of people who are investing in ammo and gold; you will soon be begging them to share their MRE's with you and they won't need your vote.

Zero is not a fair share, whether it is a migrant worker or GE who is the free rider. When Buffet, Gates, Trump, Wynn, and Carlos Slim go to lunch together, one of them is in the bottom quintile – are they entitled to free lobster bisque and a pity party? Taxing income is itself an idea so dumb they had to change the Constitution to allow it; taking at differential rates is an even worse idea that had to be stolen from the communists.

Here the tax comparison that matters. The federal government spends about 24% of GDP; if everyone paid our fair share we would each pay 24% of our income in federal taxes. Do you? Not if you are poor, and not if you are rich, not if you have deductions and exemptions, and not even if they put us all together do we pay that much.

We collectively pay about 16% of GDP in taxes; those other 8 percentage points we borrow each year is why the national debt is skyrocketing and we are speeding towards our big fat Greek collapse. That is the destination of the status quo; the goal line that is being defended at all costs against any attempt to simplify and flatten the tax system, be it flat tax, FairTax, 9-9-9, or Ron Paul's excise tax ideas.

Those who read this blog regularly know that I am a proponent of the FairTax for pragmatic reasons. In an ideal libertarian world, I would finance a Constitutionally limited government (about 20% of our current one) with a land tax and head tax – trip on that, Michelle Bachman, former IRS attorney, mother of 6, foster mother of 23, and starter of a business who has made a payroll. Even Romney's one illegal gardener would have to pay $500 to live here – consider it a cover charge for the greatest party on the planet. Can't scrape up $500? How did that tattoo get there?

But we must live in the world that is until we can create the world that should be. The two principles behind sound practical tax reform are simple: as broad a base as possible at the lowest possible single rate. Whether we tax income or consumption or both is not as important as that we stop using the tax code to reward and punish, to pick winners and losers, to advance political agendas, and to provoke class divisions. Thank you Herman Cain for taking the heat to get the ball rolling.

And for exposing politics as usual in Tuesday night's debate ambush. Do you really think that all those other smart candidates for President of the United States do not understand the difference between state taxes and federal taxes? Do you believe they don't know that people pay both state and federal taxes now? Do you think they honestly do not know the difference between a VAT and corporate income tax?

Or do you think a powerful lobby of special interests 100% vested in keeping the current system of preferences, loopholes, subsidies, guarantees, and pork in place might have put them up to it? Like perhaps the same folks who are making Ron Paul invisible, and turning this whole process into a made for TV Romney/Perry WWE main event.

They think we are stupid. They are wrong.

Ambassadors

The sun has not yet risen here in Acapulco, but in a few hours hundreds of U.S. Ambassadors will try to secure trade agreements with thousands of Mexico's most skilled negotiators.

No, it is not another round of NAFTA; I am here for the 29th International Mining Convention, an industry trade show which is held every other year. And our U.S. ambassadors are not pin-striped suiters from the State Department; we are the businessmen and businesswomen who travel the world every day selling American goods and services, creating jobs and prosperity back home and improving living standards in the developing world.

Every day all over the world, deals valued into the hundreds of millions get done without the participation of government. I didn't bring anyone from the Commerce Department with me to Mexico, and the Mexican mining executives who we will meet with at the convention do not have their government officials tagging along, either. Those guys are off having a nice Waldorf salad together in Mexico City, telling each other how important our two nations are to each other for the kazillionth time.

Here in Acapulco, we will be discussing the projects that miners are developing; the equipment they will need; the mix of technical features, price, and service that adds the most value to their operations. NAFTA won't come up; frankly, none of us have read it. The deals will be done on the basis of value added and company reputation, not government policy. We don't talk about trade; we trade. The whole world is competing for the same orders; it is a buyers' market.

Over dinner, we will discuss culture, sports, world affairs, economics, and politics – both ours and theirs. We will talk about family and faith, values and beliefs, our philosophies about managing a company, leading a community, developing the next generation of business leaders. They will laugh at my Spanish, but the attempt will be appreciated.

We will find we have more things in common than things that separate us. And I will be reminded that Mexican people love America and Americans for the products we make, for what we stand for, for the things we have accomplished, for our commitment to liberty. It is only the actions of our government and our central bank that anger them. It is the same all over the world.

Ron Paul is ridiculed by the press for proposing a defensive military posture, as if military bases and embassies are the only means of interaction between Americans and people of other nations. Big-government spokesmodels like Meet The Press' David Gregory express genuine bewilderment at the idea that less government would mean more engagement. To the business person, Paul's suggestion is self-evident. Government does not facilitate commerce; it impedes it.

When American businesspeople trade abroad, we are the face of the nation; I have been in many places where I am the only American they will ever meet in person. The world has an insatiable appetite for all things American; we are a topic of endless fascination and our founding principles are genuinely admired wherever they are understood. Most of us are happy to help them be understood, and we take our responsibilities to represent our nation seriously.

Businesspeople, students, missionaries, public health workers, tourists, educators, engineers, researchers, airline crews, technicians, interpreters, and athletes – American interests are advanced every single day by interesting Americans. Here in Acapulco, the only American government presence is the guns we sold to the narcos in Operation Fast and Furious, but that is a rant for another day.

Many misperceptions of Americans and American ideals are spread by our enemies to foment hatred. And by enemies I also mean American leftists and unionists whose only export is anti-capitalist rhetoric which paints all economic development as exploitation and assigns all under-developed peoples to perpetual victimhood.

The most effective antidote for this poison is for standard-issue Americans to interact with the people of other countries; this is the real importance of free trade. The miners of Mexico don't buy into the exploitation myth. Sure they are poor compared to the owners of the mines which employ them; there is no disputing that. But they are rich beyond their wildest imaginations compared to how they lived before the capitalists came in to develop the mines – Americans, Canadians, Chileans, Australians, South Africans.

You can't buy a bag of beans with the gold that is in the ground. Perhaps if our eco-terrorists had to live on $2 a day for a while, they would show a little more appreciation for the people who dig it up and make it unnecessary for them to do so.

20

Libertarians are often called isolationist because we would reduce the American government's footprint around the world - closing military bases, reducing embassy and consulate staff, and eliminating foreign aid programs that enrich corrupt foreign leaders with money we must borrow from the Chinese.

Reducing our government's footprint does not mean reducing America's engagement with the world. On the contrary, our commitment to free trade, tax and regulatory relief, and trans-border mobility would unleash tens of thousands more of our best ambassadors into the every nook and cranny of the world, spreading the message of liberty, democracy, and capitalism.

Of course, some will do lots of other less noble things, too, but go to either Party's convention and tell me that businesspeople have the exclusive franchise on debauchery.

A maintenance superintendent at a mine in Zacetecas State will never meet the U.S. Government's ambassador to Mexico, but he will meet with another American ambassador in an hour or so - me. It will be my pleasure to represent my country and hopefully bag some orders to keep our American factories humming.

21

And We Wonder

Liberal economist Robert Reich is all over the internet these days explaining that our economic problems would end if banks extended more credit to Americans of modest means. There's the path to prosperity - take on more debt.

And Congress has recently moved to legalize internet gambling in order to generate government revenue. Debt and gambling – this plan gets better.

A liberal friend sent me a link to a piece that advocated mandatory unionization of all working Americans. Debt, gambling, and unions – because it worked so well in Detroit.

President Obama finally got into the debt ceiling negotiations this week, demanding $600 billion in new taxes. Debt, gambling, unions, and taxes – that'll put the "gee" in GDP!

And he proposed a standard for fuel efficiency that no car can meet. Debt, gambling, unions, taxes, and no driving – look out, China! We're back!

The President also announced some convoluted public/private partnership with 11 of our largest corporations. Here's how it works: we give them billions to invent things we don't want and they take it. Debt, gambling, unions, taxes, no driving, and malinvestment – heart, heart, smiley, winkey, LOL, whatever that stuff means!

What else...oh, yeah, he wants to get rid of ATMs. Debt, gambling, unions, taxes, no driving, malinvestment, and no cash. I'm thinking Nobel Prize #2.

Treasury Secretary Geithner said we must shrink the private sector in order to grow the public sector. Debt, gambling, unions, taxes, no driving, malinvestment, no cash, and more government. Take that, Arthur Laffer!

And finally, ex-czar Van Jones is back in the news, announcing the country is not broke because you still have some money; he is forming his own Tea Party to take it from you. There's the plan – debt, gambling, unions, taxes, no driving, malinvestments, no cash, and communism.

And we wonder why our economy is in the ditch.

These are the same guys who tell us we need to increase the debt ceiling. They want us to co-sign a few trillion of new loans so can keep spending money they don't have on things we don't need. And their plan to pay it back? Debt, gambling, unions, taxes, no driving, malinvestments, no cash, and more government.

Not only does this insanity make sense to liberal economists, but they warn that if we don't let them borrow more money, there will be bad consequences. Really? Worse than the collapse of the dollar and interest rates with a comma in them? Here's a consequence, Mr. Bernanke: everything you have tried has failed; go lay by your dish.

Van Jones is half-right. The nation is not broke; it is our government that is broke. Not because we don't give them enough money; we will give them $2.6 trillion this year. It is because the twitterin' wieners on Capitol Hill spend $1.4 trillion more than that. If we gave them $10 trillion they would spend $15 trillion – and it would still be still be your fault that kids can't read. Because you are a racist, that's why.

There is no reason to pass another debt ceiling authorization; we already have one. And if the one we have doesn't mean anything, then why bother with another one?

On second thought, Van Jones is right - the federal government is not broke, it owns almost $6 trillion of land. Put it on E-bay, with no reserve. Can't bear to part with it? My son didn't want to sell his Mustang dragster either, but he had bills to pay. Man up, Geithner.

If the IRS can force Green Bay Packer legend Fuzzy Thurston to sell his Super Bowl ring to pay his debts, we can sure as hell force President Obama to sell off a few million acres to cover his golfing and Michelle's trips to Africa and the lunacy that is the Obama EPA.

So what will you cut, Mr. President – trees or tree-huggers? You're pro-choice, so make one. And leave our old Packers alone, you heartless Bear-loving Blagonad.

Are You Independent?

Our Independence Day celebration is a uniquely American holiday. And America is a unique nation, the only nation on earth whose First Principle is individual liberty. We are self-sovereigns; 310 million kings and queens whose authority over our own lives is established by Declaration and Constitutionally guaranteed.

So what about you – are you independent?

It is a legitimate question; one that you should ponder while the fireworks light up the night in praise of the America where freedom reigns and government serves. That America is under attack from within; it is our duty to restore it to its full glory. If you are *not* independent, then what will you celebrate this Fourth of July? *Why* will you celebrate this Fourth of July?

Are you one of the kings and queens, or have you chosen to be a minion? Please take a moment to think about your own independence on this Independence Day and make the Declaration of Independence personal.

"We hold these Truths to be self-evident." Do you? Do you believe in immutable truth – truth proved conclusively by its declaration and not subject to faddish interpretation?

"That all Men are created equal..." Do you believe that? Do you believe that laws should apply to every single person equally? That a majority opinion does not trump an individual right? That preference and prejudice have no place in law?

"Endowed by their Creator with unalienable Rights..." Do you understand where your rights come from? Do you acknowledge that your rights pre-exist the formation of government? That rights neither increase nor decrease by government decree, or by majority vote?

"That among these are Life, Liberty, and the Pursuit of Happiness." Who owns you? Do you own the fruits of your labors, the ideas of your mind, the charity of your soul? Who is responsible for your well-being, and who is accountable for the consequences of your decisions? Is my happiness your obligation? Is yours mine?

"That to secure these Rights, governments are instituted among Men..." Is this your first and only demand of government? Do

24

you expect more? Do you oppose government actions that deny rights to one in order to grant favors to another? Do you believe in a government strictly limited by the authorities granted to it by our Constitution?

Thomas Jefferson defined a new Nation in just 41 words; it is the greatest literary achievement in history.   Say them out loud; these are the beliefs that make us Americans.   We are not geography; we are that noble idea.

Our American notion of self-sovereignty is based on mutual respect, and you can not give what you do not have. Sovereigns must first respect our own liberty before we can respect each others'. I ask again: are you independent?

You were not put on this earth to pull another man's plow. You are a child of God, just like me; a brother and sister of equal standing, equally endowed with the gift of Free Will. It is yours to accept, and it is no one's to give or withhold.

You are free to speak, to worship, to associate, to defend, to testify, to publish, to own, and to trade as you see fit. You do not have to justify your choices to me or to a government formed to protect your right to make them. That's what independence is. It is glorious.

Conversely, you have no right to be insulated from the consequences of your choices; to force me to pay for your mistakes; or to indulge your unaffordable excess at my expense. That is also what independence is. It too, is glorious. The most unhappy people I know are those who expect someone else to buy their happiness for them.

We can each measure our freedom by the extent to which we respect the freedom of others; and we can each measure our tyranny by the extent to which we would take other's freedoms away. And we can each measure our independence by the extent that we stand up to tyranny when it presents itself.

So what about you - are you independent?   Have a happy Independence Day and remember what we are celebrating.

Banksters

It is easy to hate the banks; bankers and tax collectors have been our favorite targets since the beginning of time. Jesus threw the money-changers out of the temple, and forgave a tax collector just to show us He really did mean everybody when we were instructed to love our neighbors as ourselves.

The term "banksters" accurately describes the cabal of big New York banks who use the Federal Reserve to print their money, the IRS to collect their interest, and the regulators at Treasury to give them the cover of decency. The protesters on Wall Street did not invent that term; it has been a staple of libertarians, tea partiers, Paulista's, and NWO paranoids for years.

The demand of OWS for more regulation of the banking monopoly is well-intentioned, but misguided - the answer to government-regulated corruption is not more government-regulated corruption. You don't bust a monopoly by wrapping even more government sanction around it; you bust a monopoly by busting a monopoly. Let's shall.

It would be useful to remember what triggered the financial crisis of 2008, namely the imploding of the sub-prime mortgage industry that began to unravel in late 2007. And let us recall how sub-prime mortgages – loaning money to people who could not pay it back – came to be a big enough deal to break the world. If you know your local home-town banker, you know this is not an idea that they cooked up on their own after Rotary Club one Tuesday morning.

No, making the banks loan money to people who can't pay it back is an idea so colossally stupid that it would take an act of Congress to make it happen. That law was the Community Reinvestment Act, which required banks to loan money to unqualified lenders. It was a response to a call for more regulation in the 1970's, and its provisions were strengthened in response to a call for more regulation in the 1990's – careful what you wish for in twenty year increments.

Bank regulators wrote the rules and the banks followed. The Federal Reserve provided the money, and Fannie and Freddie guaranteed the loans against default. The sub-prime loans were so risky that there was no market for them; they had to be pooled with other investments to disguise the risk. The Wall Street banksters were happy to oblige, but only if they could charge hefty fees and be immunized from regulations that prohibited such wildly unethical behavior.

Congress and Treasury gave them said immunity, but stationed federal regulators right on their premises to insure compliance with the rules the government set down. Good sheepdogs do not spend years negotiating terms with the wolves; our government regulators did not simply allow the fleecing of America, they engineered it. I'll take my chances against the wolves.

And now they say they couldn't see it coming? And neither could Congressman Barney Frank, or Senator Chris Dodd, the chairmen of the House and Senate committees with responsibility for oversight of the banking system? The head of the SEC, the FDIC, Fannie, Freddie, the IG at Treasury – none of those guys saw that the government-induced housing bubble was going to burst and take the banking system with it?

Then how come Peter Schiff saw it coming? How come Ron Paul saw it coming? Wayne Allyn Root, Wes Benedict, Thomas Woods, Jim Rodgers, and hundreds of others who didn't have offices inside Lehman Brothers and Goldman Sachs warned us months and years before the bubble burst that we were headed for disaster. They are not clairvoyant, just economically literate.

The banksters, regulators, and currency manipulators at the Fed drove housing prices out of the reach of ordinary Americans. Their answer to each problem they created was to add another problem, including easy access to crushing debt. And now millions of Americans who bought at the peak of the bubble have discovered that the illusion of equity can vanish overnight, but debt is forever. The PSA's from HUD forgot to mention that part in either language.

To my knowledge, there have been no convictions of Wall Street bankers for violating banking laws, so it is reasonable to assume that they followed the regulations to a tee. And if the quality of regulators stationed right inside the New York banks was so bad they either didn't know rules were violated or were too timid to cite, then what makes us think that hiring more of them would help? Adding second stringers does not solve a quality problem on the A team.

We don't need government regulation to regulate greed – the market not only does it, but does it better and faster. There is no call to add internet penis pills to the portfolio of the Bureau of Alcohol, Firearms, and Tobacco; we seem be able to avoid some scams without having to call in people with windbreakers that say ATFIPP on them.

When Enron failed, the government refused to bail them out and their executives who broke the law went to jail. Correct answer; there hasn't been another Enron since and we did not run out of energy. When the banksters failed, the government bailed them out and paid them bonuses, and nobody went to jail. Wrong answer; they went right back to doing the same crazy stuff they were doing before, only now they are packaging toxic sovereign debt in with toxic mortgages when they engineer their incomprehensible derivative products. And we have run out of money.

The problem of how to protect the public from the banking cartels is no different than any other monopoly threat in the economy. The answer to the corrupting power of monopolies is not to sanction them with the even more corrupting power of additional government regulations; the answer is to use the anti-trust laws to break up the monopolies and allow free markets to cleanse the economy of its bad actors, starting with the Federal Reserve.

Big Money

Treasury Secretary Timothy Geithner is a trip. Last week he made news when he said that another financial meltdown – the thing he gets paid to avoid – is inevitable.

While it is refreshing to hear one of the temple's money changers admit they don't know what they are doing, saying it right out loud is not exactly the kind of thing that will calm a jittery market in a fragile global economy.

Or maybe they know exactly what they are doing. After all, it was a financial meltdown that got his boss the Presidency; maybe they figure another one will get him a second term. It is the kind of thing that would make sense to someone who lives in government cocoon immunized from the ravages of bad policy.

And it provided a diversion from yet another Constitutional insult; the ignoring of the statutory federal debt ceiling. The standoff between the Republican House of Representatives and the Democrat Senate over whether to cut spending, raise taxes, or authorize more borrowing was rendered moot.

Because Timothy Geithner kept King Obama's royal spending spree rolling full bore by stealing the money they want from the federal employee's pension trust fund. Seriously; that's what he did.

The sheep-media barely mentioned it, buried behind more newsworthy items like Arnold doing the help. Plus it was Oprah's last week of shows and the countdown to the Rapture; the end of the world for cultists in either camps.

It should have been big news. The Constitution only empowers Congress, not the President, to authorize debt; up against this statutory debt ceiling, Secretary Geithner's had no more legal authority to pilfer government worker's pension funds than I do. There isn't two different laws for the two different Tim's.

Liberal moralists who rag on capitalists for sport should consider that if the CEO of a Fortune 500 company tapped his employee pension funds to send cash to his friends overseas, his board would not only run him out of the corner office on a rail, but he would leave doing the perp walk in cuffs. That's how we roll. Character matters.

And what do my public-sector betters propose to do about their guy stealing their pensions? I thought so. Wimps.

When Wisconsin Governor Walker asked government workers to make modest future contributions to their pensions, all hell broke lose in the Badger state. "War on the middle class!", they shouted; "death of the working man!", they cried; "shame, shame, shame!", they chanted. And whatever it was they are still drumming in code.

But when President Obama – their own guy - outright stole from government worker pension funds, the silence on the left was deafening. No chants, no Hitler moustaches on pictures of the Great O, and not a solitary drumbeat from those righteous defenders of the only Americans who work, to hear them tell it.

What is wrong with you, liberals and government workers, and especially you liberal government workers? *Your guy just stole your retirement.* Not Walker, not Christie, not Boehner, not Bushcheneyreaganpalin. The One. He did it to you. The IMF guy is in jail for trying to do to the maid what your Dear Leader just did to you.

And how does it feel to be on the fleeced end the fleecing for a change? Do you understand the Tea Party now? Do you see why the Social Security Trust Fund is a farce? Now that your government has picked *your* pockets for a change, does our libertarian ideal of limited Constitutional government still seem wacky? Do you get the Second Amendment?

Only a fool – or a liberal - could think he could spend 60% more than he makes forever, borrowing even to pay the interest on the staggering debt he has already accumulated. President Obama thinks so; Ben Bernanke thinks so; Timothy Geithner thinks so.

But they would rather not have to steal it from pension funds; they would prefer to borrow it from the Federal Reserve, who simply creates more money by decree, and gives it to their giant member-banks to lend back to the Treasury at a profit.

Conservatives have rallied around an alternative budget developed by Congressman Paul Ryan. The Ryan budget is a step in the right direction - the direction of Senator Rand Paul, who has proposed $500 billion in immediate annual spending cuts as a condition of raising the debt ceiling.

Big Coffee

Is $4 too much to pay for a gallon of gasoline? Wait – before you answer, push your car for 18 miles and then tell me. I didn't think so.

I don't like paying $4 for gas either, but sometimes we need to remind ourselves of the tremendous benefit we gain from gasoline in exchange for the price we pay.

Gasoline is the most liberating invention of mankind since the printing press. The abundance of affordable goods and food we take for granted is made possible by gasoline. It is gasoline that allows us to live our lives where we choose, how we choose, with whom we choose, and when we choose. No wonder the socialists hate it.

And when it comes to getting mad at someone for their shameful profiteering and price gauging at the pump, I'm saving my ire for those socialists and Big Government types who pile on their costs to the capitalists' gasoline without adding any value.

They have forced their 10-15% ethanol filler, a boatload of state, local, and federal taxes, corporate taxes on the oil producers, refiners, transporters, wholesalers and retailers, the costs of boutique eco-blending at the refineries, and deeply-buried costs of all the government red-tape and mandates that burden each step of the supply chain, including Wisconsin's minimum markup law. Not to mention what it costs to run those drippy oil company public service advertisements to appease the greenies, the costs lobbying Congress, and the costs of buying off tort cases.

It probably would add up to half of that $4 we pay at the pump, maybe more. I know, I know – we are all supposed to hate the oil companies, but I don't.

Nope. I *love* the oil companies, the refiners, the rig leasers, the transporters, wholesalers, and retailers. Here is your $2 and a big thank you for risking your capital to provide me with all the gasoline I want, wherever and whenever I want it. I hope your profits stay high enough that you don't ever shut down stations, cut back hours of operation, or raise your prices back to the same fraction of my hourly wage it cost me to buy a gallon of your gas in 1975.

31

You give me tremendous value for the $2 portion that I pay you for my gas. I can drive for over an hour for less than it costs me to play one hand of blackjack at the Ho Chunk Casino in a blink. I can snow-blow my driveway for less than a buck and I can't find one of those save-the-planet kids to shovel it for 10 times that. Why aren't they hauling teenagers in front of Congressional committees for overcharging and holding back supply?

I wouldn't mind paying gasoline taxes into a trust fund for highway maintenance, but that's not where they go anymore. Government takes the gas tax money to pay for all manner of unrelated costly social programs that I disapprove of. I get less than nothing; they are beating me with my own belt.

Their ethanol adders have not only made me buy more crap gasoline to drive the same distance, but they have increased my food cost by diverting corn production to ethanol. If it wasn't for Kwik Trip still selling real gasoline, I would have torn my rotator cuff trying to start my weed-eater and leaf-blower with that watered-down swill the government makes us use.

Who is ripping me off – the oil companies that provide me with gasoline for their $2, or the government that juices the price the other $2? I think you know.

Every time oil prices rise and oil companies' profits improve, the left immediately wants to take the "windfall" to spend on their flaky government programs. Because Hugo Chavez did it, I suppose. A liberal friend sent me a link to a website that pleads the case for populist action against big oil:

"It is outrageous that our government continues to reward these oil giants with an additional $4 billion of *our money* in tax credits...", says Credo Action.

Say what? I hate to break it to you, Credo, but the oil companies' money is not *our* money; it is *their* money. They earned it. If you don't think they earned it, go work a rig in the North Sea for a month in winter and then weigh in. And adding $4 billion to the cost of gasoline will not bring the price down. Duh.

As far as I know, Credo Action, whoever that is, has never produced a drop of oil, and never sank a few million dollars of their own money into a dry well; and they have certainly never offered to push my car for 28 miles like the gallon of gas from those nasty capitalists does.

There is no Credo Action gas station that sells The People's Gas for $1.25, although there is nothing on earth stopping them from doing so. For that matter, why charge us anything at all, if it really is our money already anyway? Go for it!

Government letting someone keep their own money is not spending; spending is confiscating money from some of us to give to others of us. Unless, of course, you believe that all money belongs to the government and each American is an equal shareholder in Big Government, Inc. and entitled to the same dividend check. There is a word for that belief: communism.

I don't like communists; they ruin it for the rest of us who would simply like to live in peace and prosper. I wish Big Government would just get of our way so we could buy real gasoline for $2 from those money-grubbing, profiteering capitalists over at Big Oil.

Think a gallon of gas is overpriced? A gallon of Fair-Trade coffee at Starbucks will cost you $24, while their cost to make it is just over $4. That is cool 83% profit - more than 10 times what any oil company clears.

Let me know when the liberal lynch mob is formed to go after Big Coffee - I'm in.

Block Buster

The moment I saw it, I knew Mark Block should not have smoked in that ad.

When you engage in cloud-seeding, you can't complain about the deluge that follows. Not only did Block smoke on camera - worse than a snuff film these days - but the ad was not run on paid media. The latter, of course, is the real crime that has brought about the flash-mob hit on Herman Cain.

In the world of political punditry, Herman Cain is doing everything wrong and it is working. He is the most dangerous man in America. If this guy can win the nomination without spending hundreds of millions of establishment money and employing thousands of politicos, then the jig is up, and the whole electioneering industry is doomed. They can't have that, so they have to take him down - now.

One week into the corporate media beat down and we still don't even know what he is accused of: apparently someone told someone else about a rumor he heard from another guy about something that Herman might or might not have done or said or gestured that someone might or might not have misunderstood or might or might not have taken offense to at some time in the last century. There's your blockbuster, pun intended.

Unless you are clairvoyant, the 90 articles Politico has already devoted to this mirage add nothing to the description I just provided. All we know for sure is that Gloria Alred has not yet magically appeared like David Copperfield behind a battery of microphones in Atlanta, which is the UL listing for female victimhood.

People who wouldn't be caught dead parking the Mercedes among the F-150's and walking their facelift into a Waffle House might reach for the pepper spray if someone calls them "honey", but most of us human beings actually like it. South of the NASCAR line, it is just a word they attach to sentences without thinking – like "eh" for Canadians or "recall" for Wisconsin Democrats.

But this isn't about sexual harassment and everyone knows it; this is about money. And money does not care about truth, or justice, or fairness, or morality. Who is behind the hatchet job on Cain – Perry? Paul? Romney? Rove? Obama? Soros? DNC? RNC? The answer is...yes. Charges of skirt chasing aren't going to work on Ron Paul, so who knows what they will come up with if he puts 10 points on the pack.

The electioneering industry used to be the ultimate cyclical sector – every two years a minor bump, every four years a boom, and scratching for survival in between. So the smart guys who run corporate media and the major party apparatus figured out how to make that cycle continuous and billions have been pouring into the political sector ever since. Call it the election bubble. There is a ready stockpile of fundraisers and candidate marketers available, and they pick their candidates like waterfront hookers choose steamships – whoever is in port and has cash.

The action has been non-stop since 2007. That nomination process started a year earlier than normal – most of us were sick of it already before the first primary vote was cast in Iowa. The inauguration trash was not even picked up when they swung right into the selling of Stimulus, then almost a year of health care and the rise of the Tea Party, which bled right into the historic 2010 mid-term House flip.

In Wisconsin the hits just kept right on coming: a winter of protests over budget reforms, then judicial elections, recounts, senate recalls, and now the Walker recall petition drive which will take us right into the 2012 primary season. It is as likely to end as Cher's goodbye tour.

A lot of people profit handsomely from elections - campaign staff, consultants, PR firms, law firms, security, private investigators, travel agencies, advertising agencies, pollsters, media outlets, pundits, event organizers, hotels, food service, paid "volunteers", fundraisers, money managers, bloggers, social media managers, the guys who paint the busses, film crews, the list goes on and on.

So whoever had the idea to turn governing from a non-profit public service gig into one continuous for-profit election cycle must be the most popular guy or gal in the business - full employment and big fat checks for campaign ramrods and their menagerie of hangers-on. Palin figured out which side of the bread was buttered with c-notes. Life is good.

And then along comes this guy Cain. No prior office. No staff. No money. No plan recognizable to those who sell them off the shelf. He talks without a teleprompter; speaks without a script. He answers different questions with different answers, he wears a hat. His man Block smokes. And people love him. Ruh-roh.

35

We libertarians oppose any initiation of force or fraud. Either Herman Cain sexually harassed someone (force) or he has been falsely accused (fraud). Americans are fed up with hypocritical moralists running for office and telling us how to live our lives; and we are also fed up with the politics of personal destruction. So there is no middle ground here, someone is going to win and someone is going to lose.

The keepers of the conventional wisdom did not see 2010 coming; and still don't get it. This isn't politics as usual; we don't keep score of cheap debating points and gotcha moments. We want someone who can lead us out of our malaise. Someone is lying and someone is telling the truth; whoever is telling the truth has just won the White House this week.

We have devolved into a society where taking offense is an occupation, where feeling uncomfortable entitles us to compensatory damages. You want to see what real sexual harassment looks like? Go to Sturgis. You want to see how real women put an ape in his place without a lawyer? Go to Sturgis. You want to turn this whole country into Eggshell Nation because a few delicate flowers didn't get enough attention from their daddy? Go to hell.

If a guy makes a rude suggestion in a restaurant, the woman should slap his face. That's how we handled it before we handed the country over to the lawyers, parasites, and bedwetters. Her honor is vindicated and the cad's low character is exposed to the public and it takes a second for justice to be served.

$45,000 and a sealed agreement accomplish neither, and predation leaves a cloud over an innocent man for life. This is not progress.

Boeing, Boeing, Gone

Even the most cynical observer did a double-take last week when President Obama told Boeing it could not move its 787 Dreamliner production to South Carolina, making them build planes in Washington State instead.

No one could blame Boeing if they just keep right on going when they hit the Pacific and build their planes over in China. For that matter, no one could blame South Carolina if they secede from the union again.

On a personal level, I do not want to fly in a plane built by a second-choice reject workforce under the direction of an angry management team forced to live and work in a place they do not want to be. Let them build the President a new Air Force One out there and call it a day.

The International Association of Machinists has cost Boeing over $2 billion in the four strikes it has initiated at its Puget Sound facilities over the past 20 years. The AFL-CIO NOW! blog site proudly reports that Boeing's attempt to move production of 787's to South Carolina from Washington "followed years of production delays and an extraordinary round of mid-contract talks" that failed to reach any agreement.

Years of delays, excess costs, and extraordinary negotiations with knuckleheads who like to strike – oh yes, that sounds like the *perfect* spot to build things that can fall out of the sky over populated areas. Thank God we have our public servants to keep the private sector from making awful mistakes like hiring people who actually want to work.

It is possible – anything is – that a handful of political hacks appointed to reward powerful donor-constituencies know better than the world's #1 airplane builder where to build airplanes. But perhaps the government should try to tackle a more modest aviation problem first – say, keeping its hands off of little kid's privates or keeping its air traffic controllers awake – and slowly work its way up to the big stuff.

The head of the NLRB said that Boeing's decision was a clear violation of the National Labor Relations Act - an open and shut case where he had no choice but to apply the law. Nice try. I'm sure he will tell us later why his only scruple came to him *after* he allowed Boeing to spend $2 billion on a new plant and hire 1,000 workers.

People with no understanding of economics and no experience in commerce firmly believe that every facility siting decision is made on the basis of labor rates and union status alone. And when I was three I believed my mom stopped where her legs met her skirt hem and some other lady popped out of the neckline – so what? "Believe" and "know" are two different things; and it is never a good idea to put people with no understanding and no experience in charge of anything.

Cheap labor hasn't chased Boeing overseas, but cheap shots from partisan dipsticks might just do the trick. And when the unions are done high-fiving each other over the spanking their man delivered, they might want to check how much Boeing stock is owned by their pension funds. The right to be stupid is Constitutionally protected; but it is simply good manners to confine your idiocy to your own accounts.

Meanwhile, here in Wisconsin, conservatives are still angry at the loser of a recent Supreme Court race for her decision to waste a million dollars of taxpayers' money and tens of thousands of man-hours to learn exactly how badly she got beat.

Libertarians come at it from a different angle – we are angry that someone so petty and vindictive got to be a career superstar in the Department of Natural Resources before anyone but us seemed to care. "You peons exist to satisfy me" - this is the mentality that governs *all* of the agencies that govern our daily lives.

It is an infestation, not a lone beetle. Whether is it the NLRB, TSA, FAA, or the state DNR, the problem with government is that it always – *always* – takes a good intention and runs it right into the dirt.

Clean water turns into shutting down a lakeside restaurant; a bargaining right turns into telling a company where it can build things. If you have an uncontrollable urge to shut a business down, then by all means buy one and shut it down; but don't wait to pass the civil service exam and then do it on our dime.

I don't know if government makes petty tyrants or if it attracts them; probably recruits the talent and perfects it. Unlike the private sector, there is no competing brand of government to come in and wipe the floor with an organization whose core value is time off. Or so it thinks; China is doing a pretty darn good job, along with Brazil, Vietnam, India, Poland, South Africa, Turkey, South Korea, Singapore, Hong Kong, Colombia, and Peru to name just a few of the places that have welcomed the jobs that we have so callously tossed away as political pawns.

The Machinists Union called the NLRB sanction against Boeing a victory for aerospace workers - *in South Carolina!* There's your moment of clarity: better to have no job at all than to have one where their union can't steal a rake off your right to work. Tell me again why busting them is immoral.

What's wrong with the President deciding where Boeing can build planes? Mr. Obama is not the President of Boeing; that's what. He is not the President of the AFL-CIO. He is not the President of the Government. He is the President of the whole United States of America – all 300 million-plus citizens, the vast majority of whom choose to work and live free of union impairment.

His constituents include the non-union workers in South Carolina, the non-union employees of Boeing, the stockholders of Boeing, the customers of Boeing, the suppliers of Boeing, and the Americans who fly in Boeing aircraft each day, including those who pay through the nose for the privilege of sitting in Business Class, subsidizing everyone else's affordable coach fares. You're welcome; I'm sure the card got lost in the mail.

President Obama has no more right to decide where planes get built as he does to assign passenger seating based on campaign contributions and party affiliation. Oh, sheets - that was dumb of me to give him the idea, sorry. Probably have a Seat Czar appointed by Wednesday.

In business, we teach our young people that it is better to be humble than to have humility thrust upon you. Needless to say, our President has no business experience, so he hasn't yet grasped that concept. The light bulb will go on for him in November of 2012 – little dairy queen kind that takes an hour to warm up and then shows up all your zits. I still hate those things.

Bouffant Nation

You probably don't think of yourself as an employer, but you are: you create a job every time you hire someone to cut your hair. So let me ask you something: *why* do you create that job?

Do you create that job to help the economy recover? Do you create that job to reduce the unemployment rate among stylists? Do you create that job to correct a trade imbalance? Do you get your hair cut more often because President Obama or Governor Walker wants to create more jobs?

Would you get twice as many haircuts to earn a $5 rebate from the government? Would you go get yourself a B52-style bouffant if the government paid half through cash-for-coifs? If your state put a $100 tax on each haircut, would you pay it or create that job across the state line where there is no haircut tax? See - this employer stuff is not so complicated.

Unless you are a muttonhead, you only hire someone to cut your hair because you need a haircut – keyword need. And you hire a stylist with skills that meet your requirements – keyword skills. And you hire someone you can afford – keyword afford.

Job creation only happens when those three things come together: demand, skill, and price. No demand, no jobs; no skilled workers, no jobs; too pricey, no jobs. Can government compel those three things to heel? I think you know.

Government fiscal and monetary policy can do little to stimulate demand, as the past three years under both President Obama and President Bush have demonstrated. All the Keynesian multipliers in the universe cannot make your hair grow any faster, and deficit spending merely borrows from Friday to make Monday's appointments more expensive. See - economics isn't that complicated, either.

Government schools have diminished employable skills – reading, math, courtesy, ambition, competitive drive, achievement, standards, loyalty, discipline, accountability, respect – for decades. Government Affirmative Action programs and feel-good academic silliness have dumbed-down standards for college entrance tests, civil service exams, and professional certifications, diluting skills to achieve dubious social engineering objectives.

Government's economic interventions almost always increase the price of labor. Regulation, taxation, unionization, and protectionism all add costs, but do not add any value.

So if government cannot create demand, improve skills, or make labor more affordable, what can it do to help the private sector create jobs?

Watch it. Stand back and leave it alone; take as little as possible in the way of taxes, regulate only enough to make regular, and protect the sanctity of the exchange instead of picking winners and losers. Did you need government intervention to get your last haircut? Can you imagine how hideous a one-size-fits-all government-issued haircut would look like?

When this nation was founded, 95 out of 100 Americans grew food to feed themselves and the other 5. Today, with modern farm equipment and chemicals, 3 out of 100 Americans feed the whole nation and a good bit of the rest of the world. The industrialization of America spanned two centuries; the de-industrialization is occurring at a much faster pace. Since 2000, manufacturing employment has dropped by 63% to just over 11 million. Government has grown to 22.5 million and unemployment to over 15 million.

Our great-grandparents left the farm to work in the factories. Where will our kids go to make their dreams come true – the DMV? Subway? Paychex? Is the future going to be 10 of us driving around in Volts writing up carbon violations against the 3 of us that make windmill parts to fill up a warehouse until the tax subsidies run out and the Dutch owners close up shop? That seems to be the Obama/Biden vision. And trains, because...well, because.

The difference between the 19th century and the 21st century is that federal, state, and local government back then consumed less than 10% of GDP, so free enterprise was 90% free. Today, our runaway government spends over 60% of GDP, nags and nannies us to death, and deprives us of the energy we need to sustain our living standards based on a superstition that honest science has already abandoned.

Should we wonder why the recovery didn't come again this time around like the Easter Bunny always does? The more our governments do to "help", the more we prolong the deep recession and high rates of joblessness we have become mired in. You can't be for jobs and against the corporations that provide them.

And we cannot just be Bouffant Nation, where the Fed prints scads of money and we all cut each other's hair. We need to invent things here, to make them here, and to export them from here all over the world. That takes energy, a skilled workforce, sound money, and less government than we have now – a lot less.

The trick to free enterprise is the "free" part. Get government out of the way and we will quickly discover that American ingenuity did not die; it has been napping until the day when it can again thrive free of government interference.

Bradley or Brawley

This week's contrived liberal yawner is the choking accusation against Wisconsin Supreme Court judge David Prosser. Two words: Tawana Brawley.

On Sunday, the news media reported that two weeks ago Justice Prosser suddenly grabbed pro-union Justice Ann Walsh Brawley...er...Bradley by the neck and tried to choke her in the presence of four other Supreme Court judges.

My first reaction to the story was bewilderment. Why would liberals who filed lawsuits and complaints like a flash mob over the method of notice used in a legislative hearing hold their fire when a real live felonious assault is committed by their arch-nemesis - an old, white, conservative man?

And then on Monday we learned that witnesses to the incident (Supreme Court judges, no less) said it was Justice Brawley...er...Bradley that charged at Prosser with first raised, while Prosser defended himself from her attack. She said/they said.

There are two possible explanations for why Justice Brawley...er...Bradley did not file a complaint after being choked and why no assault charges were filed by Capitol Police who investigated the incident: a) liberals feel sorry for old white conservative men, or b) it never happened. I'm thinking b).

Besides, I watch COPS; I know how this works. The girl in the tank-top calls the cops when the mullet guy with no shirt pushes her down to get more beer from the fridge. The cops talk to each of them separately while they smoke, and then they slap the cuffs on mullet guy while tank-top girl screams at them to let go of her may-un.

It doesn't matter if she changes her mind or her story; the dude is always guilty in a case like this and he clunks his head as they push him into the cruiser. Did Prosser get his head clunked in the cruiser? No, he did not - and that's good enough for me. Besides, the mullet people don't have Supreme Court justices as witnesses, only cousins or maybe his momma if she is good for a few bleep-outs.

But now that some "journalist" has broken the Justice Brawley...er...Bradley version of events, the Capitol Police have referred the matter to the Department of Administration, who kicked the can over to the Dane County Sheriff, who will investigate the matter and make a recommendation to the Dane County District Attorney, the guy whose lawsuit was being discussed when Wrestlemania IV supposedly broke out in chambers. How convenient.

This will undoubtedly take union law enforcement weeks and weeks to sort out; after all, there are many evening newscasts to fill and papers to print before the recall elections, and the socialists need to get all of the free negative media coverage of their enemies as possible before then.

This shouldn't take weeks. My mom and dad could figure out which of us three boys was lying and which one was the instigator in minutes. In fact, I bet every parent reading this could spend 10 minutes with Justice Prosser and 10 minutes with Justice Brawley...er...Bradley and get this caper solved with plenty of time left for a lecture to the perpetrator about lying. Am I right, moms and dads?

I'll tell you who is in a choke-hold; it is the people of Wisconsin who are forced to watch the hysterical over-reactions of the lefties in this state week after week. These nimrods have lost control of their bowels ever since they lost the election in November and can't tell the rest of us what to do anymore.

What's next, commies? You going to throw acid on our face and scream "if I can't have you nobody can?" I know what is really bothering you; Walker and his Republicans are making fixing your mess look easy. This one's easy to fix, too: Supreme Court judges wouldn't go around charging at each other now that their adversary might be packin' heat under that robe. You're welcome.

It is, of course, possible that Justice Prosser actually choked Justice Brawley...er...Bradley. Just as it was possible in the beginning that somebody actually hacked Weiner's Twitter or however you say that with a straight face. Did you believe him, even for a minute? Me neither.

Maybe at the socialist sing-a-long down at the Capitol they should add "What A Fool Believes" to their repertoire. Seems appropriate.

Bunnies and Small Children

The math is deceptively simple: minus one plus one equals zero. Government cannot add a single dollar to the economy that it has not first taken out of it.

The economics are even simpler: people spend their own money more carefully than they spend other people's money.

The spectacular failure of "Green Economy" poster kid Solyndra will cost the taxpayers over $500 million. More important than why we gave them those loan guarantees is why they were needed in the first place. They were only necessary because no one would use their own money to back the venture.

States and local governments do it too. In Wisconsin, tens of millions of taxpayer dollars were wasted on incentives to lure Talgo, a Spanish train car company, to locate a factory here that never built a train. In the city of Oconomowoc, the government is planning to spend $10 million, roughly its annual budget, to build a community center that will offer wedding receptions in competition with private firms.

Now, if there was a critical shortage of reception venues in Oconomowoc, don't you think entrepreneurs like Rick and Rudy Eckert at Olympia Resort would expand their space to meet the demand? By the way, if you do not know of the Eckerts, you should; liberty has no greater friends in the Badger state. And if you live in Oconomowoc, you should find out what on earth is going downtown and what it will do to your property taxes.

Or if it made economic sense to build railcars in Wisconsin, don't you think someone a little closer than Spain would have done so with their own money? Should I name them, our industrial entrepreneurs who put their family names on the line? Do you think they have lost the instincts that made them wealthy beyond even their own imaginations? No, it was those experienced instincts that told them not to put their own money - real money- into any of these losing propositions.

And I would be curious to know just how much Al Gore lost when Solyndra went bankrupt - I would bet he didn't put single penny of his own money where that big mouth demands the government puts ours.

"But we need the jobs", the public works lobby will plead. Indeed we do need jobs; precisely why government needs to get out of the way of those who create real ones.

The statists' promise of jobs created by emptying public coffers on this or that high-minded project ignores the far greater numbers of jobs that were killed by filling up those coffers in the first place. That $500 million that the government tossed down the Solyndra rat hole took more like $600 million out of the economy (it takes a lot of overhead to piss away someone else's money).

What would taxpayers have done for themselves with that $600 million? Add a deck on the house, buy a car, invest in a business, take a vacation, buy a Gibson guitar, perhaps? I did, just to say screw you to our President and all the union job-killers who have thrown in with him. Are going to come and take my rosewood fretboards, too, boys? Bring your lunch.

Taxpayers would have spent or saved their own money on something more economically viable than Solyndra. More jobs are created, more businesses prosper, and more incomes rise when economic exchanges are voluntary and people who earned the money decide what to do with it.

Voluntary exchange only occurs when both parties gain more than they trade away. No one needs an extra incentive to make a smart deal; it's only the stupid ones that need a government subsidy.

The amount of capital is finite, even if the amount of government currency used to measure it is not. Government does not create capital; it only diverts it to purposes other than which its rightful owners would have put it. The rich did not get that way by making bad financial decisions, and government did not go broke by making good ones.

The crowd squeals with delight when the magician pulls a rabbit out the hat; we forget that behind the curtain some child is crying her eyes out wondering where her little cuddly bunny went.

Clearly, President Obama hates bunnies and small children; he wants to take away $470 billion of their parents' money to fund more stupid politician tricks like Solyndra, Talgo, and the Oconomowoc public wedding chapel. If we love him, he tells us, we should pass his bill.

I never thought about it before he brought it up, but I guess I love bunnies and small children more than I love some slick magician from Illinois. The only trick that worked so far for the Great O is the one where he talks into a teleprompter and makes the jobs disappear.

So here's a better idea: let's love ourselves and our neighbors and not pass the bill. The President will be fine in the love department; he has a wife and two daughters and the whole crew over at MSNBC to rub his feet.

The government can not pull rabbits from hats and it cannot create jobs; it can only create an environment in which job-creators flourish, or convince them to invest elsewhere. If the President would quit unwisely picking the latter, he would not need to beg us to love him.

Chi Ni De Dou Xi, Obama!

I finally discovered a way to listen to President Obama's economic team without risking my sanity - watch them on TV in China.

In English, their incomprehensible gibberish is an offensive mix of spin, blame, Keynesian superstition, guess, bravado, rubbish, half-truths, and full-out lies. In Mandarin Chinese, it is just incomprehensible gibberish. Upgrade.

Zhengzhou is an industrial city of 9 million people in Henan province in the heartland of China; that is where I happened to be when Standard and Poor's dropped the hammer on the debt-mongers at Treasury and the Fed last week, downgrading U.S. sovereign debt from its long-standing AAA rating.

The local news showed U.S. officials responding to the downgrade, their comments dubbed – sort of like a Kung Fu movie in reverse. With a little imagination, you could pretend they were actually making sense. Ok, with a lot of imagination.

Whatever spin they were pitching, the Chinese were having none of it. Commentators' body language gave away their disdain for our official excuse-making, Chinese officials harshly scolded the President and Congress for their fiscal irresponsibility, and the Chinese people were angry at their own government for buying so much lousy U.S. debt in the first place.

On the plus side, I learned a new phrase, "Chi Ni De Dou Xi, Obama!" (eat your own peas, Obama!).

They are living the American dream over in Henan Province – incomes are rapidly rising as productivity skyrockets and labor skills improve. People are grateful to their industrialists, entrepreneurs, and traders who rescued them from four decades of spreadin' the wealth around and the poverty, famine, war, oppression, and death it brought to China. They revere American businessmen, and it was frankly refreshing to be appreciated.

The entrepreneurial industrialists of Henan Province are young – in their 40's mostly, and running the firms they founded in their 20's. Their squeaky-clean factories are filled with new machine tools, overhead cranes, computer controlled production lines, state of the art environmental protections, automated material handling systems, and six-sigma black belts. Want to make a

Chinese factory worker laugh? Explain the word "exploitation" to him.

That investment capital comes from the 30% savings rate of the new Chinese middle class and the low tax rates on corporate income and capital gains. Factory workers don't want a union; they buy stock in their firm, share in its profits, and look forward to striking it rich in a future IPO. They get it; and they learned it from us.

Less than two decades of movement towards free-market capitalism has repaired the damage Mao and his brand of hope and change did to China. Economic liberty is bringing with it greater personal liberty, prosperity, and peace. My trip was an eye opener; I could not find the slave labor sweatshops I expected to see, my Facebook was not blocked, and the only government official calling for suppression of free speech was U.S. Senator John Kerry's call to silence the tea party.

An Op-Ed in a Chinese newspaper denounced Kerry's idea, while the American press remained sock-puppet silent. At a private dinner with the Mayor of Zhengzhou, he called me "genius" (granted, his vocabulary is limited); that same day Joe Biden called me a terrorist. There is your moment of clarity.

China is not what's wrong with America. Freaks like Biden, Geithner, Bernanke, Obama, Pelosi, and Reid are what is wrong with America.

Throw in McCain, Bush, McConnell, Boehner, and every other Republican statist masquerading as a conservative at election time. And include the growing legions of loafing sacks who think the world owes them because they breathe; eaters, Henry Kissinger called them. People whose idea of justice is to share your money equally among themselves – that is who have brought us low.

Since 1985, we have bought over $3 trillion of goods from China; in doing so, we have saved over $3 trillion in lower prices for those goods. I just spent two weeks looking at what the Chinese did with their $3 trillion - new factories, machine tools, power plants, roads, bridges, mines, dams, cars, refineries, stores, offices, railways, ships, ports, vocational training, private schools, and new jobs by the tens of millions.

Where did ours go? More government, foreign wars, bad loans, domestic partner benefits, TSA gropers, six miles of orange cones leading up to 8 guys watching the 9th drive a blacktop roller,

Viagra for public pensioners, 19 new czars, tens of thousands of pages of new regulations, bank bailouts, more drug prisons, government agencies suing each other, bone-headed recall elections - stuff like that.

The Chinese are not kicking our ass; we are parking it on their foot.

Did we really think we could sustain a debt economy where some of us flip houses and the rest flip burgers? Did we really think our private sector would thrive under the thumb of an expanding army of government workers whose career goal is time off? Did we think taxing and regulating our industries off-shore would make us better off than the countries who welcomed the jobs we chased away?

While we slog through the third year of the Obama depression, China's economy is growing at over 9%; you have to go there to truly appreciate the joy of real prosperity. Sound money, lower taxes, less regulation, available energy, hard work, entrepreneurship and invention, labor mobility – there is no magic juice. The Chinese are simply following the capitalist game plan that they learned from reading American economic history and watching it work in nearby Hong Kong and Taiwan. It is not China's fault that our guys don't read Milton Freidman.

I visited a shipyard in Nan Tong City where tens of thousands of skilled tradesmen are newly employed building semi-submersible drill rigs for Brazil's booming off-shore oil industry. Those jobs should have been created in our own Gulf coast yards and those rigs should be operating in our own waters; China only got into the game after Obama shut down our domestic off-shore oil industry.

It is not the difference in wages that caused those jobs to be lost to Brazil and China; it is the difference in Presidents. Theirs are better. Chi Ni De Dou Xi, Obama!

Church and State

The First Amendment to the Constitution prohibits Congress from making any law that establishes a religion or bans the free exercise of a religious belief.

That notion of religious tolerance has served us well for most of our history. It is not so difficult to comprehend, and it frankly not so difficult to put into practice. The separation of Church and State is no trickier than the separation of Work and State, or Family and State, or Club and State.

The question of whether government should hold dominion over religion or vice versa was answered by Jesus himself, who said, "render unto Caesar that which is Caesar's, and unto the Lord that which is the Lord's".

I know people with just about every possible religious conviction, including atheists, wiccans, and naturists. I have yet to meet someone who is genuinely offended by a religious display or reference in the public arena. A group of atheists in New York City objects to a street sign honoring first responders who lost their lives on 9/11 because it contains the word "heaven". They say they are insulted; I bet they are not.

And so what if they are? I can find you a dozen people who are offended at anything; should we all stop living because a few of us can't cope?

NBC edited out the phrase "under God" from the Pledge of Allegiance in a piece aired during the U.S. Open. In the world of the politically correct statist, it is probably not the "God" part that irks as much as the "under" part.

That is what chafes the tender bottoms of those infants who believe in the supreme and omnipotent State. It is not that God is acknowledged by those of us who believe; it is that we refuse to put their God – the Omnipotent State – before Him.

But that is exactly where the framers put the State – second fiddle. "Congress shall pass no law..." Public religious expression is explicitly protected by the First Amendment – all of it, everywhere, and regardless of who might pretend to be offended by it.

51

Citizens United

A good friend and fellow traveler in the liberty movement recently asked my opinion on last year's U.S. Supreme Court's *Citizens United* decision. The ruling still generates controversy, especially when its effects are described as "chilling" - conveying personhood onto corporations and equating money with speech.

The notion that corporations are separate legal entities – i.e. "persons" - is not new; it is a foundational concept in commercial contract law and torts. It is what spares us from having to get each of the stockholders of ATT&T to sign our cell phone service contract among other useful considerations. And when President Obama is preparing to spend over $1 billion in his re-election bid, money *is* speech, whether we like it or not. Color me "not".

While all rights belong to individuals, the individual right to free speech can be amplified via the companion right of association. A corporation is a form of association; and while we think immediately of huge multinationals, most corporations are small and many are non-profits. If we think of McCain/Feingold as muzzling the family farm or a local co-op, the Court's decision to strike it down takes on a whole different cast.

We all tend to forget the specifics of landmark legal cases. Citizens United, a non-profit advocacy corporation, tried to buy advertising for its documentary film about Hillary Clinton within the window that McCain/Feingold banned corporate purchases of "electioneering" speech – 60 days before an election and 30 days before a primary. It was their law, not the Court decision, which equated money with speech.

Citizens United challenged the law on constitutional grounds – freedom of speech, freedom of association, equal protection. Amicus briefs supporting Citizens United were filed by Heritage Foundation (conservative), CATO Institute (Libertarian) and the ACLU (liberal). I thought that alignment was a sign of the end times.

And the court ruled in its favor, deciding 5 to 4 that it is (duh) unconstitutional to ban free speech selectively - only certain forms, only at certain times, and only to certain types of associations. Previous cases had struck down other provisions of McCain/Feingold, so another defeat should come as no surprise.

The criticism from Democrats and media was predictable – McCain/Feingold protected incumbents from competition and created a virtual monopoly for the mainstream media – themselves big and powerful corporations – to control the narrative during the weeks when regular people actually pay attention to elections. The stacked deck was unstacked by the *Citizens United* decision and the deck-stackers are still whining.

Not my team, but I don't imagine that the Republican establishment was all too happy with the ruling, either – it enabled 2010 tea-party candidates like Rand Paul, Marco Rubio, Allan West, Nikki Haley and dozens of others to break through against the old-guard of the GOP and a media openly hostile to the liberty movement.

Feingold himself was defeated by a novice, and McCain barely survived an insurgent primary challenge. 60 new faces went to Congress and changed the trajectory of the debate on spending, deficits, and debt. Could the 2010 revolution have succeeded under the old rules that bought Barack Obama his victory? Maybe, but I doubt it.

What I find most troubling about the *Citizens United* case is that the dissenting opinion of the four liberal judges did not rest on any constitutional principle; rather it questioned the wisdom of rejecting the "common sense of the American people...who have fought against the distinctive corrupting potential of corporate electioneering since the days of Theodore Roosevelt." Say what?

This is quite remarkable, yet almost never remarked upon. First of all, it is not the job of the Supreme Court to judge the wisdom of laws, only the laws themselves. Not to mention that the collective common sense of the American people is vested in its elected representatives, not in 4 partisan jurists appointed for life. Finally, the theories and ideologies of the early progressives (Roosevelt) are not the standard against which constitutional challenges are to be judged – the Constitution is the standard.

During my own fleeting campaign for Congress as a Libertarian Party candidate, I would have loved to have some corporation write me a check for $100,000 so I could take a full swing at socialist (c'mon, just admit it) incumbent Tammy Baldwin – better yet, a dozen of them. I would have worn their logos on my suit like a NASSCAR driver so you all know who it is that loves liberty enough to send it a check. I would be happy to modify my stump speech: "I want to be your Congressman, not your Mommy...and buy all your ammo at Todd's House of Guns."

And Congresswoman Baldwin could have worn her backers' logos, too – knowing Tammy, I'm sure she would do so with pride, as would Republican challenger Chad Lee. That debate would have been refreshingly honest, transparent as all get-out, and, heaven forbid, fun. Are we better off with processed-cheese candidates marketed on TV like timeshares and bankrolled by billionaires who have been sanitized by 7 layers of McCain/Feingold facades?

Isn't it better to just know the truth than to hide the money trail through a labyrinth of PACS, 427s, 501c, foundations, institutes, associations, and all other mutant forms of "independent expenditures" that only exist to protect incumbents, insulate the two establishment parties, and seal the deal for entrenched special interests?

The best campaign finance reform is a blank piece of paper; let individual donors – and only individuals - give to individual candidates and put the entire sham-ethics industry out of business.

Milton Freidman argued that corporations should make no donations of any sort, as it deprives shareholders of dividends that rightly belong to them. I agree. Let individual shareholders decide what causes, candidates, and charities are worthy of their donations, and remove all limits on their generosity. And ditto for individual union members.

It doesn't concern me terribly that corporations seek to influence government; what concerns me terribly is that government has enough influence that they would bother. It was not supposed to be like this. Government was supposed to limited, and the "general welfare" was supposed to be the handful of things that are good for everyone, not favor one minority interest at the expense of another.

And the Supreme Court was supposed to set the boundaries for the political process, not be an extension of it. The 5-4 Court did not split over how to apply the Constitution in *Citizens United*; it split over whether or not to bother. That is chilling.

Class Warfare

While the civil war between taxpayers and taxeaters rages on across the nation, the battle here in Wisconsin has devolved from class warfare to a war on class.

Even the Democrat State Senators who went AWOL (the opening salvo in the war on class) have had it with the juvenile antics of their fellow unionists and entitlement cranks. It's pretty bad when you annoy folks who think running away is the grown-up thing to do.

Last week a couple of moonbats bike-locked their heads to the railing in the Senate chamber and tried to shout down the pledge of allegiance. The week before, a group dressed as Zombies inserted themselves into a ceremony honoring Special Olympians. Classy.

The head of the state's firefighters' union held a press conference after the state Supreme Court upheld the legality of the Budget Repair Bill to drop an F-bomb or two and warn us taxpayers to get our "knuckles ready" for a fight. That same day, a State Senator's office was stink-bombed. Very classy.

Wisconsin's Democrat Secretary of State is delaying the publishing of the budget bill to allow local unions to sign contract extensions before it goes into effect, forcing more job cuts than necessary and pinning the cuts on Governor Walker. And gay activists, apparently worried that they were not being obnoxious enough in the Segway era, have now taken to throwing glitter on those who disagree with them. So classy.

A tent city called "Walkerville" has popped up on the Capitol square, and a journalist filming the activities there was accosted by a guy in a pink dress. And what would a week of protests in Madison be without another round of death threats and profanities emailed to legislators who voted for a balanced budget. How classy.

This one's nice: a teacher made her children draw pictures of Governor Walker as the devil. And over the weekend, veterans returning from the war had their homecoming marred by Walker protestors who could not stop the pity party for even one hour out of respect for those who have given up months and even years of their lives to protect our freedoms. How very classy.

Disrupting blood drives, elementary school classrooms, Special Olympic ceremonies, veterans' homecomings, and legislative proceedings is not what democracy looks like; it is what pathetic losers look like. Your mommies must be so proud.

Look, Democrats, I know how much it hurts to lose elections - I'm a Libertarian, remember? But get over it, like we do. You are losing votes in the next one with each air horn blast and profanity-laced drool. And you are making the whole state look bad by disrupting events that have nothing to do with you and your pay.

Besides, I can't imagine that you have persuaded a single person to come around to your way of thinking by your obnoxious and offensive behavior. Maybe Governor Walker is the jerk you say he is, but not if we are grading on a curve – you guys got the whole d-bag honor roll sowed up.

When the Republicans cratered on Constitutional Carry, did you see us gunners out spray-painting the entrance at Bed, Bath, and Beyond? No, you did not. Because we are responsible adults, that's why. All it takes is to listen to that little voice in the back of your head that says, "don't be a 'hole".

By all means, protest and rally to your hearts content – it's still a free country, despite your best efforts to turn it into a socialist adult day care. Fill up Camp Randall, blow your horns, and beat your drums until your fingers bleed.

But let the people who live and work around the Square have some peace, for God's sake. You have been disturbing it for months now, and they have done nothing to deserve you. And leave our returning veterans and their families alone; you do not deserve them.

And speaking of the working class, I hope you tentwads don't have the misguided notion that all your no-class antics are helping working people. Any business thinking of moving to Wisconsin or expanding here gets a daily reminder on YouTube of the lunacy that lurks just one election away from running the state again.

And if you don't think that businesspeople take things like that into account when deciding where to invest and create jobs, then you are too dumb to be carrying something as dangerous as a bike lock.

In fact, I think the legislature should pass a law that requires a permit and training to carry a bike lock, since more people locked their own heads to railings last week than shot themselves accidently with open carry. Guns are much safer.

Give it up, already. Walker won, Prosser won, the recount is over, the courts ruled, the budget passed, and the recalls aren't going to mean squat. It's over.

Rest up for Right To Work, because that's the big enchilada – it will determine the economic trajectory of this state for the next 50 years. And when the time comes, let's fight that fight with some class. Our kids are watching.

Comparable Worth

The confrontation between Wisconsin taxpayers and their public sector unions has been focused on what we pay them. But yesterday, the Department of Education (President Obama's, not President Bush's) turned our attention to the more important question of what we are getting for our money, when it sanctioned the Madison School District for inadequate quality.

Yes, the People's Republic of Madison - crème de la crème of liberal progressivism, the state-workers' paradise, greener than thou, smarter than thou, more just than thou, holier than...oh, wait, that would be a religious reference and probably against a city ordinance...gun free, smoke free, bike-ridin', drum-beating, sandal-wearing, tent-camping Madison, where 2+2=tax the rich.

It turns out that Madison teachers and administrators – the ones who took off work on fraudulent doctors excuses to protest the budget reform bill that saved thousands of their jobs - can't teach very well, either. They are very well paid, enjoy a stacked school board, and work under extended contracts that preserved their sacred WEAC monopoly benefits; they are the poster kids for the status quo.

Poster kids, indeed. Madison is one of only six districts in the state of Wisconsin that could not meet the minimum national (that would include Mississippi) standards for tested student proficiency. That is six out of the state's 420 school districts – only 1.4% that couldn't cut it. You take the numerator and divide it by the denominator, and...oh, never mind.

Predictably, Madison school officials and leaders in the capital's educational community blamed the test, apparently oblivious to the embarrassing fact that over 98% of school districts in the state managed to achieve the national (that would include Texas) standard that Madison could not.

No, the problem is not with the tests or with the kids. The problem is with the people running the schools and the classrooms in the 1.4% of districts that are inferior (big word, lots of syllables, means not as good) to the districts who have focused on their own kids instead of obsessing over some other school's mascot.

We teach our young business leaders that losers will reveal themselves in the language they use. The radars should go off when you hear the "three F's": it's not Fair, it's not my Fault, and it's not mine to Fix.

In the Wisconsin State Journal article on the sanctions today, Adam Gamoran, Director of Wisconsin Center for Educational Research, said that standardized testing "made no sense" (it's not fair); superintendent Dan Nerad said the district is following the plan approved by state Department of Public Instruction (it's not my fault); and State Superintendent has asked for Congress to change the testing law (it's not mine to fix).

Danger, Danger! Warning, Will Robinson! Hand sign to forehead, loser alert.

This year's national (that would include Alabama) standard was only 80.5% proficiency for reading, and 68.5% in math. Do you know what the proficiency requirement is for entry-level work in our factories? 100%. Many, if not most, employers administer the same or even tougher basic testing for applicants, and there are no stickers, stars, or do-overs when a job is on the line.

Why? Because we cannot take on the safety risk of hiring someone who can't read a warning label, and we can't afford the scrap costs from employee who can't measure or calculate or know when a computer result is in error. What value can someone offer in exchange for a wage if they cannot even fill out their timecard correctly? We are not the remedial class for schools who won't educate their kids.

I intentionally said "won't", because it is a choice. Three school districts in this state – Madison, Milwaukee, and Racine - make up the bulk of the 228 individual schools which failed to meet the national (that would include Arkansas) standards. There are 2,072 other schools that met those national (that would include North Carolina) standards. They did their job, so no one can say it can't be done.

Those Madison kids who can't read or cipher will not work in high paying jobs; they will be looking up at the person who operates the cash register, if they work at all. Our middle class is not shrinking because a few people make too much; it is shrinking because less and less people coming out of school and into the workforce are able to acquire the skills that are worth middle class wages.

Mr. Gamoran tells us that the 2014 goal of 100% proficiency in math and reading is "unrealistic". I agree with him to a point; under the current system of union-run government monopoly schools led by people who believe they cannot win, that assessment is 100% (that means 100 out of 100, Madison school system graduates) accurate.

But then we part company. Every single child is teachable, and every single one deserves to be proficient in reading and math. That is why we need to bust the union-government monopoly on education and provide every Wisconsin parent with real school choice.

Choice and competition will increase the quality of education and lower its cost. We can't afford to throw another generation away to indulge the fantasies of the ideologues that have been running our public schools into the ground for decades.

There is no shortage of sanctimonious world-savers posing and preening and lecturing us about civic morality in our state capital; my advice to them is to turn down the volume and narrow the scope – see if you can save Leopold Elementary School first and then work your way up to the whole world.

And while you are at it, take some time to watch the pictures and video clips of today's union protests in Madison. Watch them over and over and over. Those folks dressed up as zombies and disrupting a Special Olympics ceremony to stick it to...who even knows who you losers are trying to stick it to anymore...those are the minds you have molded; they are your work product; that is your team.

They busted on the Special Olympics. You must be so proud to know that you were able to take children entrusted into your care and use your positions of authority to turn them into soul-less human garbage. Two words: Own It.

Constitutional Carry

We had such high hopes in Wisconsin for this new Governor and this legislature. Conservatives, libertarians, and constitutionalists had a few priorities that we did not think would be difficult to achieve in short order, chief among them being removal of the unconstitutional restrictions on carrying firearms.

We are not asking for much; only that law abiding citizens be afforded the same opportunities for self-defense that criminals have enjoyed in this state for decades.

Criminals do not have to secure permits, endure training, buy licenses, or track ammo. Criminals are not subject to restrictions on the caliber, magazine size, or firing mechanism of their weapons. When criminals find themselves in need of a firearm for self-defense, they do not have to dial 911 and then wait for a police officer to show up with one. Criminals have no waiting period; no forms to fill out.

We are only asking that non-criminals be afforded equal rights. The fact that oh-by-the-way concealed carry reduces violent crime is a bonus, but we should not have to prove to anyone that there is a benefit to them in order for our rights to be secured.

The bill to remove *all* restrictions on owning and carrying firearms in the state of Wisconsin should have been written on one page, debated for a minute, and passed on the first day of the legislative session. You either believe in freedom or you don't; you either believe in the Constitution or you don't; you either believe in unalienable rights or you don't. Liberty does not accept amendments or earmarks.

Wisconsin's Constitutional Carry Bill, LRB 11-2007-1 has finally been introduced and is co-sponsored by Dr. Pam Galloway, a citizen legislator with whom I was privileged to share a panel during the health care debates of 2009-10. It strikes down all of the provisions of Wisconsin law that infringe upon the right to keep and bear arms. Bravo, Senator Galloway and all who support her.

But her more experienced colleagues have subsequently introduced competing bills which introduce new requirements for training, registration, licensing and other infringements. The author of one of them, Rep. Donald Pridemore, argues that his added red tape is "a reasonable compromise between an individual's second amendment rights and a modern day application of these rights".

Dear Rep. Pridemore: no compromise of a right is ever "reasonable". But thank you for helping me point out the difference between a Republican and a Libertarian. We Libertarians are quite *unreasonable* when it comes to compromising on unalienable rights. It is a heck of a word to say, so we tend to mean it.

The Constitution of the United States does not grant rights to citizens; it limits the powers of government to infringe on the rights which have already endowed upon us by our Creator. One of those is the right to keep and bear arms, to defend our persons and property in any manner we see fit.

In fact, guns are the *only* product or service mentioned anywhere in the Constitution. While we also clearly have a right to keep and bear food, healthcare, clothing, shelter, and many other necessary things, the framers did not deem any of them important enough to warn the government against any form of infringement – only guns. Think about that.

Who do you imagine they had in mind that needed to be expressly warned by the 2nd amendment? I'm guessing the same folks who are being warned "hands off" in the other nine. Was the 4th amendment aimed at your neighbor, requiring a warrant before he comes in to borrow a cup of sugar? Was the 5th amendment needed to limit the power of your priest at confession? Was the 1st amendment meant to keep the auctioneer from ignoring your bid?

No. It is government that the founders feared enough to bind by the Constitution and the Bill of Rights; and their worst fears of government encroachment on our liberties have come true in our lifetimes. The purpose of the second amendment is to protect us from our government; we will not negotiate the dinner menu with cannibals.

Government officials who swear to uphold and defend the Constitution, and who are expressly prohibited from *any* form of infringement on the citizens' rights to keep and bear arms, have amassed so many unconstitutional prohibitions in violation of the oath that it takes Dr. Galloway's bill 19 pages to list all of them which will be struck moot by adhering to the Constitution in Wisconsin. It is time for us to correct this wrong, and to do so in one fell swoop.

The thing about gun rights is not the guns part, it's the rights part. We do not require citizens to buy a license and pay for training to vote, speak, worship, assemble, secure their homes, serve on a jury, or petition for redress. Constitutional carry is liberty's demand, not mine; call your representatives and remind them what they were sent to do last November.

D-I-V-O-R-C-E

Crank up the Tammy Wynette, the Congressional Super Committee on deficit reduction failed. Irreconcilable differences, I think they call it.

Like an estranged married couple enduring court-ordered counseling because they had to, the Republicans and Democrats recited their irreconcilable differences, whined about how hard they tried to go the extra mile, and blamed each other for the breakup. For those of you who find the language of fiscal negotiations incomprehensible, let me translate for you.

The Democrat position: "he is an uncaring cheapskate sonofabitch who doesn't care about me or the kids or anything but himself and that goddamn stock portfolio. I gave up everything for this family now that my looks are gone he wants to cut me off? Fat chance, a-hole."

The Republican position: "that frigid bitch spends all day eating bon-bons and running up the credit cards on stuff we can't afford to impress her European friends. I work my ass off and she spends twice whatever I make on implants and Jimmy Choos. I'm cutting my losses."

It's a little more complicated than that, but not much. We independents are like the kids watching mommy and daddy rip each others guts out; hoping against hope that they really love us, even when we know they are fighting for custody just to get the alimony and child support. We hate 'em both, and would like to just move in with the neighbors next door who have a pool.

Our Counselor-In-Chief was a no help making this bad marriage work, as usual. He didn't even come to a single session, just yelled at everybody and called the whole family lazy, as if it wasn't HIS family, but let's not start that whole birther thing up again now that we finally got Trump off TV. The President got his teleprompter replaced just in time to tell us it was all the Republicans fault; sort of like having Gloria Allred decide who's telling the truth about Herman Cain.

This whole Super Committee thing was stupid from the start. Thank God it failed; maybe now we won't be tempted to try something so idiotic ever again. They preened and postured and pretended and in the end, kicked the can down the road. No surprise there; that isn't dysfunction in Washington, it is political science. That is how they roll, it's what they do.

There is no Constitutional authority for such a monstrosity as a Super Committee, and let's be honest – those were not the 12 smartest folks out of the pool of 535. The Super Committee as more like an expanded Village People; dressed up caricatures to entertain us with some predictable shtick and a bit of narrative in between songs – I expected John Kerry to break into "In The Navy" at any moment.

Actually, I don't consider it a failure that they couldn't agree on anything – not even how to end their silly charade. Because they couldn't get their job done, spending will supposedly get cut by $1.2 trillion; that is $1.2 trillion more than anybody else has come up with. Failure is when these ninnies actually pass something – like Obamacare, for example; that is when the system lets us down. Because 9 times out of 10 what they pass is unconstitutional, and the tenth time it's bad policy.

C'mon. Does anyone seriously believe that any of these "automatic cuts" will ever happen? They don't kick in until after the next election, so a new Congress, one that is not bound by what this one pretended to do, will meet to decide which of the dozens of tunnels and ladders left for them in the debt ceiling bill to use to breach the "firewall of austerity".

We all know this: Mommy and Daddy are never going to work it out. They both want to be married to somebody else – anybody else. Us kids have fended for ourselves long enough that frankly we don't care if we never see either one of them again. I don't want to go to the circus anymore on Dad's weekend and Mom's home cooking tastes a lot like last week's KFC microwaved. Don't bother.

But here is a practical solution to the budget stalemate, if anyone cares anymore. Start with this: we have been taxed enough, and you don't get anymore taxes from the people who already pay them. Argue over how to spend it; that is the role of Congress in our system. If you want to spend more, then get the money from well-head taxes on new oil production and pipeline fees on the one they want to bring down from Canada.

You want to spend more? Fine – then give us cheap gas. You don't want us to have cheap gas and energy independence? Fine – then cut spending and go sequester yourself. Let us know what you decide.

Dear Occupiers

Dear Occupiers: You are absolutely right to fight against the corrupting influence of corporatism in our political system, but your 13 point demand list is a victory dance for the very guys you are drumming against.

Do you want to actually do something worthwhile? Then cut your list of demands down from 13 to just these 2: abolish the Federal Reserve and enact the FairTax.

The Government could not spend 60% more than it takes in without someone loaning them the money. Would you loan your own money to a deadbeat who had neither the wherewithal nor the intention of ever paying it back? Let me rephrase that. If you had any money, would you... And neither would the rest of the world, which has pretty much quit buying U.S. debt.

So the Federal Reserve steps in and prints money out of thin air, virtually gives it away to those Wall Street banks, which turn right around and loan it to the government at 3.7% interest at the Treasury auctions, a damn fine profit for the couple of nanoseconds it takes to process the two transactions on their servers. You can't rack up billions in profits one $2.00 ATM fee at a time, you know; people take too long to push the buttons.

And what do you occupationists' demand? Even more government spending - which means more borrowing, which means more counterfeiting of currency, which means more profits for the Wall Street banks, not less. They are secretly cheering you on behind those brass doors you are hollering at. And all that fiat money inflates the currency, raising prices and depressing real earnings. You would already be making a living wage if the Fed hadn't turned your dollars into dimes; your ideas turn them into pennies faster than they are headed already.

Here's an analogy the stoners among you might understand – it's not fair that your street dealer has such fine rims and a smoking hot girlfriend so your answer is demand even more addicts. Wrong. Abolish the drug cartel (Federal Reserve) and shrink the number of addicts (Government programs). Here's what will happen; drug prices drop (currency normalization) the girlfriend leaves (externalities) and the guy in the wife-beater has to make an honest living (real GDP growth). There is a little more to macroeconomics and monetary policy than that, but not enough to warrant taking out another student loan.

You are wasting your time on the wrong street, my friends. You aren't even in the right town, unless Timmy Geithner still has an office there. Go down to K Street in Washington D.C. if you want to stop corruption in politics. That's where all the lobbyists hang out, and that is where the actual corrupting takes place.

There are more than 14,000 lobbyists in D.C. and their job is to take the money from special interests (meaning the other guy's association, not mine) and spread it around to Congressmen and regulators, who gladly provide a return on that investment in the form of tax breaks, subsidies, boondoggle spending, and regulatory preferences, which further enrich the special interests, who give even more money to lobbyists, who spread it around like manure – and round and round it goes, getting deeper and deeper with each lap of the spreader.

Who do you think will put an end to it – those guys? The status quo is a win-win-win for the revolving door of special interests, lobbyists, and politicians sucking away at the public teat down on K Street. One day you're the nipple, the next day the lips; and the taxpayer gets milked – there's your moment of clarity.

Those Wall Street banks are just the errand boys that move cash from the Fed to the government to the special interests to the lobbyists to the regulators and campaigns of the folks desperate to operate the machinery for next four years. Rich errand boys to be sure, but errand boys nonetheless.

Want to put an end to the racket? Then join us to enact the FairTax – a national sales tax which replaces all other federal taxes and abolishes the IRS. With no tax breaks to give, there is no reason to lobby, and no purpose for the special interests. Just like the dealer with the spinners, everybody with their snout in the trough down on K Street has to go get honest work.

And we save $400 billion in compliance costs that the current tax system extracts from the economy each year. Hit the bong and contemplate that one for a moment; that is a $400 billion job stimulus - not just this year but every single year until hell freezes over. C'mon President Obama, say it just once, I double-dog dare you - "Pass This Bill!" I didn't think so; there is a campaign war chest to fill.

If abolishing the Federal Reserve and implementing FairTax is a little too radical for you (in which case I have no idea why you are reading this column), then Herman Cain's 9-9-9 tax plan and re-purposing of the Fed mandate onto sound money is the next best thing. Keynesians mock it and Arthur Laffer loves it; good enough for me. Mr. Cain's plan takes the best of the FairTax, the best of the Flat Tax, and levels the playing field for all businesses while improving our global competitiveness.

And if you want to close your own personal income gap, go occupy North Dakota. The place is busting out at the seams with the oil boom that is going on there; 3.4% unemployment and jobs going to the highest bidder. You lefties drew your line in the sand on fossil fuels – the unemployment line. If you want to make a living wage, put down your bongos and get your butts out to Williston.

We just lost Steve Jobs – my generation's Thomas Edison. The guy secured over 300 patents and unlike the politicians and charlatans who heap praise upon themselves, he did literally change the world. We lose phones with more computing power than the million dollar mainframe computers he liberated us from. And he got mad, silly, stinking rich doing it. Should we hate Steve Jobs because he climbed to the other side of the income gap? No, we should thank our dear Lord for him and people like him with each click of the mouse that he invented.

Dear occupiers: the liberals who have promised you hope and change don't have either to give you. You are waiting for a bus to prosperity that will never come. Start walking; you will be surprised how fast you can catch up.

Death and Taxes

Now that the Super Committee foolishness is behind him, President Obama can focus is full attention to the more serious business of blaming all of his failures on George W. Bush.

Let me say at the outset that I am no fan of George W. Bush. One of the worst things he ever did was attach his name to a sensible economic policy that worked. Yes, worked. I thought it might be useful to pre-empt the next year of carnival-barking with a number or two for my liberal friends who prefer their economics to be delivered to them in slogans.

Start with this one: the FY2003 budget deficit was $377 billion. The significance of that milestone is that it is the year when the Bush tax cuts were implemented. Four years later, in FY2007, the deficit had fallen to $161 billion. The deficit shrunk by 57.3% in the first four years of the Bush tax cuts; you will not hear that on TV, in schools, or on the campaign trail in the next 12 months. You're welcome.

And it didn't happen because of those famous "draconian spending cuts" Senators Clinton and Schumer made a fortune complaining to their base about back then. In fact, government spending *increased* over those four years by 26% - more than double the rate of inflation. Two wars, No Child Left Behind, Katrina, the Patriot Act, and Medicare Part D will do that for you. The deficit was reduced in spite of all that spending because tax receipts *rose* by 44%. That is what reducing tax rates on producers will do for you.

In FY2003 receipts were $1,782 billion, and in FY2007 they were $2,568 billion. Yes, MSNBC junkies, tax receipts went *up* when top rates went *down*; just like Arthur Laffer said they would. Go ahead and hate Bush as much as you want, but don't take it out on math.

And don't even call them the Bush Tax Cuts, as I can't imagine that he sat down one day by himself and wrote up changes to the tax code. He was not the only one who understands the difference between tax rates and tax revenues, and besides it is Congress, not the President, who levies taxes and controls spending. Amazing what you can find out when you actually read the Constitution.

Bill Clinton lowered capital gains rates (seriously, he did) and the resulting surge in tax receipts caused the balanced budget that

69

Democrats and Newt Gingrich now take credit for. Clinton knew what Margaret Thatcher, Ronald Reagan, and John F. Kennedy did – like the people who own it, capital will move to where it is punished the least. And capital formation is the necessary predecessor of job creation.

And if you don't like those stubborn facts about deficits during the Bush years, don't get mad at me; take your grievance to Office of Management and Budget – President Obama's OMB – who publish the numbers on actual receipts and actual outlays. Cash flow doesn't lie, and receipts and outlays are the bottom line of fiscal policy.

Tax-the-rich obsessive-compulsives will still complain that tax receipts fell as a percentage of GDP from 2003 to 2007 and they will be correct. But so what? Would you turn down a 44% raise because mine was 60%? The sad thing is, there are a whole lot of Americans who probably would; such is the state of the coveting class these days.

In case you missed it, Bush has already been punished by the voters. Too much spending, debt, and war weariness cost the Republicans both houses of Congress in 2006. Taking office in January of 2007, Nancy Pelosi and Harry Reid inherited a 14,000 point Dow, a 3.5% growth rate, and unemployment at 4.4%. They promised to do much better and they got their chance, starting with the FY2008 budget.

But they did not even wait for the budget process to begin; they announced their economic agenda right off the bat – increase taxes on the wealthy, increase taxes on corporations, cap and trade, card check, tariff increases, more government regulation, nationalization of health care, "green" mandates, restricting energy production, and commandeering the nation's student loan programs.

Their war on capitalism was declared while the movers were still hauling boxes in and out of the Capitol. Mission accomplished, to borrow a phrase. In FY2011, after four years of Pelosi/Reid budgets, the federal government's deficit is now $1.3 trillion - almost *ten times* what it was when they took over. 15 million Americans are unemployed.

So let's recap: Republicans controlled the House and Senate and enacted tax cuts; four years later their deficit was reduced by 57.3%. Democrats controlled the House and Senate and declared war on capitalism; four years later their deficit was increased by 819%. And they call George W. Bush dumb.

To be fair to the Democrats, the financial system melted down on their watch. And to be fair to Republicans, terrorists flew planes into buildings on theirs. Neither party asked for the trouble that dropped in their laps; none of us ever do. But we don't pay our elected officials to be lucky and we don't pay them to make excuses; we pay them to fix things.

President Obama's idea of fixing things is to repeatedly threaten to punish job creators by repealing the "Bush tax cuts". He creates investor uncertainty every time he opens his mouth and then he blames the investors for their risk-aversion. The President himself is the risk that investors are avoiding now, and many have finally come out and said so in recent weeks.

Here is what they know that the President apparently does not: the knife cuts both ways. If cutting the top selective tax rates increased tax revenues by 44% and reduced the deficit by 57%, then what do you think will happen when those tax rates are raised? That's right, revenues will plummet, the deficit – already obscene – will blow up even worse, and the economy will crater.

The $2 trillion that has accumulated on corporate balance sheets is not being hoarded to punish the working man; it is being saved for a time where it can be responsibly invested, when returns and risk can be reasonably estimated – in other words, when Mr. Obama is gone.

Here is the difference between political science and economics: mastery of the former will get you elected, while ignorance of the latter will get you a Presidential pension after just four years.

Don't Ask, Don't Tell

Many libertarians are pleased that the Defense Department's policy of Don't Ask, Don't Tell has been rescinded. I am not one of them; in fact, I was hoping that DADT would be expanded in scope to cover every single means of categorizing people for differential treatment, and expanded in breadth to bring every single department and agency in government to heel.

The Fourth Amendment specifically prohibits government snooping: "The right of the people to be secure in their persons, houses, papers, and effects, against unreasonable searches and seizures, shall not be violated."

Don't Ask.

And the Fifth Amendment specifically protects us from having to answer the government: "...nor shall be compelled in any criminal case to be a witness against himself..."

Don't Tell.

That is how liberty is supposed to work. They can't ask about gender, race, age, sexual preference, religious affiliation, party membership, health status, disability, business ownership, housing status, occupation, income, charitable contributions, source of income, place of residence, firearm ownership, vehicle choice, diet, intoxicant choice, number of children, insurance status, travel destination, vaccination history, or smoking preference. But they do anyway.

They can't ask us what's in our home, our cars, our boats, our tackle boxes, our computers, our phones, our pads, our emails, our phone calls, our mail, our diaries, our health records, our checkbooks, our account balances, our businesses, our transaction histories, our bank boxes, our churches, our clubs, our land, our pockets, our purses, our shoes, or our briefcases. But they do anyway.

Given the tens of thousands of laws, statutes, ordinances, and regulations that exist, it is hard to imagine what might *not* be a potential criminal case these days. One day you are a freeman making guitars at Gibson, the next day you are a criminal for doing exactly the same thing. How do you think the government knew how many trucks to bring when they shut that factory down? Who was forced to fill out all the forms that told them? We are being beaten with our own belts.

Think for just a moment about all of the personal information that the government has already accumulated about you; imagine how much more they will learn when your health records are "consolidated" under ObamaCare. We worry that identity theft may allow criminals to ruin our lives, yet they can access only a fraction of the information the Nannycrats in government have at their disposal. Membership in the entitlement society is not free; the cover charge is your liberty, the rent is your privacy, and the dues are collected in pride.

Article I, Section 8 of the Constitution lists the specific things that the federal government is empowered to do. Section 9 lists things the government is explicitly prohibited from doing. Section 10 prohibits the states from doing things we have assigned to the federal government, and the Ninth and Tenth Amendments prohibit the federal government from doing things reserved for the states and for the people. It is not complicated; unless, of course, you are a liberal judge.

Nowhere in the Constitution is the government permitted to ask without a specific cause and warrant, and everywhere we are protected from self-revelation. The whole document is a job description for a servant government, one who respects its masters' privacy and keeps its own mouth shut. The meanings of the words in that job description are plain; it is just that they mean things that people who seek unlimited government power to advance their own agendas wish weren't in there.

Go get your copy of the Constitution and read Article I, Section 8 again to see if you can find a single one of those enumerated powers that would require the government to profile us in order to do their job. Why would the feds need to track the calibers, serial numbers and clip capacities of our handguns – to maintain Postal roads?

The Don't Ask, Don't Tell policy was enacted to protect the rights of homosexuals who wished to serve in the military. DADT is the same policy that is applied to heterosexuals everywhere - except when your wife is trying to set up one of her girlfriends with your buddy who hates football, takes his shoes off in the house without asking, and wears socks that match his sweaters.

"Must Ask, Must Tell" is not the relationship between the citizens and their government that was envisioned by the framers of the Constitution. And that pesky little Constitution is the only thing standing between you and the people who wish to deprive you of your liberty in the name of their "public good". Every abuse of power ever undertaken was justified by some noble-sounding public purpose.

Don't Ask, Don't Tell will forever go down in the lexicon as a symbol of discrimination, and that is indeed unfortunate. It should be the battle cry of a new generation committed to restore the liberty their parents squandered in a fool's trade for the empty promises of an entitlement society whose benefits are unaffordable and a security apparatus that only keeps military spending safe.

Downward Wisconsin

We used to make things here in Wisconsin.

We made machine tools in Milwaukee, cars in Kenosha and ships in Sheboygan. We mined iron in the north and lead in the south. We made cheese, we made brats, we made beer, and we even made napkins to clean up what we spilled. And we made money.

The original war on poverty was a private, mercenary affair. Men like Harnischfeger, Allis, Chalmers, Kohler, Kearney, Trecker, Modine, Case, Mead, Falk, Allen, Bradley, Cutler, Hammer, Harley, Davidson, Pabst, and Miller lifted millions up from subsistence living to middle class comfort. They did it - not "Fighting Bob" La Follette or any of the politicians who came along later to take the credit and rake a piece of the action through the steepest progressive scheme in the nation.

Those old geezers with the beards cured poverty by putting people to work. Generations of Wisconsinites learned trades and mastered them in the factories, breweries, mills, foundries, and shipyards those capitalists built with their hands. Thousands of small businesses supplied these industrial giants, and tens of thousands of proprietors and professionals provided all of the services that all those other families needed to live well. The wealth got spread around plenty.

The profits generated by our great industrialists funded charities, the arts, education, libraries, museums, parks, and community development associations. Taxes on their profits, property, and payrolls built our schools, roads, bridges, and the safety net that Wisconsin's progressives are still taking credit for, as if the money came from their council meetings. The offering plates in churches of every denomination were filled with money left over from company paychecks that were made possible because a few bold young men risked it all and got rich. Don't thank God for them; thank them that you learned about God.

Their wealth pales in comparison to the wealth they created for millions and millions of other Wisconsin families. Those with an appreciation for the immeasurable contributions of Wisconsin's industrial icons of 1910 will find the list of Wisconsin's top ten employers of 2010 appalling:

Walmart, University of Wisconsin–Madison, Milwaukee Public Schools, U.S. Postal Service, Wisconsin Department of

Corrections, Menards, Marshfield Clinic, Aurora Health Care, City of Milwaukee, and Wisconsin Department of Veterans Affairs.

This is what a century of progressivism will get you. Wisconsin is the birthplace of the progressive movement, the home of the Socialist Party, the first state to allow public sector unions, the cradle of environmental activism, a liberal fortress walled off against common sense for decades.

There is no shortage of activists, advocates, and agitators in this State. If government were the answer to our problems, we would have no problems. The very same people – or people just like them – who picketed, struck, sued, taxed, and regulated our great companies out of this state are now complaining about the unemployment and poverty that they have brought upon themselves. They got rid of those old rich white guys and replaced them with...nothing.

Wisconsin ranks 47th in the rate of new business formation. We are one of the worst states for native college graduate exodus; our brightest and most ambitions graduates leave to seek their fortunes elsewhere. Why shouldn't they? Our tax rates are among the worst in the nation and our business climate, perpetually in the bottom of the rankings, has only recently moved up thanks to a Governor who now faces a recall for his trouble.

In 1970, the new environmental movement joined unions and socialists in a coordinated effort to demonize industry. When I was in college, the ranting against "polluting profiteers" was like white noise – always there. Here is the price of their victory: in 1970, manufacturers paid 18.2% of Wisconsin's property taxes – the major source of school funding - and in 2010 those who remained paid 3.7%.

So who is it that caused the funding crisis in our schools and the skyrocketing tax rates on our homes? It is the same ignoramuses who are sitting on bridges, pooping on things, and passing around recall petitions. The unemployed 26-year old in the hemp hat looking for sympathy might look instead to the biography of Jerome I. Case, who started his business at the age of 21, miraculously without an iPhone 4s.

Case got rich by asking people what they want and making it for them. He did not get rich by telling people what he wanted and waiting for them to do something about it. If you want to declare war on your own poverty, memorize that.

In the last decade alone we have lost 150,000 manufacturing jobs in this state – 25%. And it's not just jobs that have been lost; the companies that provided them are gone. The 450,000 people who still work in manufacturing in Wisconsin are now outnumbered by people who work for government. A significant number of the latter are tasked with taxing, regulating, and generally harassing the former. While it is true that many manufacturers chased low-wage opportunities on their own, many more were driven out of the state by the increasing cost of doing business here.

It is a myth that unions raise wages. If you consider only the 1,000 jobs in a closed shop, you might think an average union wage is, say, $30/hr. But if you add in the zero wages of the 10,000 jobs lost in companies chased out, the average of all 11,000 union workers is reduced to $2.72/hr. Do you know the average wage of union iron miners in this state? Zero. And the left is fighting hard to keep it that way in Northern Wisconsin. Looking out for the working man, they call it.

It is also a myth that free trade causes job losses. Over the past three years, U.S. manufacturers sold $70 billion more goods to our Free Trade Agreement (FTA) partners than we bought from them. Conversely, we suffered a $1.3 trillion trade deficit with countries where no FTA's exist. I doubt that kids are going to learn that in our government-union monopoly schools – it doesn't fit the narrative.

No one wants to see another person suffer in poverty, and liberty is the best economic policy there is. The great industrialists of Wisconsin took less than a generation to lift millions up to a life of dignity, pride, prosperity and good will. When enterprise was free and government was limited, we all prospered. Those great men of industry were not anointed at birth to be rich; they rose from nothing to great wealth through their own hard work and the value they added to their employees and their customers through choice, competition, and voluntary exchange. That is the only sure path to real prosperity; the debt economy is a temporary illusion.

Look again at the list of our famous industrialists and the list of our current employers. Who would you like your child or grandchild to grow up to be? Who do you think did more good on this earth – Jerome Case and his tractors, or the Coordinator of Supplier Diversity at MPS.

If you chose MPS, then apply now – that job is open, and it pays up to $72,000 plus benefits and early retirement. Save the world.

Eat My Peas

The next time somebody tells me we must all sacrifice to save our country, I am going to tell them, "eat my peas". Thank you, President Obama, for a great line.

First, let's get something straight - soldiers and sailors and marines and airmen sacrifice to save our country; nobody else does. This whole shared sacrifice thing is a crock - the cannibal demanding a shared sacrifice at dinnertime.

Where was the shared sacrifice when the businessman quit his job 30 years ago and double-mortgaged his home to take a chance on a dream? Did any teachers come and work in his firm during their summer off so that his wife and kids could have a week of proper vacation? Did anyone donate their savings so she would not have to work two jobs to support the family during those start-up years?

And who was it that shared the sacrifice of the medical school or law school student – did the IT tech at the Department of Motor Vehicles babysit for free so that single mom could sleep for a few hours before the bar exam? Who was their brothers' keeper back then, comrade?

Why are we only all in this together when the it-takes-the-village-people want to tax the dentists, doctors, lawyers, businesspeople, financiers, investors, entrepreneurs, inventors, visionaries, workaholics and all who have risen to the top of their professions into oblivion? Why do they wait 30 years and then come after our stuff?

And sacrifice for what? To cop an overused phrase, let me be clear: it is not the country they want to save, it's the government. More specifically, it is their cushy government jobs and their generous government pensions and perks. When any partisan says we all need to sacrifice, he or she is saying that *you* need to sacrifice so they don't. There's your moment of clarity.

Not them, not their team, oh no. They are victims, martyrs, lambs who have already been slaughtered. $100k per year to watch porn on the job and you want me to eat peas? GE doesn't pay a dime in taxes but you expect me to pitch in the other arm and the other leg? Eat *my* peas, buddy.

Shared sacrifice means we give and they take; that is the sharing formula. Last night I saw another ugly advertisement where the

Cannibal Party candidate in the Milwaukee area recall election told me we all have to share in the sacrifice. Eat my peas, lady.

I don't even know who you are, and I don't know the lady you are running against, but I know she was elected fair and square. This recall nonsense in Wisconsin is a farce – a union election, run by out of state union pimps. Anyone who has been through one knows the familiar feel.

They get enough signatures to call an election, use the NLRB (oops, GAB) to rig the rules in their favor, schedule it faster than the management side can react, bring in the goons and the cash from outside and then lie, threaten, bully, bribe and cheat to win at all cost. Been there, done that - won all four times.

How low will they go? How about paying kids to lie in advertisements? The very first one they ran in Milwaukee shows "local" kids blaming the pain that the Milwaukee teachers' union inflicted on its own members – layoffs, larger class sizes – to their opponent. The kids weren't even local, and the script was so bogus my dogs walked out of the room.

Using kids to spread lies – JFK would be so proud. What's next, some pre-teen crying in a wheelchair? "Alberta Darling eats children and she closed all of the schools so that my mommy would die." And when the director yells "cut", the little princess jumps out of the wheelchair, puts on a flannel shirt, grabs a fishing rod, tucks the pony tail under the cap and pretends to be a boy from Rhinelander: "Kim Simac sold all the hospitals and schools to the Taliban so they can ban country music and dump nuclear waste into the Wisconsin River."

"Paid for by friends of Agenda 21". Eat my peas, Soros.

A liberal apologist for those over-the-top ads said they are thought-provoking. Here's a thought - who in their right mind would spend millions to win a job that pays $49,000 per year? Or this - which did you lose first, your scruples or your marbles? And what on earth do they want to do to us that they want to win bad enough to force kids to lie? That's what those skanky ads made me think about.

As a Libertarian, I had fully intended to stay out of the Wisconsin recall fray. It is a purely partisan peeing contest that will have no impact; and as one of my Facebook friends keenly observed, Republicans' and Democrats' top priority is to punish each other. It's a stupid game, and I didn't feel like playing. Using kids to lie changed my mind.

So please, vote Republican, no matter who it is. Not because I love Republicans; I don't. But while Republicans are un-libertarian, Democrats are anti-libertarian. The modern-day Democrat Party stands for nothing; it is the party that pays kids to lie. It's the Government Party, seeking more government for the sake of more government. Watch their ads in the recall, if you can stomach the bullsnot, and tell me what they stand for, besides not being Scott Walker. And paying kids to lie.

We already did not-Scott-Walker. A decade of not-Scott-Walker left us $3 billion in the tank with the 4th worst business climate in the nation, 39% proficient schools, a smoking ban on private property, tax hikes every year, unilateral personal disarmament, some useless train cars, and a ban on organic milk sales in the Dairy State.

You want me to sacrifice some more for that? Eat my peas.

Fair Share

April is the month we all like to discuss who is not paying their taxes. If you watch MSNBC it's "millionaires and billionaires" and if your watch FOX it's "the bottom 47%". Either directly or by implication, their respective house-band pundits will tell us our nation is broke because their favorite someone-else did not pay their fair share.

For the record, the nation is not broke; our government is broke. It is our pool boy that can't pay his bills; not us freepersons who own the mansion. I know the pool boy has convinced his friends he owns the joint, but it is ours - the Constitution is our deed.

Let's be honest. It's not how much the rich pay in taxes in taxes that makes liberals' teeth grind, it's that they are too stinking rich in the first place. To liberal economists like Robert Reich and Paul Krugman, the increased concentration of wealth in the hands of a few in recent decades is proof positive that Republican economic policies have looted the middle class in order to enrich the wealthy.

Democrats, write this down: I agree with those guys completely on the numbers. I own it. Over the past 30 years, the top 1% of Americans increased their percentage of the nation's wealth; relevant statistics are sourced very well on Inequality.com website, one of yours. Surprised? Don't make assumptions about what others read.

But the fun begins when I ask for your theory of operation for *how* all that wealth was transferred from the "middle class" to "the rich". It is a serious and civil question and one of my favorites: just how did the money move from one of your bank accounts to one of theirs? That's what "concentration of wealth" means.

Here's how: U.S. household debt *doubled* from 60% of disposable income in 1975 to 127% in 2005, while the wealthiest 1% reduced their debt ratio by nearly 40%. Didn't that just suck: the rich got richer by lending us money. You can't make that sound evil even if you lace it with F-bombs or say it in drum.

The principle is easy to illustrate in the economy of two: we each start with $2,000 – no wealth gap. Then I borrow $1,000 from you for 10 years at 15% simple interest ($150 per year). At the end of the term, you will have $3,500 and I will have $500 –

82

wealth gap. Did you screw me over, you rich, capitalist shameshameshame?

No, you lent me the money I asked to borrow. A well-raised person would say, "thank you"; an ungrateful lout would hurl obscenities and demand you pay their taxes, too. Rather, rinse, repeat that borrowing for 30 years with boatloads of zeros and commas added and there you have it – the flow of wealth from the middle class to the rich.

Who else did you think was loaning you the money to buy that 4-head VCR you just hadda hadda hadda have - the kid calling in the authorization on the phone at Radio Shack? Did you think he was asking his mom to run over with $240 from his sock drawer to cover the till because he thought you were "good for it"?

Visa isn't a gift card from the Tooth Fairy; it is a handy little device that makes it unnecessary to drive all the way to Warren Buffett's house every time you want to buy another book at Borders. Don't blame him because you used it.

Would you rather swipe your card at the Walgreens and have the little box talk back to you, "Sorry, Susan, but Michael Moore can't live with himself any more over this whole wealth concentration thing. Put back the Gold Bond and ProActive and bring cash next payday...oh, and Right On!"

The rich got richer since 1975, true enough. And here is what else happened since 1975: Visa, MasterCard, Discover, American Express, Paychex, Check-N-Go, Countrywide, Lending Tree, Quicken Loans, GM credit, Ford Credit, GE Capital, Kohls, Menards, Best Buy, and all those barbarians in your wallet. The national savings rate plummeted from 10.1% to -2.1%. The financial services sector – i.e. the debt industry - is *double* the percentage of GDP as it was back then.

Six Presidents, three from each party; half of them increased taxes on the rich (Carter, Bush Classic, Obama) and half cut taxes (Reagan, Clinton, Bush Dance Remix). It may make us feel good to blame someone else for our economic circumstances, but the laws of economics don't know or care how we feel. Debt impoverishes the debtor; same as it ever was.

Barring true calamity, we choose our relative wealth for ourselves; and we move up or down the rankings as we discover how high is up for us. Some will deny that relative wealth is a choice; and in doing so they have already made theirs. Upward mobility is the gift of capitalism, but it does you no good unaccepted and unopened.

Libertarians oppose taxing income on principle, but until we convince the rest of the nation, the only practical way to tax income fairly is a flat and equal percentage, either when it is earned (Flat Tax), or as I prefer, when it is spent (FairTax). Our current tax system cannot be fixed by partisan tinkering; it must be scrapped and replaced, and the sooner the better.

Not paying taxes isn't enough to make you rich – ask the bottom 47%...or Wesley Snipes. You get rich by spending less than you earn, earning more than you did, and developing skills that people value highly. And yes, it is that simple.

Children, teach your parents by saving and investing – and stay out of debt. May you live long and prosper.

Fiat Math

I have finally figured out how to attain my ideal weight. I will have a council of economic advisors say that I am 6'4" tall, and a special commission report that I weigh 185 lbs. That's how the government does it – fiat math.

As long as I do not pass by a mirror in my clingy Under Armor or listen when you point at me and laugh, I can just pretend that my Keynesian diet plan – eating 1.6 trillion extra calories to stimulate my metabolism – is working. Besides, Joe Biden assured me I have already lost or avoided over 3 million pounds.

Last week was an especially bad week for the truth.

CBO reported that the $39 billion in Republocrat budget "cuts" described only a week earlier by President Obama as "historic" were 99% fudged. All that remains is for the *real* President - Ashton Kutcher - to jump out from under the podium, spin his hat around to the front, and yell "Punk'd!" Good one, Ashton.

It gets worse for those who shovel fictitious economic data for a living. Turns out that inflation, which we all knew is running over 10%, really *is* running at 10% if we count it as we did when I studied economics in college. And if we measure unemployment as we did back then, it is at 20%, give or take the margin of error. If I would have known we were going to have to do this for ourselves, I would have paid more attention in class; check that, I would have *gone* to class.

But government is sticking by its new and improved fiat math formula, calling unemployment at 8.8% and inflation at 2.1%. Add the two and those delivering the misery come up with a misery index of 10.9, while those on the receiving end are feeling the 30 points you get when you actually include unemployed people in the unemployment rate and things people buy in the inflation rate. I know, I know – hairsplitting.

And none of us knows what is happening with the money supply anymore, another one of those econ things we had to study by torchlight on our chiseled stone tablets. The Fed's answer to its critics was to simply stop reporting weekly M1-M6 a few years ago. The new procedure is for Congressman Ron Paul to sue the Federal Reserve, who loses and appeals up to the Supreme Court. Two years after the fact we finally get our chance to gasp in horror. Transparency.

But wait - there's more. A new study shows that women really make 8% *more* than men, turning 40 years of feminist propaganda and government EEOC policy on its head. And for the umpti-eth week in a row, the government's economic models forecasted the wrong number for new jobless claims - not even close. Finally, GDP was again oh-by-the-way revised downward from what was previously reported; a story so boring it doesn't even make the papers anymore.

Two words: toldya!

So let's recap: the government's smartest people, with unlimited funds and an army of minions at their disposal, do not know what government takes in or what it spends; do not know how many of us are working, what we earn, or what we produce; and do not know what things cost, or how much money they printed.

Those are the smartest people. The second tier of our know-betters rely on that lack of information to decide what we can buy, what we will pay for it, how much we can earn, how much we can keep, what we can weigh, drive, watch, read, learn, teach, carry on a plane, do with our cell phones, heat with, shoot, and a thousand other things that are none of their business.

And the third tier is getting ready to run for office again in 2012.

It should surprise no one that a government unable to count has made a mess of everything we have entrusted it to do. The only thing either Party remotely cares about is votes, and they can't even count them right. It goes straight downhill from there.

The only reform that will improve the federal government is to jettison large chunks of it. With all due respect to Congressman Paul Ryan, there was no need to develop a fiscal "roadmap" to save the nation; we already have one called the Constitution.

Start with a budget of zero, then take Article 1 Section 8 and add the amount needed to perform each of the enumerated powers; stop when you hit Section 9. There's your federal budget; about a quarter of what we are spending now, probably less.

Show me your plan to get *there*, leaders of either party, and I will support it. Until then, I'm with Joe Biden – let's just take a nap until they get serious. It is frankly offensive to be lectured by middle-aged adolescents about the other guys' "real" motivations. I'm quite certain Congressmen with autistic children do not secretly want to give them to billionaire cannibals for tax write-offs. And I doubt that the President's real goal is third world nation status; that would be the first thing he set out to do that is actually working.

The legitimate negotiations over the size and scope of the federal budget were completed when each and every member of Congress swore an oath to uphold and defend the Constitution. It's what they say next that makes clear just who it is she must be defended from.

Flavored History

California recently passed a law requiring public schools to teach gay history. The law has produced the predictable disproportionate reactions from the gloating left and the outraged right.

I myself am simply bewildered - what the heck is gay history? If a person's contributions were historically significant, then they will already be recorded in the history books. So does gay history mean simply going through the text and highlighting the people who were/are gay?

No, the state decrees that new content must be added, which means the purpose of the mandate is not simply to recognize the legitimate achievements of gay people, which would be fine, but to elevate accomplishments and add significance to events that historians have not accorded to them on the merits. Artificial flavor added.

Here is a touchy question for the gay historians of California: what will you say about Jeffrey Dahmer? And will children learn about Congressman Barney Frank's culpability in the collapse of our financial system? Will gay men be honestly cast as perpetrators in the AIDS epidemic? Will the scandal of gay pedophile priests in the Catholic Church be included? Are you telling the story or selling a movement?

Flavored history is not history; it is advocacy. The problem is not just that it promotes a slanted political agenda to vulnerable minds, but that it perpetuates the very segregation and discrimination it purports to overcome. Gay history - like black history, women's history, Hispanic history, union history, and any other of the flavored varieties – reinforces separateness, and separateness is what leads to hate.

American history, properly told, is the triumph of individual liberty over separateness. We are the melting pot. We are the nation that ended slavery. We are the nation that championed women's suffrage. We are the nation that institutionalized charity. We are the nation founded upon religious tolerance. We are the nation who faces and corrects our defects. Our history does not need artificial flavoring – it is pretty darn good right out of the tap.

In 1969, my American History text acquainted us with the historic contributions of Susan B. Anthony, Carry Nation, Abigail

Adams, Clara Barton, Amelia Earhart, Rosa Parks, Grace Hopper and dozens of other women who changed the course of American history. Their achievements inspired boys and girls alike.

By 1994, my son's American History text had been "improved" by a mandate to include "women's history". The first page of the now separate chapter on women was adorned with a picture of Marilyn Monroe. A text insert on her life was larger than the space devoted to Thomas Jefferson. Artificial flavor added.

The importance of historical figures is found between their ears, not between their legs. It is the uncommonly great ideas that change the course of human history, not the biological configurations and physical urges of the bodies that house those magnificent minds.

Being a woman is no accomplishment – one out of two people are; one in five is black; one in fifty is gay. A mind like Thomas Jefferson is one in a billion. Or how about Ayn Rand – her book, "Atlas Shrugged" has been named as the second most transformational in history after the Bible.

Did my son learn about Ayn Rand in "women's history"? No, he learned about Ayn Rand from me. I hope he learned a lot of other things from me – including that we should treat each and every person with equal respect and kindness, regardless of their race, gender, age, orientation, disability, or parent's wealth.

I hope he learned that collective victimhood is a choice, and that inequality of outcome is proof that equality of opportunity exists. I hope he learned that success is achieved through hard work, good character, a positive attitude, and a commitment to excellence. I hope he learned to admire real achievement, and to celebrate, not covet, the success of others.

I hope he learned that liberty is a birthright from God and not a grant from government. I hope he learned that charity is its own reward; that humility will be thrust upon those who do not impose it upon themselves; that each of us will be remembered for what we did and not for what we hoped someone else would do.

I hope he learned all that from me; because he did not learn it in public school.

Several years ago, I was invited to sit in on the annual faculty meeting of a large public university. The keynote speaker encouraged them to imbed overtly anti-capitalist teachings into each and every one of the courses they taught, and he received a standing ovation for this blatantly unethical idea.

Not just flavored history, but flavored mathematics, astronomy, psychology, accounting, nursing, physics, art, and even flavored business administration. Everything flavored with Marxist propaganda – "look there kids, that is the big-oil-is-bad dipper".

When I asked afterwards why Marxist philosophy should not be confined to political science, history, or economics curricula where it seemed more appropriate, the response was, "the objective is to imbed ideas, not to debate them".

That was an honest answer. Propagandists and ideologues are not interested in debate; nor are they interested in truth, tolerance, accommodation, balance, objectivity, proportion, or rationality. They are only interested in forcing your acceptance of their belief system. Key word: force.

Forced conformance is not education, and those who indoctrinate are not educators. Opponents of indoctrination do not hate gays, women, or minorities; we have long ago cleansed our souls of discrimination and prejudice. Try as some might to project their own vile thoughts into our heads, we won't waste our time on their unresolved guilt. That angers them.

It is said that a mind is a terrible thing to waste – especially on self-indulgent ideologues and self-absorbed bureaucrats. History is history. The truly historic achievements of individuals *of all flavors* stand on their own merits; no embellishment is necessary.

Forgive Us Our Debts

Congressman Ron Paul has identified the best solution to the debt ceiling crisis by calling out a central fallacy of our national debt - $1.6 trillion of it is owed to the Federal Reserve, an arm of the government for all intents and purposes.

Forgive the debt to the Fed, says Rep. Paul, and we get our borrowing line back without raising the debt ceiling or a tax hike. Simple.

Those who think Congressman Paul's idea is whacky should say the alternative out loud: the government owes money to itself, so it pays interest to itself, which is returned to itself. But rather than forgive itself its debt to itself, it will require itself to pay itself, plunging the world into chaos and destroying the dollar.

Now who sounds like a wing-nut? But Congressman Paul's simple solution does not have a snowball's chance in hell. Why? Because twads run our government.

"Twad" is a densely compacted contraction of the words "nitwit" and "dickwad". It is not an economic term; it is something I learned up North in the 5th grade. We were not allowed to cuss, so our vocabulary of creative slurs is quite highly developed.

Speaking of twads, when it was time to enrich his UAW buddies in 2009, President Obama didn't hesitate for a second to repudiate the debts Chrysler owed to its bondholders. Those were billions of real losses he inflicted on real citizens back then, but now when it's the Fed he won't even consider what amounts to an internal bookkeeping entry.

The Federal Reserve is off limits because it is the vehicle that enables excessive government spending and debt; it is the President's no-limit credit card and he has no intention of ever cutting it up. Neither do the rest of the twads; they are all promising to go on a fiscal diet in ten years while ordering the cheesy fries now.

The Fed and Treasury are the right and left hands of monetary policy run amuck; they are like two children who lent billions in monopoly money to each other and are now demanding that Mom and Dad pay them real-money interest before we pay the light bill. Or in the President's case, before we send social security checks to seniors.

91

Who didn't see that one coming? Debt addiction withdrawal causes some mighty ugly and bizarre behavior. The Democrats now claim to have discovered a right to borrow and spend without Congressional approval in the 14th Amendment of the Constitution. The bizarre part is that they found a copy of the Constitution.

Launching a stealth operation that would make Seal Team Six proud, they helicoptered right over the hostile territory of the enumerated powers in Article I, Section 8; and dodged the suppressing fire of the first, second, fourth, fifth, ninth, and tenth amendments; and scaled the wall of the first three sections of the 14th itself to snatch up just six words from the whole of section four before returning to base to cobble up perhaps the stupidest argument in the history of argument.

They claim that that the disconnected phrases "public debt" and "shall not be questioned" give the President unlimited borrowing authority. The chunk they cut out in their truthendectomy contains the qualifier, "authorized by law", which is more than a little significant since they are debating the law that would...um...authorize debt. Still think "twads" was a bit harsh?

We better not let them get anywhere near the Lord's Prayer, or it will come out "Father...lead us...into...evil...forever, Amen." And speaking of religion, Congressman Charles Rangel claimed that Jesus would weigh-in on the Democrat side of the debt ceiling debate had He returned to walk among us this summer.

Now, I hate to break it to you, Tax Cheat Charlie, but Jesus is more likely to descend in glory to spank your bony ass all the way back to Harlem for taking His name in vain than He is to fly wingman for President O-bysmal's fiscal insanity.

"Forgive us our debts" does not mean what you think it does, Congressman, and the IRS won't forgive yours even after the Rapture comes. If you were trying to scare them off by name-dropping the big J, you don't know your tormentors very well.

Here is a simple-guy question: if that trillion dollar stimulus was a one-time investment to get the economy moving, then why can't the President cut spending by a trillion dollars this year? He said it worked, and doesn't one-time still mean less than two times?

President Obama told us that he had to reluctantly add a trillion dollars of one-time spending in 2009 to make up for the stupid mistakes of the guy who was President the year before. Since he now says we have to spend more than that every single year through the end of his second term, I presume he has concluded he is even more stupid than his predecessor and plans to remain that way every year.

Who am I to argue with the judgment of the President of the United States?

And you can throw in that gang of six, the leadership of both parties in both chambers, and the front runners for the GOP Presidential nomination. These guys are all unserious about cutting spending, shrinking government, and reducing the debt. They want to finagle some pixie-dust "framework" that dupes the talking heads (not too difficult an assignment), and then get back to the important work of fund-raising and earmarks.

The only budget that matters is the next one - Fiscal Year 2012, which begins October 1. Cancel your August vacation and balance that one, twads.

Friend or Foe

A single day does not pass that I do not receive many e-mails telling me that one or the other of the Republican candidates for President is an imposter to his/her cause - not really a conservative or not really a libertarian, as the case may be. It is frankly very annoying.

The tactic is ineffective, and the underlying premise – that political piety exists – is deeply flawed. Political orientation is not digital - 1 or 0, left or right, approve or disapprove. Think of it as a continuum with utopian socialism anchoring one end and utopian libertarianism at the other.

Each of us first chooses one of those directions - State or Self – and then discovers a comfortable destination along the route we travel in search of our core beliefs. Our resting places have names - progressive, liberal, moderate, blue-dog, centrist, neo-con, conservative, paleo. Those fixated on labels will drill even deeper, pursuing their happiness by defining sub-categories of sub-categories of sub-categories.

Too many of us judge each others' politics by the absolute distance between our places on the spectrum. This seems unnecessarily divisive and is mostly counterproductive. Some hairs are too fine to split, and purity exists only in the mind of the purist. No two people will agree on every single issue unless both have surrendered their brains to an ideology they have memorized.

Years of living over here on the libertarian lunatic fringe have taught me to define others by the direction of their steps, not by the number it would still take for them to reach me. If I can see your face as you travel, you are my friend; if you have turned your back on me we will be adversaries. These days, when each election is a virtual referendum on the Constitution, it does not have to be much more complicated than that. It's ok for conservatives and libertarians to be good neighbors; we don't have to be family.

Free trade, limited government, individual liberty, private property - is there any conservative or any libertarian who does not embrace these four principles? More importantly, is there a single liberal, progressive, or socialist who does not oppose them all? The choice of trajectories is so starkly opposite that such surgical sub-species labeling as "neo-progressive post-libertarian anarchist" serves no practical purpose. But if you are one of these, I hope it makes you happy.

We already know there will be a Democrat incumbent President running for re-election in 2012 who hails from the left-most nether regions of the spectrum. We know he is an anti-capitalist, a statist, an internationalist, an anti-constitutionalist and an interventionist. We know that we will never see his face from where we stand; he will never travel in this direction. Not ever.

We know that he fears liberty enough to extinguish it; what we don't know yet is who liberty will choose to defeat him.

While we each may have a preferred candidate among this year's lineup of challengers for the Presidency, it is foolish to think our favorite can win our country back by tearing down the others. To imagine our guy or gal is the only one who can lead a nation of self-sovereigns is to deny self-sovereignty at its essence. We are not electing a savior; that position has been filled for all eternity.

The first primary is still months away. The process of nomination is long and arduous for a reason; it will show us what we don't know now about each of those who seek the office. It is a contest that must be played out, not a coronation ritual staged for TV ratings months before the first vote is cast.

We will discover the true character of the candidates. We will observe their leadership style in the management of their campaigns. We will judge their stamina, consistency, and temperament. We will see how they handle disappointment, victory, deception, unfairness, adulation, and defection. We will watch to see if their positions can mature without abandonment of principle. We will study their gaffes, their recoveries, their missteps, and their strategic prowess. We will see them get angry, and judge them by what they get angry about. We will watch them gloat and judge them by what they gloat over.

Those of us who have left the Republican Party should not tell it how to pick its standard bearers. But we should remind our GOP friends that they cannot win elections on their own. They will need all of us tea partiers, independents, Libertarians, Constitutionalists, patriots, and disaffected Democrats to secure their victories.

And we will not blindly support whoever they select; fitness for office is more than simply being the least unfit in the herd. If a third-party candidate draws large numbers of votes in 2012, it will be the fault of the GOP fielding a bad ticket that could not win us over.

Republican activists working on campaigns are not making that job easier on themselves by sending out daily emails telling us what a lying, corrupt, unprincipled poser this or that one of their rivals is. At this point, any one of them could find themselves at the top of that ticket, and words are not so easily eaten in the internet age.

President Obama has proven that you cannot lead this nation on a last-guy-bad platform. All of the GOP challengers have said they would repeal Obamacare on their first day in office – we get that. If they want to move up in the polls, they should start talking about day two.

Generic Marriage

Considering that the media refuses to cover Ron Paul's campaign and has stoned Gary Johnson from any airtime at all, it is understandable that most Americans are unaware of the growing split in the libertarian community between the supporters of the congressman and former Governor, the two libertarian candidates in the race.

Yeah, I know, a split among libertarians is like civil war in Lichtenstein, but even a single cell must divide for an organism to grow. We don't get too many chances at this multiple candidate stuff, so cut us some slack, ok?

It is getting a little nasty, and the central issue seems to be Congressman Paul's refusal to support federal gay marriage legislation. To some libertarians, support for legislated gay marriage has become a litmus test, with those who oppose it relegated to some impure un-libertarian designation, "paleo-conservative" being the most popular. At the risk of being so branded, I don't think this is the right issue to purge our ranks over.

For thousands of years, across all cultures, religions, and government forms, the understanding of marriage and family has been unchanged. Marriage is a sacrament in many religious traditions, a union ordained by God. It does not seem to be a matter for our current government to define what it is or it isn't. And legislating gay marriage is exactly that - government re-defining for the people what marriage is.

Libertarians reflexively object to government imposing itself into private matters, so it is difficult to understand how this issue has come to drive a wedge into a movement which is way too small to be dividing itself up. I don't see any conflict in defending the individual rights of gay people (I do) while opposing a legislated redefinition of a term that has had one universal meaning since the beginning of time (I also do). We would not redefine the word "children" because some kids want to live at the neighbors.

Our founding fathers, the classic liberal philosophers, and the icons of libertarian thought in the last century – none of those great libertarian thinkers, as far as I know, advocated legislated gay marriage. Are they un-libertarian? Do we now disown them? Its not like homosexuality was just invented by Elton John – they must have thought about it back then. And, perhaps like me, they came down on the side of none of my business, live and let live, don't ask don't care.

I get the whole disparity of government benefits thing, but that is a problem of unconstitutional and unjustifiable bloated government benefits. When black people were denied jobs by law, the remedy was not to add another federal law that redefined the meaning of white. We changed the labor laws that caused discrimination.

As far as I know, there is no law that prohibits any religion from sanctioning same-sex marriage now. If two men or two women want to get married, they can find a church and a minister perfectly happy to oblige. There – you're married. Whether it is a blessed sacrament or an abomination to the Lord is up to you and Him; neither Ron Paul or Gary Johnson or any other candidate have a say about that.

You don't get any more married because the government writes it down on a piece of paper. And if you think that county clerk's stamp on a license is what keeps heteros together, spare your friends the cost of the his-and-his bath towels and fancy wedding card, because you guys won't outlast the warranty on the toaster. When even the threat of Hell-fire can't keep the wrong pants from dropping in unison, don't expect a dusty paper in a safety deposit box to inspire fidelity.

Let's try and solve this. Enact FairTax so there are no tax ramifications of being married or not being married. And give every adult person the right to designate a single co-owner of assets and property rights, including succession in death – a turbo POA, basically. Married people will designate their spouse or test that succession process, I suspect. We already have child custody arrangements figured out for every conceivable configuration short of invertebrates; no more laws are needed.

Now what's the problem? And we all know the real answer: there is a militant homosexual agenda whose advocates use government to force acceptance of a lifestyle that a majority of Americans find immoral. Let's quit pretending this is an argument about something else. And using government force to impose moral judgments is inherently un-libertarian. Our government did not define marriage; it is not compelled to re-define it.

Here is the basic problem for generic marriage: if the gender of the partners in a marriage is unimportant, then why is the number? Is 3 ok? 5? A couple of these, a few of those? And

98

what is magic about 18 years of age, or 17, or 16 or younger? Brothers, cousins, moms, daughters, moms and daughters – if we can't leave the line where it has been drawn for millennia, then why is it ok to draw a new one?

Reasonable people can disagree about where to draw the boundaries of marriage without being haters. But it is no less libertarian to support a traditional definition of marriage than it is to draw the line anywhere else along the spectrum of possible unions. It is certainly not an issue to tear a movement apart that is finally gaining some mainstream traction.

So let's not tear ourselves asunder over this one, libertarians. And go easy on my man Ron Paul – he was liberty's only friend for a long, long time.

Goodbye

Joanne Kloppenburg announced she would not challenge the results of the recount of her defeat in the April election for a seat on the Wisconsin Supreme Court in the courts. Here is the significance her decision: none.

The recount was an insignificant event, and she is an insignificant person - an empty vessel with a shiny surface that reflected the unionists' hatred for Governor Scott Walker back to them. That was the glow; there never was anything more to it.

The Kloppenburg saga captures perfectly the essence of what so many of us find most objectionable about the state of affairs of our politics these days: insignificant people we don't care about get in our face and stay there 24/7. Should we be grateful to Ms. Kloppenburg that the beatings have stopped? Sure. Thanks. Bye.

Most of us are not political crack-heads, jonesing for our daily fix of victimhood, partisan spin, overhype, and payback. We prefer to focus on our families, homes, businesses, jobs, neighborhoods, churches, clubs, hobbies, schools, sports teams, meals, clothes, entertainment, charities, and friends.

Here is how this is supposed to work; candidates campaign for a job and then we vote on who gets it. Voting is the end of the job interview; you got the job or you didn't. Go fix a bridge if you won, and go lay by your dish if you lost. Either way, just leave us alone until the next time we have to decide who will represent us.

We are sick of the relentless drama. It started in 2007 with the contest between Hillary and Barack, then their fight over Florida and Michigan delegations, which ran us right into the Presidential campaign, which flipped immediately to GM bailouts and trillion dollar stimulus, which bled right into a whole year of health care, which fired up the Tea Parties until the 2010 elections were upon us, which ran right into the lame duck session and tax showdown and...

[We interrupt this rant to thank the Green Bay Packers for their fantastic playoff run and Super Bowl victory, which gave us a one month reprieve from the self-absorbed crack-head pols and the coverage of their machinations by the pom-pom press.]

...then on to Walker's Budget Repair Bill and six weeks of insanity and paralysis at the Capitol and then the Supreme Court election in April, which should have been a yawner but instead we endured Scylla and Charybdis bombarding us day and night, and then the mistaken count, and then the real count, and then the canvass, and then the recount, and then the wait for the decision on the court case, and then it will be the recalls and then it will be time to crank it all back up again for 2012. The partisan bickering is not amusing anymore; it is exhausting.

The libertarians' best argument for much less government is made every day by the incompetence and insincerity of the big-government advocates in both parties who fiddle and futz and waste money they do not have on things that do not matter. Like, for example, a recount that never had a prayer.

I don't hate anyone, including Joanne Kloppenburg. What I hate is that Ms. Kloppenburg, and people like her, force me to stay engaged in the political process day after day when I have 100 more productive things I would rather be doing.

I hate it that I have to defend my rights from the very people I pay to protect them. And I hate it that I have to explain my rights to someone who came within a whisper of sitting on the Court that is my last line of defense in this state.

I hate it that young people discover truths about liberty in my column that they were not taught in school. I hate it that journalists are so biased and ignorant that I have to read eight papers to get a fair idea of what is going on in this world. I hate it that people who don't work claim to speak for those of us who do.

I hate it that Joanne Kloppenburg made her problem our problem and indulged her appetite for a vendetta at our expense. I hate it that she was the best the Democrat Party could come up with to sit on the Supreme Court. And I hate it that the Republican's best candidate could only beat her by a few thousand votes.

Goodbye, Ms. Kloppenburg. Thank you for exiting the stage. Please stay gone.

Good Riddance

There isn't a lot left to say about the killing of Osama Bin Laden last Monday by U.S. Special Forces. "Good riddance" for him; "thank you" to them.

Today, I attended the christening of the U.S.S. Michael S. Murphy, named in honor of the Navy SEAL who won the Congressional Medal of Honor for heroism in Afghanistan. Lt. Murphy was a warrior; he died fighting enemy soldiers in battle. Osama Bin Laden was a coward; he died hiding after sending boys on suicide missions to kill civilians.

The media's post-game obsessions with details of the mission this week have ranged from irrelevant to asinine. The Obama administration has bungled the release of information on the raid as ineptly as humanly possible, but so what? What is the difference how he died, when he died, what he was carrying, who was with him, how long it took, what caliber the bullets were, how he was buried, how the DNA was matched or where the pictures are?

Bin Laden killed Americans for personal glory and we finally found him and killed him; the rest is noise. We should neither celebrate nor apologize for exercising our right of self-defense. Bin Laden signed his own death warrant many times over by killing innocents on five continents for over two decades. He recognized no legal authority on the planet, so justice has not been denied by delivering him to the Judge of us all.

Why does the left fret over the message it might send to the world if we say this or that or do thus or such now that he is gone? Here is your message, world: we will spend whatever it takes and do whatever it takes for as long as it takes wherever it takes to defend ourselves. Just know that.

And know this, too: 3 billion other unarmed humans were *not* killed by U.S. Special Forces on Monday. Those of us who do not spend our time blowing up Americans have nothing to fear from SEAL Team 6 – they are not coming for me next just because I write a blog that is critical of their Commander-In-Chief.

When we killed the Somali pirates, there was no orgy of speculation, no weeklong frenzy of hand-wringing and bed-wetting; just relief that the bad guys were taken down without casualties on our side. Piracy on the high seas and terrorism are similar threats to our security in that non-state actors prey on innocents from sanctuaries beyond the reach of sovereign legal systems and the international treaties that set the boundaries of conventional warfare.

Our defensive capabilities must also extend beyond sovereign legal systems and wartime conventions. And yes, it is disturbing to know that small and secretive lethal forces are necessary to keep us safe. It is far more disturbing to keep sending standing armies to occupy foreign nations as our only means of response. Even more disturbing to be defenseless, trusting that lawyers torturing the meaning of words in court to maximize their billings might somehow deter the guys in foreign lands who are planning to blow us up. Naïve becomes stupid when implemented.

It is not anti-libertarian to defend ourselves when we are attacked; the means by which we do so are not for others to choose. The time to ponder the consequences of killing American civilians is before, not after, aggression is initiated. If you don't want us to trespass into your yard, Mr. Pakistan, then don't hide the wolf that ate our children in your garden shed. Get it? Diplomacy is only complicated to diplomats.

What is the backlash we fear from the killing of Osama Bin Laden? Will the bombs of radical Islamists take our oil wells out of production? Our Department of Interior beat them to the punch. Will Al Qaeda do something to destabilize our currency? The FED is way ahead of them. Could we be assaulted in airports? TSA even has a manual for how to do it. The greatest threat to our liberties works in cubicles, not caves.

We can honor the lives lost in 9/11 and on the battlefields of Afghanistan and Iraq by reclaiming the liberty we have given up in the name of the war on terror, the liberty we have given up in the name of economic crisis, and the liberty we have given up in the name of "social justice". It is our freedom that Osama Bin Laden hated; it was our lives, our liberty, and our pursuit of happiness that he sought to take from us.

Men like Lt. Michael S. Murphy remind us that this is still the home of the brave; let us honor their service by making it once again the land of the free. That is victory.

Greatly Disturbed

Planned Parenthood has been defunded by four states, igniting the shovel-ready protests of the abortionist lobby, which called the budget actions (yawn) a "war on women".

Well, half-right. It's actually just a war on women who feel entitled to a do-gooder merit badge on somebody else's dime.

Teri Huyck, President of Planned Parenthood Advocates of Wisconsin, issued a statement which said, "It is greatly disturbing to me that some politicians' personal beliefs are trumping our shared responsibility to make sure women and men have access to reproductive health care…" blah, blah, blah.

Just stop it.

First of all, there is no shared responsibility to provide access to reproductive health care or any other product or service – none whatsoever.

Secondly, the personal belief at work here is the personal belief of Ms. Hyuck that you and I are obligated to pay for someone else's abortions. Not.

Thirdly, it was not "some politicians", that voted to cut funding for Planned Parenthood, it was a majority of the legislators elected by the people.

So apparently what is "greatly disturbing" to her is that duly elected representatives "trumped" her personal belief in a budget priority decision. How dare they?

I would suspect what is really bugging Ms. Huyck and her pals is that she knows voluntary donations will not be enough to pay her salary and provide the budget for "advocacy" that gets her name in the papers. Without a public subsidy, her profession is unsustainable. They must not tell them that in advocacy school.

Priorities become evident in crisis; Planned Parenthood's response to reduced funding has been to keep its abortion clinics open and increase spending on political advocacy, while closing clinics that perform those other health services they try to lay the guilt trip on the rest of us with. That is how much they care about cancer screening, teen counseling and low-income women.

Conservatives want to defund Planned Parenthood because it is the nation's largest abortion provider. Libertarians want to defund Planned Parenthood for all the other things it does. Liberals want to increase funding for Planned Parenthood on principle – the principle that liberals are entitled to always get their way on someone else's money.

The idea that government is obligated to provide "reproductive health care" is ludicrous – there is no right to any product or service. There is, however, an explicit right to bear arms – so why aren't Ms. Hyuck and her fellow professional advocates out there marching to get me the Beretta that I deserve? Why are there no ammo clinics? Huh? Huh?

Better yet, try this minor change to her statement: "It is greatly disturbing to me that some politicians' personal beliefs are trumping our shared responsibility to make sure women and men have access to Tim Nerenz' new book, *Capitalista!*

What's that you say? People have to buy it themselves? The state won't give them one on demand? Damn you, Scott Walker and your War on Reading! I am greatly, greatly, greatly disturbed! Where's my drum? Recall them all!

This whole "it takes a village" crap of the shared-responsibility left is asinine. Look where it got Africa, where the saying originated. The continent with the most natural resources on the planet is also the poorest, the sickest, the most corrupt, the most violent, and the least free. That's what you get when the individual is surrendered to the collective.

For the first 50 years of its existence, Planned Parenthood somehow managed without public funding. It was not until 1970 that Richard Nixon opened the door for them to get their snouts in the public trough - as if we needed one more reason to dislike the guy.

And no surprise, government intervention into the family planning business has been an unmitigated disaster. Teen pregnancy rates have shot through the roof, illegitimacy is the norm, STDs are rampant, and tens of millions of lives have been aborted. The institution of marriage has been weakened, and all manner of social pathologies have been the result. If that's what planning does, give me chaos.

Before there was government, there was scorn. Avoiding shame was how families were planned, along with those old-fashioned notions of love and commitment and sacrifice.

It worked a lot better and it was free. The consequences of sex were the responsibility of the two participants; not a village, and not a line item in a state budget. It was shameful to get knocked up, or to do the knocking, or to contract a disease, or have to endure the smirks at a shotgun wedding.

Boys had bad ideas and girls had the final say; it was a sneak preview of married life. For most teenagers, it was our introduction to personal responsibility on a major scale – the first problem mom and dad could not fix; our first life-changer.

For thousands of years, billions of people have figured out the dynamics of love, sex, child-rearing, families, and health without the need for professional advocates funded by government. We amateurs have done much better at it with the help of our families, churches, friends, and neighborhoods, frankly.

Getting government out of the family planning business is a good thing. That's one down and about a thousand other industries to go. Let the whining begin.

Great Teachers

The ultimate libertarian solution to the education crisis is to abolish government-run schools altogether; in the meantime, we can improve public schools, and it is not as difficult as the entrenched education bureaucracy has made it out to be.

First, abolish the federal Department of Education and the state Departments of Public Instruction. Next, cut funding from the current roughly $11,000 per student we pay now down in Wisconsin to $8,000. You're welcome, taxpayers.

Divide that sum equally between the teachers and the principal. With a nominal class size of 30 students, a teacher's baseline salary would be $120,000. You're welcome, teachers.

Then multiply the teacher's base salary by the rate of student proficiency he/she produces as measured by standard testing. We're not talking straight A's here, just proficiency. You're welcome, suddenly proficient students.

A teacher that produces 100% proficiency would earn $120,000; a teacher that achieves only 40% proficiency would earn only $48,000. Both would be compensated fairly. You're welcome, good teachers; talk to the hand, bad teachers.

Here's the tricky part: the balance of their unpaid baseline is rebated to the parents...*of the kids who were proficient.* Call it No Parent Left Behind: either take responsibility for your kids' education or pay more. You're welcome, responsible parents.

And to you irresponsible parents: you have been dragging the rest of us down for too long. Shut up, man up, and get your kids educated. Do your job.

Did I mention teachers must pay their own retirement savings and health care costs? A married couple of great teachers would earn $240k; they can afford it. If they can handle a class size of 35 they could bring home $272k. Teachers will be drumming for the Bush tax cuts to be permanent.

And don't tell me a good teacher can't make 35 kids proficient. Mrs. Lindroth did it in Ironwood with a bunch of un-medicated, demonic 6th graders in 1966. Back then, she did it without teachers' aides or social workers or iPads. She taught and we learned; that was the division of labor.

But what about the teachers' unions? What about the conventions? What about the masters' degrees? Knock yourself out, teachers; you can spend their own money on anything you think will improve your skills. Who better to judge the return on investment than the teacher making the investment?

The other $4,000 goes to the principal to run the school. A school with 300 kids will get a baseline budget of $1,200,000 to pay administrators, maintenance, and facility expenses – capital budgets will be handled separately via bond resolutions. The principal gets a salary of $120k plus half of whatever he/she saves from the budget baseline. You're welcome, principals.

Just like the teachers, principals' baseline salary is reduced according to the aggregate proficiency of the school. That's what prevents greedy and stupid cost gutting; overhead will not be cut if it legitimately improves proficiency. You're welcome again, proficient students.

So there you have it, teachers - compete for your salary like the rest of us. Your income will be based on your ability to get those kids to perform, just like ours is when they come to work in our factories and firms after you are done with them.

I think most of you are great teachers and would quickly max out if we got the government and your unions off your back and out of your classroom. That is, if you are reading this you are great; the slackers are off sulking and whining about how bad they got it under Walker.

Screw 'em; the slackers have run the show for long enough. They will quit after the first year their pay is cut, and then we will be done with them for good. You're welcome, everyone. That will make room for someone with talent and passion that actually wants to teach. Oh, yeah, and make $120k with summers off. Teaching will attract the best and brightest again. Competition will bring out the best in everyone; it always does.

While monetary incentives may seem crass and unseemly to education elitists, they work. That is the only reason we use them to drive improvements in business performance. And to be blunt, good intentions haven't done squat for public education; a half century of steady decline in world rankings tells us so.

Great teachers deserve great compensation, and so do great administrators. And we all deserve great schools; especially our children, whose success in life will be no greater than the proficiencies and values we have equipped them with. How do

108

you improve educational proficiency? Pay for it. And don't pay for anything else.

Does anyone think a better plan will come from the protest tents surrounding our state capitol this summer? From the federal Department of Education? From the Department of Public Instruction? From the Governor's office? From the Legislature? From WEAC? From any school board or superintendent in the State?

Me neither. That is why ultimately, we need to get the government out of the education business altogether and let choice and competition work the magic. In the meantime, let's pay for proficiency and not lose another generation to ignorance.

Hate-baiters

Liberals call conservatives many things: racists, heartless, greedy, selfish, sexist, homophobic, and now...haters. Last week a popular liberal blogger announced that calling conservatives haters will be the Democrats election strategy in 2012.

Like most other things, the standard for hating has been dumbed-down in recent times; it used to be that you had to actually hate someone to be a hater. Nowadays all it takes is to oppose increased funding for any government program, or in the case of DADT, merely oppose a policy, or in the case of the Tea Party, merely gather.

And if conservatives are haters simply for what they believe about government, then we libertarians must be drooling, vein-popping ragers. We don't just hope to restrain government programs; we would prefer that most of them be abolished altogether.

Sure – I'm a hater. I hate ignorant talk like calling people haters for no reason. I hate the partisan demagogues who profit from peddling such blatant nonsense. I hate the stifling of speech, the intimidation of opponents, and the suppression of dissent that the hater-card is intended to accomplish. I hate the arrogance that Statists display by playing it.

How weak is the mind that would conclude the only possible explanation for policy disagreement must be an opponent's hatred for whole classes of people? How blithering must be the idiot who can see only two possible sides in a debate – his own and you-are-hater? How flimsy must the case be when the best argument to support it is "you hate". How dreadfully stupid must be the second-best?

Yes, my dear Govbots - it is possible to question government programs without hating people. A transition from Social Security to private ownership of retirement accounts would increase pension income six-fold; why would we advocate for it if we hated old people? Or why do we work for school choice if we hate children and parents?

Why defend the right to carry if we hate the people who live in the most dangerous neighborhoods? Why fight for sound money if we hate poor people living on fixed incomes? Why push pro-growth economic policies if we hate the unemployed? Why oppose the welfare state if we hate the minority communities which have been decimated by it? Why uphold the Constitution if we hate all the citizens it was put in place to protect?

The idea that anyone who comes to hold an un-liberal belief arrived there by hate is so middle-school that it deserves an equally juvenile response: "He who smelt it, dealt it."

If you think everyone else is racist, it is probably because you are. Ditto if you think everyone hates homosexuals, or women, or men, or Jews, or Muslims, or blacks, or illegal aliens, or poor people or whoever you want to lump together into a herd. In fact, it is that herd mentality that gets people started down the road of hating.

And if you smell haters everywhere then chances are you are dealing that yourself, too. It would never occur to me that someone who comes to a different political position than mine got there because he/she hates. I've never heard anyone suggest such a thing, because I know very few people who hate. Life is too short.

For some reason, the anti-hater left especially hates the Tea Party, citing their boisterous rallies and too-white demographics, as if that should seal the deal.

I have been invited to a few Tea Party events, and found them to be less hostile to opposition views than the Milwaukee Brewers fans were at Miller Park Saturday night – that poor girl did not even say anything, just wore a St. Louis Cardinals jacket.

And the racial make-up of the Susan B. Komen Race for the Cure on Sunday was no more diverse than the Tea Party events that I have attended. SBK is not a government program - do we hate women because we chose to participate?

I have to believe that every conceivable political and religious viewpoint was represented in the lakefront crowd of 20,000 as well as in the large group of breast cancer survivors who were honored. Does anyone really think that half of them hate on the other half of them? Anyone?

And yet, that's what the hate-baiters on the left would have you believe – that half of those nice people wearing pink hate the other half of those nice people wearing pink, ergo you should vote for a Democrat, any Democrat.

That is their victory strategy for 2012? That's the big idea? The scary thing isn't that they think it will work; the scary thing is that they paid somebody to think it up.

Heartless

A reader called me "heartless" recently for my libertarian view that three sacred-cow entitlement programs – social security, Medicare, and unemployment compensation - should be abolished as we return to Constitutionally-limited government.

I didn't take personal offense; the bar has been set pretty high for fighting-words by liberal elected officials who have recently called me a terrorist, declared war on me, called me a lyncher, and told me to go to hell. "Heartless" has been downgraded from its previous AAA rating.

As difficult as it might be for the unquestioning govbot to imagine, life without these safety-net programs would not simply be possible, it would be better – much better. The market mechanism for insuring against calamity is called, conveniently, insurance.

In a 1995 study, Cato Institute concluded that if a worker born in 1970 would purchase private insurance with the money paid into social security taxes each month over a working lifetime, the annuity benefit paid at retirement would be six times higher than the benefit he will receive from social security. Six times higher.

Tell me, govbots, how is increasing the retirement benefit six-fold heartless?

Let's try Medicare. Most of us are covered by employer-provided insurance, or were until President Obama decided to screw that up. If the Medicare taxes we paid over our working lifetimes would have been invested into private accounts, the annuity stream at retirement would purchase health insurance far superior to the Medicare benefit we will receive from the current government program.

Tell me, govbots, why is better health insurance for seniors heartless?

Unemployment compensation already is insurance; employers pay your premium into a state-run insurance fund. We are just starting to get socked with premium increases in response to the high numbers of unemployed and the extended periods of benefits doled out by the government. Don't kid yourself that you are not paying; those increased premium costs reduce the money available for wage increases or in extreme cases force layoffs.

How much better for each of us to purchase his/her own unemployment insurance suitable for our circumstances and desires; think AFLAC without having to injure yourself. It would be risk-weighted, just like car insurance or property insurance; people with stable work histories would pay far less, while people who have trouble holding jobs would pay far more. Employers with lousy layoff history would have to pay higher wages to attract workers. You – not the State – would decide the amount and duration of benefits you would receive and you could insure your full salary if you choose to. I would.

Tell me, govbots, what is heartless about giving workers control over their own income continuation plans?

I'll tell you what is heartless: forcing people into a crappy government pension program that pays one sixth the annuity of private plans is heartless. Forcing people into a crappy government medical insurance program that costs more, delivers less, and drives the best doctors out is heartless. Forcing hardworking people to subsidize chronic job-droppers in a crappy government salary insurance plan is heartless.

What is cruelly heartless is that our government officials knew these entitlement programs were unsustainable 15, 20, even 40 years ago and decided to ride them to perpetual re-election all the way into bankruptcy. Lying to young people about the certainly of their benefit, lying to old people about the security of their next check, lying to the nation about a trust fund that was raided years ago – now that's heartless.

Government is heartless, not me. I'm a hunka-hunka burnin' love compared to the Republocrats who continue to promise benefits that can only be paid if Ben Bernanke succeeds in turning dollars to nickels over there at the Fed's printing presses. Speaking of things that we would be better off by abolishing...

Liberty is compassionate, and don't let any overeducated simpleton repeating 1930's talking points tell you different. If social security were abolished, you could receive six times the retirement benefit. If Medicare were abolished, you could have more money to spend on health care. If unemployment insurance were individualized, you could continue your weekly pay while you looked for a new job. And if the Fed were abolished, you would receive those benefits in real dollars. What sucks about that?

But you can't, because the government won't let you. They don't need a reason.

Chile privatized their public pension program years ago. Even those who transitioned in mid-career received double the benefit in retirement than what would have been paid under the old government social security system. Doubled it - top that, Congressman Ryan. Why are we trying to save ours?

Are the Chileans inherently smarter and more responsible than Americans? I've been there; they seemed pretty ordinary to me. If Americans really are too stupid to fend for ourselves, then for Heaven's sake let's quit hiring us for government jobs where we will have to take care of some other human being, too. Let's just hire nothing but Chileans from now on. Maybe that's the President's next jobs plan.

The choice is not liberty or compassion; it is liberty or government. You must decide whether you wish to govern yourself or be governed by someone else.

In Wisconsin we get an up close and personal view of just who that someone else is nearly every week, as they disrupt Special Olympics, vandalize elementary schools, harass food pantries and sheltered workshops, threaten school boards, occupy public buildings, hound the children of elected officials, slander judges, target businesses, abuse the court system, stalk elected officials, and discriminate at parades they insist be given in their honor.

Even if that guys was right about me, heartless still beats mindless any day. I choose liberty.

Hookers and Heroin

These GOP Presidential debates on television do very little to educate the public on the principles, positions, and policies of the various candidates. A 30 second response to a "gotcha" question allows 10 seconds to throw off a sound bite, 10 seconds to mischaracterize an opponents' position, and then 10 seconds to change the subject.

So-called moderators seem to be especially bent on hanging Ron Paul with ridiculous questions intended to belittle principled libertarian positions on matters of individual rights or personal responsibility. No one remembers his answers; the indictment is made with the questions.

Breathe easy, America. Libertarians would not require all Americans to relinquish their health insurance, then go into a coma and die. Nor would we take all the money from Social Security and give it to Iran to build more nuclear bombs. And we would not force you to use hookers and heroin.

A younger Congressman Paul would have handed Chris Wallace his lunch when asked that vapid hookers-and-heroin question in the first GOP candidate's debate. If I may be so bold as to suggest an answer that would have still left 10 seconds to change the subject:

"Yes, adults should be free to choose their own intoxicants and personal services. No, the government should not regulate either of them. Yes, that means you should make the choice of things like hookers and heroin for yourself, Mr. Wallace. And no, you should not expect the rest of us to keep you from making bad choices; you have a mom and a wife for that."

As a practical matter, we are going to have to tolerate hookers and heroin whether we like it or not; no civilization has yet succeeded in exterminating either one. The only question is whether or not we are willing to pay a great deal of money for ineffective random and arbitrary prosecution of a tiny fraction of those who break laws prohibiting both.

The libertarian response to unwanted hookers and heroin at your doorstep is the same as the libertarian response to unwanted Girl Scouts and Girl Scout cookies: "no thank you, sweetie." Do Americans lack even that much spine now? That seems to be an incredibly dismal view of the character of our friends and neighbors. And the question itself trivializes the principle of liberty. Why hookers and heroin?

Why not ask us who should choose our schools, charities, means of self-defense, medical care, food, travel destination, occupation, guitars, energy source, transportation, investments, currency, curricula, worship locations, insurance coverage, student loan source, pension option, taxation rate, public debt obligation, property use?

Libertarians do not advocate immorality; we argue that the cost of government regulation of morality – our loss of all those other liberties – is too high.

And who is it that encourages dangerous behavior – the libertarian who declines to imprison you for it, or the statist who relieves you of responsibility for its consequence? And who prescribes the more effective deterrent - Republicans who would put you in jail at taxpayer expense, Democrats who would put you in treatment at taxpayer expense, or Libertarians who would leave it to your spouse to extract retribution at your own expense? I know which I fear most.

Personal morality is not a suitable subject for legislation, and government is a poor substitute for family, church, and community in regulating personal morality. If all vice laws were struck down tomorrow, the authority of the wife, husband, mother, father, child, sibling, pastor, friend, in-law, and neighbor would not diminish one whit.

The hookers-and-heroin question is only intended to divide libertarians and conservatives. It defends the progressives' stake in state-regulated choice by reducing self-ownership from a noble ideal to a coarse pursuit. It presumes that freedom will bring out the worst in us, rather than our best. It assumes that only persons employed by the State are capable of making correct moral choices.

That notion of morally superior government would require that only morally superior people are selected for government service, or that somehow government service induces moral superiority in those selected. Not a day goes by that belief in such nonsense is shattered by a news story of corruption, abuse of authority, personal debauchery, criminal activity, or betrayal of public trust committed by those whom the statists insist must regulate choice for the rest of us.

Sin is a bi-partisan activity practiced in Washington, D.C., and in statehouses, county seats, and city halls across the country. Although an argument could be made that their experience and expertise qualifies them to regulate immoral behavior, they should concentrate on defending our rights and upholding the Constitution instead.

It Ain't Me, Babe

President Obama is taking a break between vacations to cram in a little work this week – a three-day bus tour to explain why nothing is ever his fault. When my son was a boy, he could do this without hiring a bus.

I'm not sure who the warm-up act is on his Blame-A-Pallooza tour - Lindsay Lohan would be a good choice – but I have a suggestion for his theme song: "It Ain't Me, Babe", by the Turtles. He could sing "it ain't me, babe" part, and then we all join in on the "no, no, no!" that follows. Let him get used to the sound of it before 2012 rolls around.

At his first stop, the President said that just because people are frustrated with the political system doesn't mean they should lose faith in the government's ability to confront the country's problems.   I agree: it is the government's inability to confront the country's problems that should cause us to lose faith in the government's ability to confront the country's problems.

I was out of the country when the debt ceiling debacle went down, but I have read that the White House called it a "tea party downgrade", as if that would scare us into standing down. Team Obama now claims it was all the tea party talk of default that led S&P to de-rate our sovereign debt.   That takes gall of the unmitigated variety.

The only guys I recall talking about default were the President, his minions, and his lackeys in the media. They were the ones who said if they did not get their way they would default on the debt, stop paying social security, suspend Medicare, and quit paying the military, remember?   Default was his choice, not ours.

We were the ones who said we should pay the interest on the debt to avoid default, pay our uniformed military, pay social security (as if the government could figure out how to stop it anyway), and pay Medicare reimbursements, then cut spending across the rest of government to bring expenditures in line with revenue.   Not increasing the debt would have protected our nation's AAA rating, not caused its downgrade.

We just have to keep banging away at it until they get it. You don't solve a debt crisis by taking on more debt. You don't solve a spending problem by spending more. You don't revive a flat-lined economy by taxing it. You don't fix a too-big government

119

by making it bigger. And you don't cure fools by listening to them.

The fools continue to state the federal government's debt as a ratio of national income – now exceeding 100%. That is like calculating my debt as a ratio of all my readers' incomes. The federal government's debt is almost *seven times* its own income. That is why the S&P downgraded it from good-as-gold to better-buy-gold.

Let's say you make $70,000 per year and your debt is $490,000 and rising by the month. Is your low credit score the tea party's fault? Can you fix it by borrowing more and spending more? Do we all have to sacrifice so you can keep living large? If your last name starts with "O" and ends with "bama" the answer is yes, yes we can. Sorry, but no, no we won't; that was the message of the 2010 mid-term revolution, and it was reinforced this past weekend in the Iowa straw poll.

The President says we should raise taxes because our federal tax revenue is at an all time low of 15% of GDP, and that proves we are not paying our fair share.   No, what that proves is that unemployment is at an all time high and a whole lot of people aren't paying any taxes at all.   The rest of us are paying plenty.

Try this, sir: fire half of your White House staff and see what it does to the WH share of taxes as a percentage of GDP. Now, go to the people still working there and explain that you must double their taxes to maintain the historical White House fair share. Sarah Palin would beat you in a West Wing straw poll.

Speaking of fools...Ben Bernanke stunned the world last week when he stated he will extend the Fed's zero interest rate policy for two more years. You can mark on your calendar the date that the economy will start to improve – 25 months from now at the earliest.

Recessions last 12-16 months, and ours started in the fourth quarter of 2007, the first year of the reign of Queen Nancy Pelosi and her socialist Congress. A President in a coma would have presided over a recovery shortly after inauguration; unfortunately, our guy was wide awake and surrounded himself with economic witch doctors plucked out of central banks and academia.

Their potions and chants entertain a clueless media and dupe the economic illiterates who measure prosperity by the size of their free lunch, but the President's Keynesian superstitions and unionist/socialist ideology have dragged out the Obama depression for three years now with no end in sight.

Not to hear him tell it. According to our Blamer-In-Chief, Bush did it, the tea party did it, racism did it, rich people did it, Walker did it, corporate jets did it, BP did it, the tsunami did it, global warming did it, the Constitution did it, guns did it, Congress did it, Wall street did it, the Church did it, AFP did it, S&P did it, the Supreme Court did it, Fox news did it, Arizona did it, China did it, people with Ron Paul stickers did it, talk radio did it, guns did it, his caddy did it.

Good luck selling that soap in Iowa, where tea party favorites Bachman and Paul lapped the field in the straw poll over the weekend, where Perry went to kick off his bid for the Presidency, and where Herman Cain finished in the upper chart. Best not bash the tea party in tea party country.

Unless the President's new economic plan is to add an ethanol mandate to Obamacare and spot the Hawkeyes 21 points in every Big Ten contest this fall, Blamezilla might as well stay on the bus and head back to D.C. What is the fuel efficiency of a bus, anyway? Why isn't he driving a Prius or peddling a bike or riding a solar skateboard or something? How come we have to use those Dairy Queen light bulbs while he tours the heartland at 3 miles per gallon?

Come to think of it, "It Ain't Me, Babe" might be the perfect theme song for this President, because the lyric continues with, "I'm not the one you're looking for, babe." Got that right.

121

Jack and Jill

Jack and Jill went up the hill to fetch a pail of water. Jack fell down and broke his crown, and Jill became a libertarian. What the...?

Here's how it happened. First, the IRS took half her water in taxes. Then the Department of Justice took her bucket because it might be made out of illegal wood from India. Then the DNR fined Jill for disrupting the habitat of some creek guppy no one ever heard of.

The NLRB ruled Jill could only fetch water in Washington State and had to pay union guys to do it. TSA did a full cavity search and a double pat down of her mommy parts; that had nothing to do with the bucket of water, they just get off on that stuff. When she gasped, the EPA fined her for an excessive carbon dioxide emission.

Then Bruce and Lance named Jill in a class-action lawsuit because she got to inherit her husband's bucket of water while they couldn't even get married. She was banned from the Labor Day parade in Wausau because Jack never joined the water-fetchers union and voted Republican once. The USDA had her detained when a tip came in that she might have raw milk in that bucket.

President Obama decided Jill had more water than she needed, and said we would all be better off with him "spreadin' the wet around". Joe Biden later claimed he hydrated or moistened over 2 million Americans. One solar panel company took 365 million gallons of government stimulus water and then moved to China. Al Gore made a Power Point movie that showed Jill boiling polar bears in her bucket on coal-fired stove. He made billions off the fakery.

An angry mob stalked Jill wherever she went because she wouldn't buy their water, shouting "shame, shame, shame" and drumming for months. When she suggested they could just Segway up the hill and fetch a pail for themselves like she did, the Congressional Black Caucus called her a racist and Maxine Waters told her to go to hell. Jimmy Hoffa said he would take sons of bitches like her out; she was pretty sure he didn't mean on a date.

Afraid for her life, Jill went to buy a handgun but had to wait five days. Then she found out she could not carry it in her purse in

Wisconsin until November anyway. While she counted the days down, a teen flashmob beat and then pistol-whipped her after the state fair. "Wow – how'd you guys get your training and permits already?" she marveled, spitting teeth. Jill was a little naïve about criminals and guns.

Meanwhile Ben Bernanke started printing trillions of new bucket-o-water redemption certificates, and Jill's bucket of real water shot up in price from 300 certificates per fluid ounce to over 1,900 of the bogus Fed water-coupons. Ron Paul and Peter Schiff said "toldya" while Michael Moore made a movie about Jill's obscene water-wealth entitled "Koch Whore." When Jack Jr. got suspended from school for calling some gay kid a "teabagger", Jill wondered why all those liberal commentators on TV still had jobs.

And then Jill started to notice that fewer and fewer people were hiking up the hill to fetch their own heavy pails of water, while more and more people sat at the bottom of the hill, demanding government quench their thirst. After a time, they did not even know where the water came from; and they did not care. They just wanted more; they said they were entitled to it.

They elected politicians who promised them free water. Her government blamed the rich water-fetchers like Jill for the thirst of those who sat at the bottom of the hill in poverty. That same government took and more of Jill's water away from her in taxes; they forced her to pay fetching permits; they regulated her route; they mandated airbags for her buckets; they forced her to buy insurance she did not want; they invaded other countries and sent her the bill.

And they did not stop at taking her property. They told her where she could send her kids to school and what they must be taught. They made her pay a union in order to fetch buckets of water for herself. They told her what she could eat, drive, smoke, own, sell, buy, wear, drink, study, build, party with, heat with, light with, listen to, watch, flush, shoot, visit, record, say, write, and marry.

They told her she could not be trusted to make those decisions for herself; and they built new prisons to hold her if she made choices they did not like. One Party told her this is what democracy looks like; the other Party couldn't even come up with a catchy slogan for it.

Both Parties buried the nation in debt so deep that neither Jack Jr. nor Jack III would ever see it paid back. They spent Jill's money on themselves and their friends; then they had the nerve to call her greedy and heartless for wanting to keep what she earned for herself and her children.

And then one day, Jill had a moment of clarity. She read somewhere that liberty is the absence of government in choice; that government is the absence of liberty in choice; that tyranny is the absence of choice in government. The dairy-queen light bulb finally went off for Jill.

She saw tyranny for the first time in the good intentions of those who would take her liberty for her own good. She never asked them to save her, and they never asked if they could. Jill discovered they did not care about her. She remembered that her rights were endowed to her by her Creator, not created by any legislature. She realized that they only took as much liberty from her as she gave away.

Jill reclaimed her liberty. She made liberty her first principle - that is what it means to be a libertarian. Did she live happily ever after? No, that only happens in fairy tales and in the imaginations of empty heads who believe the lies of politicians who promise happiness they cannot deliver.

But she did live free ever after; she owned herself. And so should you.

Jobzilla

Let's play "Who wants to be a CEO?" Ok, you are about to create or save a $50,000 job just to claim that new $780 one time payroll tax credit when the Department of Justice comes blasting into your office with guns drawn and confiscates all your raw materials.

Do you a) thank the President for his bold leadership in job creation, b) blame the Tea Party for foiling his perfect and most wonderful vision of our nation, or c) move your plant to another country where they need warrants to seize your property. Ding ding ding ding ding ding!

Let's stay with No-Brainers for $400, Alex. Ok, you are about ready to place orders for a few million dollars of new capital equipment that you don't even need just to take advantage of the President's one-time accelerated depreciation rule when the NLRB forces you to abandon the billion-dollar plant you just built in South Carolina and move the work to Washington state and overpay union guys who go on strike a lot.

Do you a) praise Mr. Obama for tinkering with an obscure accounting rule in order to benefit Wall Street banks, b) blame the Republicans for not doing it first, or c) build your next plant in a country where mobbed-up union bosses don't threaten to "take you out" when they welcome the President to their stage. Ding ding ding ding ding ding!

Bonus Round: You are trying to decide where to site a new industrial facility that will employ thousands when you learn that EPA has passed arbitrary rules that will shut down over 20 power plants, double your energy costs, and cause rationing of electricity. Do you, a) salute the President for his commitment to his donors' green job subsidies, b) blame George W. Bush for global warming, or c) build your plant in Brazil where they will sell you all the energy you need at low costs. Congratulations – you just won an all-expense-paid trip to Sao Paulo!

I must confess I did not watch the President's speech last night, I just read a transcript this morning. While he was putting lipstick on his recycled 2009 stimulus pig, I was driving home from a meeting with Wisconsin Governor Walker at one of our plants up north. What a contrast.

President Obama told us (again) what Congress needed to do to create jobs, as if they could; Governor Walker asked us how we create jobs in our company. The President dictated incentives and demanded we hire more workers; the Governor asked us what government could do that might matter to us.

President Obama encouraged everyone (again) to go to college. We talked with Governor Walker about the shortage of skilled trades and technicians and the high-paying jobs that we can't fill for lack of qualified candidates. I learned that most students at Wisconsin's two-year technical colleges have four-year degrees (and a mountain of student loan debt) in fields where there is no demand.

President Obama promised to plug school budgets and increase teacher pay for a year (again); Governor Walker asked us what Wisconsin students need to learn in school to be employable. The President lectured a room full of professional politicians; the Governor took questions from our plant employees – and he answered them.

Our Governor came to learn; our President hasn't learned a thing.

The President's words don't really matter anymore, because his actions are pure Jobzilla. Stomp – Obamacare. Stomp - repeal of the Bush tax cuts. Stomp – union card check by executive order. Stomp – drilling ban. Stomp – EPA edicts. Stomp – $1.4 trillion deficit.

But here he goes again with the roads, bridges, and schools shtick - $150 billion to rebuild our infrastructure after he just threw $800 billion down that rat hole with nary a single new road, bridge, or school to show for it. Here's a clue: 15 million unemployed Americans aren't going back to work on roads unless President Jobzilla has 15 million surplus CAT D7 bulldozers stored with the cheese in those government warehouses of his.

And am I the only one that sees pure hypocrisy in the President's "payroll tax holiday"? You realize, I hope, that the payroll tax he is talking about is your Social Security withholding. So not only are you contributing less, which might reduce the amount of benefit you will receive when you retire, but your "holiday" will be taxed at ordinary income rates come the end of the year.

Not to mention that those payroll taxes are what funds Social Security, an already broken system that Republican Rick Perry correctly called a "Ponzi scheme" in Wednesday's debate. That "tax holiday" money was supposed to go into the Social Security

Trust Fund, the pot of money they keep saying is really there for you even though they spent it all on other stuff like teleprompters and tour busses from Canada.

The President just proposed to defund Social Security by 50% and not one liberal went hysterical on him. Not one drum, not one "war on the middle class", and nothing but gurgling coos from the infants at MSNBC. If a libertarian did that (or Paul Ryan) all hell would break loose. And how did Social Security get so flush with cash all of a sudden that President Obama can afford to defund it for a whole year? A month ago, we didn't even have enough money to cut checks to recipients without raising the debt ceiling and borrowing more money – remember all the wheelchairs going over the cliff on August 3?

I'm not sure if our Jobzilla President even knows how any of this stuff actually works. The advance hype for his big speech said Mr. Obama would solve our jobs problem with over $400 billion of "tax cuts and spending increases that would be paid for by deficit reduction." Three letters: W, T, and you-pick-em. That statement would need a lot of editing just to be upgraded to stupid.

Here is what is so sad: someone with a college degree wrote that talking point, dozens of people with college degrees approved it, and hundreds of journalists and editors with college degrees printed it. And our President thinks even more people should go to college.

I think less people should go to college and more people should learn to drive bulldozers and graders. And build them and design them and service them and make parts for them, and mine the iron and make the steel and drive the trucks and drill the oil wells and refine the diesel fuel and build ships and nuclear power plants and windmills and appliances and foundries and factories and all the cranes and machine tools to fill them up.

The only jobs plan we need is to get the government off our back so we can do all those things here again. That will put 15 million Americans back to work.

Judge Tim

Silly me, I thought that it was the job of the legislature to make laws, the job of the executive branch to enforce them, and the job of the judiciary to keep the Constitution between those first two and me.

Had I known that the job of the judiciary in Wisconsin is to overturn the decisions of the legislature, prevent the executive from carrying them out, and impose their own personal ideology on the whole state, I would have never wasted my time running for U.S. Congress. I would have aimed high and gone straight for county judge right off the bat.

And I know the perfect county for a libertarian judge - Iron County, home to the city of Hurley, "where Hwy 51 ends and the fun begins!" We have a cottage near there in Oma Township, otherwise known as the Kingdom of Oma. Libertarian Judge Tim from the Kingdom of Oma would be your best friend or worst nightmare, depending on whether you are a freeperson or a taxeater.

Dane County Judge MaryAnn Sumi didn't like the way the legislature passed Governor Walker's budget repair bill so she put it on ice. Well guess what - Judge Tim doesn't like the way the legislature passed the income tax; so that will be my first injunction and we can all stop withholding tomorrow.

You know what else I don't like? Bar time. Do you have any idea how many bad marriages can be traced back to the pressure of finding someone before the lights came on and the music stopped? In the Kingdom of Oma the party won't stop until you run out of cash.

And I would put the ki-bosh on that smoking ban, for sure. If you are not old enough to walk out of a too-smoky bar, you are not old enough to drink. In fact, the drinking age in the Kingdom of Oma will be when you stop whining; Dane might be our first dry county. Back when I was on the tour, my tri-fecta package was a Black Russian, a bottle of Rolling Rock for a wash, and a Marlboro. Two out of three is like ZZ Top without Billy Gibbons. Glad I quit when I did.

Want to bet on the Badgers, the Packers, or the over/under on how many voters rise up from the dead in the Kloppenburg recount? You won't have to drive to an Indian Casino; you can place your wager at the Kwik Trip...or the M&I bank. I'll order that one out of spite.

Know what else you can do at the KT? Fill up your SUV, ATV, and Jet Skis with high octane, no ethanol, manly gas. For about a buck a gallon, because Judge Tim doesn't like gas tax, either. Want to run your Prius on corn? Put the bikes on the rack and move to Iowa; they are addicted to the stuff over there.

But how would we pay for the DNR with all those tax cuts, you ask? Simple answer: "you're welcome". Here's how the DNR would fare in Judge Tim's court: "Attorney Kloppenburg, show me where your name is on the deed to this property...I didn't think so...now sit down and shut up. And buy this guy's pier; no, buy him two just for being a dork."

And don't even think about boycotting our fine businesses up here in the Kingdom of Oma, because Judge Tim knows how to spell extortion and throw your miserable butts in the hooskow for 20 hard. While I'm at it, I think I will rule that the Federal anti-trust waiver for unions is nullified in Wisconsin. There – now your whole amalgamated brotherhood can drag your knuckles back home to Illinois. And as long as we are nullifying...sayonara, Obamacare! You have just been *injunctified!*

I like guns, don't you? Concealed carry, open carry, locked and loaded and ready to defend against the dirtbags and gang-bangers who are already packin'. Not just allowed, but mandatory, just like recycling used to be before Judge Tim ordered the prisoners in jail to sort the garbage so honest citizens didn't have to waste our time doing it. What's that, ACLU - sorting trash is cruel and unusual punishment? I know! I know!

Let's see, what else don't I like?...seat belts, car seats, dairy queen light bulbs, out of state college kids voting to increase taxes they will never pay. Drink raw milk if you think you should, don't worry about motorcycle helmets, and consider the speed limits on rural interstates to be suggestions. And of course, I'll be reversing any injunction Judge Sumi issues. I'll get an app for my iPhone to alert me.

You think Obama has power? Hah! Judge Tim can make a hundred thousand people suddenly get glaucoma just by making medical marijuana legal, and then cure them all when I end prohibition altogether. Just don't come into my court expecting unemployment when you flunked your drug test at work, stoner. Judge Tim has no sympathy for slackers.

If you think the people in the Kingdom of Oma will vote me out over pot, you've never been to Hurley. Did I mention I would Voter ID the whole state by decree and make everyone cast their ballot in gun shop, church, or Harley dealership. Think of it as affirmative action, making up for a century of liberal home-field advantage voting in public schools. Besides, once I order the state give every parent vouchers, there won't be any public schools left to vote in.

Now, I know that my liberal opponents for county judge will point to my lack of judicial experience and say I should start out on the Supreme Court until I know what I am doing, like their guys do. And my conservative opponents will be lecturing about impartiality and temperament and separation of powers and things that people under 40 never learned. That is noble.

But I'll wipe the floor with them both. There won't be no Franken re-counts when Judge Tim stands for re-election. You know why? Because freedom is popular, just like Ron Paul says. And free people would rather live in the Kingdom of Oma than the People's Republic of Madison.

It's too bad they don't have the choice.

July 5th

Most Americans think of our 4ᵗʰ of July holiday as a celebration as the birth of our nation. In one sense, that is correct, but Independence Day has much deeper significance; it commemorates the birth of an *idea*.

That noble idea is that man's natural state is the absence of government. We call that state Liberty. The Independence that was declared in 1776 was the independence from government, from *being governed*. In the state of Liberty, we govern ourselves; we are responsible for our own choices and their consequences.

Self-sovereignty was once so universally understood that Thomas Jefferson described its truth to be self-evident. The Declaration of Independence does not argue for self-sovereignty; it simply states the fact.

The truth that all men (and women) were created equal, that no just law could favor one over another, did not require an explanation then; it does not now.

The truth that our rights were endowments from our Creator, not permissions from a government of men, did not require an explanation then; it does not now.

The truth that we own ourselves did not require an explanation then; it does not now.

We have a right to our life, not the life of another; we have a right to our liberty, not the liberty of another; we have a right to pursue our happiness, not the happiness of another. A nation-state is not independent; independence from government can not describe a government.

The only independence that can exist in a nation is the independence of its citizens. Protecting that independence – the pre-existing rights of the individual - is the only rightful purpose for government. That is what our Declaration declared.

Are we independent? Do we demand that our laws apply equally to every single person? Do we nullify laws that do not? Do we reject the demand of our government to claim our liberties and license them back to us? Do we accept the claims of others upon our property, the fruits of our labors?

Our leaders have confiscated the language of liberty and have substituted their own meanings for the words of our founding documents.

They lie, saying that dependency is independence, that freedom from responsibility is liberty, that privilege is right, that right is permission, that private property is public resource, that partisan privilege is general welfare.

The American Revolution was a tax rebellion. The rate of taxation imposed by the King of England on the colonists was 10.9% of GDP; that was enough for blood to be shed. Today, the Kingdom of Washington, D.C. extracts 24% of GDP from its 50 colonies. Half of the nation demands that it take even more.

That half of the nation will not save it; they have lost the desire to be independent. They demand to be fed, housed, educated, cared for, and sustained by the work of others. They even lack the initiative to do the looting themselves; waiting instead for government to do it for them.

But the other half, those who work and produce in surplus,

Laboring Daily

It is unfortunate, yet oddly fitting, that the abysmal August job numbers came out right before the Labor Day holiday. The least-working President in American history had to endure yet another economic wedgie to add to his unprecedented string of epic fails.

Or maybe it is a grand design. Liberals have been working for years to take Christ out of Christmas, Thanks out of Thanksgiving, Independence out of Independence Day, Memorials out of Memorial Day, so maybe it is just a reflex action for them to take American Labor out of Labor Day.

Labor Day parade organizers in Wausau, Wisconsin banned Republicans from the holiday parade this year because the GOP stood up to public sector unions – the principle of the thing, don't you know. Less than a minute after the city informed them they would have to pay for the parade themselves if they made it a partisan event, they relented. Principle just ain't what it used to be.

But at least have what that first principle of liberalism is: I am entitled to celebrate my own bad self at your expense. That pretty much sums up what they do every day of the year in cubicles and conference centers and vans with red plates; they call that daily celebration of their own bad selves at our expense "government".

Funny they should claim Labor Day for their own; it should be about doing work, not avoiding it. Last week, the govbots got on their horse in one Wisconsin school district to defend the "right" of teachers to take 20 sick days off during a school year already punctuated with union holidays, winter and spring breaks, summers off, and conferences galore. In another district, anger boiled over at the suggestion they up their work day by 30 minutes and put in a (gasp) full eight hard. No, really – and for as many as five straight days in a row. I know, I know.

In yet another pre-Labor Day noogie from our vacationer-in-chief, Mr. Obama's EPA issued a slew of regulatory pronouncements designed to choke the life right out of the American industrial and energy sectors last week. The President had to quickly back off and rescind his own edicts, deciding we really can't afford to enact job killing regulations right now.

Which begs the obvious question: when could we ever afford to enact job killing regulations? A month ago, when the President gave his EPA the go-ahead to unleash their regulatory kick in the nuts? Did he think that was a good time to enact job killing regulations? Please don't tell us that Mr. Obama just figured out this week that we need jobs. Although that would explain a lot.

I read that some Congresswoman from California took the opportunity of the upcoming holiday to blame the high rate of black unemployment (16%) on racism. Three words: Crock.

I forget - was it the KKK or the skinheads who drove vocational educational programs out of public schools? And whose idea was it to pass kids that can't read to the next grade so we don't hurt their self-esteem? Who was it that replaced basic skills with a curriculum full of politically-correct pabulum? Who was it that insisted on bi-lingual education and tried to get Ebonics recognized as a language? Who sued and sued and sued until all moral instruction and teaching of traditional values were driven out of the school systems? Who taught situational ethics and cultural equivalence?

Who blocks school choice and prevents inner city kids from having a fighting chance to be educated and employable? Who was it that tried to replace grades and awards with stickers and hugs for everyone? Who was it that insisted that unions run the schools? Who was it that packed school boards in order to negotiate work rules with themselves?

Liberals, that's who. A half-century of unionized government monopoly schools has produced an unemployable underclass who can't read or cipher and lacks the basic social skills to win and hold a job. You guys expect us to throw you a parade for that?

And who was it that taxed employers out of the cities? Who didn't want those icky, icky factories in their gentrified Chardonnay neighborhoods? Who shut down the offshore oil industry? Who cut off the water to California's agriculture industry? Who was it that increased the minimum wage and drove black teenage unemployment to over 50%? Who was it that forced banks to give mortgages to people who could not afford them and now can't move to where the jobs are because they are handcuffed to upside down mortgages?

Liberals, that's who. They have ruined public education; they have ruined the economy; they have sacrificed our jobs on their altar of environmental guilt fantasy; they have chased producers overseas; they have unionized the public sector and increased both its bloat and its sloth. You guys expect us to throw you a parade for that?

I don't know why you think this is your day. You are the enemies of work; the job killers. They should throw you a parade in China; you have delivered world industrial leadership to them by driving it out of America. Enjoy your bratwurst.

Those of us who work rings around you are not ceding Labor Day to you just because you have the arrogance to claim it for yourselves. 93% of private sector workers choose to work free of union interference. Labor Day is our holiday, too. More of us are left-handed than belong to your unions. You are not even the most popular lefties in the workforce anymore.

Work is freedom of association put to the purpose of mutual prosperity. The exchange of one's labor for capital is the most basic of capitalist transactions; it is the daily proof that we still own ourselves. That is indeed something to celebrate.

Celebrate workplace liberty this Labor Day.

Lather, Rinse, Repeat

Wisconsin's teachers' union (WEAC) announced this week it is cutting 40% of its staff, a move it blames on Governor Scott Walker's "union-busting" budget reform bill. I re-read the bill a couple more times, and nowhere could I find a single provision that reduced WEAC's membership by a single person. Nowhere.

The AP news article covering the WEAC announcement did not cite any drop in membership, nor did it state that membership dues have fallen. So why would a teachers' union cut 40% of its member-support jobs in Wisconsin right before the start of a school year, especially this year where so much is changing?

Since it offered no other explanation for its actions except that it is unhappy about who was elected Governor last year, it seems pretty clear that WEAC cut 40% of its workforce solely for the purpose of grabbing an anti-Walker headline the day before the recall election of two Democrat state senators. A compliant media gladly obliged, broadcasting the smear as if it were fact-checked.

Who treats their employees like dirt? Not the evil corporations or greedy CEOs the left rags on mindlessly day after day, but the very unionists who make their living fleecing the public and conning the soft-headed into thinking they care a whit about the working man. Not just any union, mind you, but WEAC - the posers who would have us believe they are all kindergarten teachers in calico dresses holding kittens and humming lullabies to sick children. Ok, except for that death-threat lady.

If a prominent Wisconsin company announced a 40% job cut without showing any loss of customers or citing any reduction in revenue, the screams of corporate greed and exploitation would rattle bratwursts off the grills all the way from Kenosha to Superior. By the way, WEAC's executive director – the sackmeister - makes more than most CEO's in Wisconsin; drum on that, comrades.

Recently, the head of the NEA stated openly the teachers' unions do not care about kids; the actions of Milwaukee and Madison locals made it clear they do not care about teachers, either; and now we learn that WEAC doesn't even care about their own workers. 42 jobs were tossed to influence a meaningless recall election. Own it, teachers. That is your union; that is what your

136

dues have purchased. You paid to be represented by ruthless fools, and you got represented.

Governor Walker took bold action to reform the public sector workplace, and WEAC is now running the bully's retreat. Walker should turn his attention to reforming the laws that govern private sector employment in this state. Lather, rinse, repeat. If he is serious about creating jobs in Wisconsin, he should pass Right To Work legislation now.

The moral argument for RTW is simple enough; involuntary association is an offense to liberty, and sanctioned extortion is still extortion. From a practical standpoint, compulsory unionization stifles innovation, punishes excellence, rewards sloth, protects incompetence, and promotes mediocrity.

In the private sector choice and competition drive innovation and excellence; free trade in goods, services, labor, and capital improve the quality, cost, and selection of articles for consumption. The abundance we enjoy was not legislated or voted by a simple majority; it was invented for profit and optimized through choice and competition in the free market.

Company price-fixing is illegal, and for good reason; fixing the risk of loss allows greed to run unchecked. But union labor price-fixing is exempt from anti-trust laws, and the result has been predictably devastating. In company after company, industry after industry, wherever unions thrive, companies and jobs die. Union membership has been in a free-fall for five decades in this nation; not because the deck is stacked against unions in elections, but because the parasite inevitably kills the host.

93% of private sector workers now choose to work free of union interference in their workplace; not because they are unaware of their right to form and join unions, but because they are acutely aware of the threats that unions pose to their livelihood and their liberties. The Obama administration is working urgently to rig the rules so that unions can be more easily imposed on unwilling workers. Time is of the essence.

Right To Work insures that each of us can exercise our Constitutional right to either join a union or work union-free. It prevents *me* from setting the terms and conditions for the exchange of *your* labor. It preserves your ownership over your own self. It protects us both from extortion – the forced payment of tribute to a third party.

There is no third-party "right" to seize profit from an economic exchange between free people. The right of association in the workplace has three facets: the right to form and join a union, the right to work union free, and the right to choose to bargain with a collective or with individual employees.

These are not privileges granted by government and subject to majority rule; these are individual rights that precede government. They are the Creator's endowment to a free people. The question for Governor Walker is: when will he enact legislation to recognize it? We are waiting.

Lay By Your Dish

We went past the straw breaking the camel's back some time ago; we are now spearing its humps while it writhes on the ground in pain.

Of course I am referring to the Obama administration's decision this week to tax Christmas trees. This, apparently, is what he meant by going around Congress to get things done for the American people. Because...um...taxing Christmas was what we were all clamoring for him to get done. Right.

And I still can't figure out which is dumber – taxing Christmas or trying to balance the budget 15 cents at a time. What kind of fool adds a three-nickel tax? All that does is make the guy in the tree both take his glove off to count 85 cents change that I will drop in the snow. Besides, at 15 cents a pop, you would have to clear-cut Canada just to pay for the Fannie Mae and Freddie Mac bonuses we paid last week.

The timing of this new tax is impeccable; millions of still-unemployed Americans must be thrilled to know there will be even less money for their children's toys this Christmas so that the Agriculture Department won't have to postpone their bonuses, raises, and staff additions. I'm sure we will all start with government when we list the things we are grateful for this Thanksgiving.

It's all part of the President's own 9-9-9-15 plan: 9 percent unemployment, 9 trillion in new debt, 9 wars all at once, and a 15 cent tax on joy just to show Boehner who gets tops.

This decision to tax a religious symbol raises the obvious economic policy and Constitutional law question: what the front door is wrong with these people? No seriously...where do they get off putting the government bite on our Christmas? If Christmas is so bad it has to be taxed, then why are they all going to take the day off to celebrate it?

Here is what I want from government this Christmas: plow the snow, arrest a criminal, and go lay by your dish. Just leave us alone; read the Constitution and see if you can find anything in there that authorizes you to do even half the stupid things you do to us. And then read the Bill of Rights again – pretend it applies to you.

The unsolvable problem with too-big government is that there aren't enough smart people to run it, and taxing Christmas trees just proves the point.

You can't fix people who think it is a brilliant idea to tax Christmas trees. You can't protect us from these cretins by holding their budget increases to half the rate of inflation over the next decade; you have to abolish the Department that employs them. If the GOP candidates ever decide to start talking about real issues again, why don't they all list the departments and agencies they would abolish if we give them the job? If they can't come up with one, let them pay our Christmas tree tax out of their own pocket and then ask them again.

Abolishing most of the federal government would be a mercy killing. Whatever bunch of nut-balls sat in a conference room and decided to serve the American people by taxing our Christmas needs to be set free from the shackles of government service, along with the whole bureaucracy that approved it. Remember, this is the best idea they came up with that day; it could have been a lot worse if tree-tax genius would have been off on a sick day looking at condominium foreclosures with her friend from HUD.

And of all the things to punish; Christmas brings out the very best in people. Charities, professional organizations, businesses, unions, the military, churches, schools – we cheerfully give billions to help those less fortunate than us. We buy toys for kids, and necessities for families, and feed the hungry and shelter the homeless and reconcile family differences, our churches are packed.

There is no law that compels us to give. There is no regulation that mandates generosity. We do not need to apply for a permit and attend a class. There is no fee, or license required. There is not a Democrat Christmas and a Republican Christmas. No one is forced to celebrate Christmas, and no one is punished if they choose not to. The smiles at Christmas are what the safety net looks like when government is not involved; that is what every day would look like if made government go lay by its dish.

But government won't go lay by its dish. It won't leave us alone for a minute. God forbid we would just do things for each other by ourselves and feel good about it. It must have driven them crazy to know that we would spend an hour with our families picking out a tree and not obsessing about their politics; they had to find one more way to inject their craving for drama into our private time.

And for what? We could bring a lot more revenue into the federal government if Buffet and Gates just paid those higher tax rates they said they ought to be paying. Well go ahead, boys. Hear that bell ringing in front of the K-mart? Pretend it is the Agriculture Department, stuff a billion into the IRS kettle and get them off our backs.

They taxed Christmas trees. You can't even say that without getting angry, whether you are Republican, Democrat, Libertarian, Independent, or just a person with a shred of decency left in you.

Leave Me Out Of It

The libertarian position on social issues can be summed up in five words: leave me out of it.

I have heard libertarians described as economic conservatives and social liberals; I prefer socially neutral, as liberals do not seek freedom on social and cultural issues, they demand state approval and subsidy of their specific moral choices.

For example, liberals do not simply propose tolerance of gay couples; they demand that the state approve and sanction those unions as marriage, and provide a plethora of taxpayer-funded benefits. Conservatives seek legislation prohibiting gay marriage, demanding the state defend the sanctity of traditional marriage.

My libertarian approach to the issue is simple: be as gay as you want, just leave me out of it. Don't ask, don't tell, don't care. Don't care about your choice of partners; don't care to re-write the dictionary; don't care to pay for your LGBT agenda.

Many social conservatives would find "be as gay as you want" to be unacceptably tolerant; and many liberals would "leave me out of it" to be homophobic and hateful. My response to both is: be as intolerant or as indignant as you want, just leave me out of it. Have you detected the theme here?

You pick the issue, and my answer is going to be the same: be as fill-in-the-blank as you want, just leave me out of it. Be green, be socialist, be churchy, be feminist, be whatever, just don't make me approve of your choice or pay for it. You have a right to tolerance; you have no right to approval.

I don't care what you choose to eat, smoke, drive, worship, own, defend yourself with, party with, listen to, read, heal yourself with, weigh, say, buy, sell, own, save, invest, gamble, teach your kids, do for a living, or anything else, particularly. It's a free country...used to be, anyway.

Not wanting to tell you what you can and can't do – how did that get to be a radical political philosophy? And not wanting to pay for your lifestyle choices – how did that get to be a matter of public morality?

Live how you want to live and leave me out of it; and then give me the same respect back. Believe what you wish and tell me why it makes you happy. But don't use the power of the state to shove your beliefs down my throat.

Don't tell me I can't send my kid to school with a brown bag lunch and don't tell me I must pay for NPR to make a version of "Sesame Street" for Pakistan. You want to buy school lunch and fund a Muslim Big Bird, go right ahead; just leave me out of it.

Morality is its own reward, and immorality is its own punishment; the state does not have a dog in the fight when it comes to most of the social issues that define the "culture war" that rages in this nation. If you covet, lie, steal, murder, disrespect, aggress, and commit adultery, you will be miserable and impoverished all on your own.

I will have no sympathy for you, and it pisses me off that the state would intervene with my tax dollars to try in vain to insulate you from the consequences of your own choices. Prohibition does not prevent bad behavior; acceptance encourages it.

It's not that us libertarians dismiss the importance of public morality; quite the contrary, we find values and traditions to be far too important to trust them to government. Most social issues get down to religious convictions; sin and salvation are the business of churches, not government.

When God wants to set you straight He will come and find you, speaking from personal experience. And He is not about to subcontract the job of soul-saving to a mob of self-absorbed partisan hacks whose only priority is grinding axes and feathering their own beds.

Government does the worst possible job of instilling moral values, preserving cultural traditions, and providing a common framework of civility. Would you describe government employees, statists, and unionists as "civil" in the budget debates all across the country in recent weeks? Not me. A different word comes to mind.

While I generally avoid profanity in my writing, the Thesaurus provides no suitable alternative for the word "asshole". If the suppository fits, wear it.

Those are the people we are entrusting with development and enforcement of public morality. Those boobs in SEIU shirts making fools of themselves are who government is. The argument against intrusive government is best made by exposing

143

the public to the people who will be doing the intruding. I've seen quite enough of them, haven't you?

Betting our potholes on the 'holes is one thing; it is quite another to hand them our children, our culture, and our values. If you still trust them, go ahead – but leave me out of it.

Libertarian Haiku

It is my money
You go piss up a rope
Shame on you, wood tick

Do not take my gun
You will find it is unloaded
My other is not

Leave me alone
Hey! I said leave me alone
Leave me alone, asshole

Do as you wish to
You are none of my business
Quit making it so

Live out your conscience
Celebrate all your choices
Don't send me the bill

I hear your crying
Your pain is felt by the sun
I will call the government for you
Because I care

Drum, balloon, pink slip
What could be more urgent?
Badgers at 4-0

Could you be my mom?
I see you are not my mom;
Quit telling me what to do

Where were you hiding
From me when I earned it?
Jerk

Who owns you, I ask?
Again, I ask – who owns you?
You don't even know

My life is not yours
How brief is our encounter
Thank God it's over

Have you fixed the bridge?
Leave my money, guns, and stash
Go lay by your dish

Living Wage

Here is the truth we all hate: we get paid what we are worth. Plus or minus a temporary distortion that will be restored to equilibrium by the market in due time, of course.

And everyone earns a living wage, too – just not equal to the living we would like to do. We all would like to get paid a lot more for doing what we like, but the value of what we do is only determined by what someone else is willing to freely pay for it. Riding around on a Segway and yelling is just not worth very much, no matter how good you get at it.

Those who advocate for a government-mandated living wage should instead focus on increasing the worth of those whose labor is not worth very much. A law cannot turn $5 worth into $10 worth or labor, it can only make $5 worth of labor *cost* $10. That's why the jobs aren't coming back.

Whenever we read about some CEO or Wall Street trader making tens of millions of dollars, we compare it to our income and think it is grossly unfair that anyone should make that much. Instead, we should ask ourselves what those guys and gals do that is worth $20 million more than the law requires someone to pay them.

Can you manage a multi-billion hedge fund that will beat market returns? I can't. Do you even know who derivatives work? I don't. Can you run a profitable multi-national corporation with tens of thousands of employees? Not me. What did you do last year that you should have been paid millions for? Perform delicate surgeries? Arrange a merger? Host a hit TV show? Invent a new drug? Build a killer app? Cure a disease? Run a casino? Win the Super Bowl? Me neither.

If you make $20/hour, it is because the value of what you produce in that hour of work is $21 or greater. If the value of what you produce is only $10, then guess what – you aren't going to make $20. And certainly not $20 million, regardless of what Oprah makes, and regardless of what her opinion of a living wage is.

The notion that every job should pay a living wage is one of those emotionally satisfying ideas that make no rational sense. Whose lifestyle are we entitled to – Lindsay Lohan's or some monk who eats pond grass? And what does what we would like to spend have to do with what our work is worth, anyway?

If two people both make the same widgets at the same rate, should the one with 6 kids and a bad nicotine habit get paid four times as much as the single person with frugal tastes? What does the chain smoking family man do that is worth four times more? And who will pay four times as much for his widgets? Not me.

Get ready, Wisconsin, because the news media loves to sensationalize boring government budget issues with the heartbreaking stories of people at the margins who will be shattered by any proposed reductions in the size of government. "How can I live on $15,000?" pleads the tearful mother who is paid only minimum wage.

We are supposed to be moved to give her another $5,000 or $10,000 or whatever the magic number liberals have attached to the term "living wage". We are called greedy and uncaring if we even question the premise that it is our duty to subsidize her family. Tell me, what is so caring about people who earn six figures demanding those who earn seven subsidize those who earn five? Generosity is when you give your own money. Looting is when you give someone else's.

They ignore the reality that the $5,000 or $10,000 must be taken away from working people with families of their own who are struggling just as hard to live on their wages. No one writes their story; there are no zombies publicizing their cause, no drummers banging out their grievance, no chanting and rallies and boycotts on their behalf.

"How will I live?" is the wrong question for that mother to ask, and we are the wrong ones to be questioned. The right question, the one she needs to ask herself, is, "why is my labor still only worth $15,000 after 20 years of working?" Hoping to be paid more, expecting to be paid more, even demanding to be paid more will not make that mother worth more.

She needs to acquire skills and develop competencies that will pay her three or four times what she is worth now. She will not acquire those skills from food stamps, rent subsidies, Badger Care, the EIC, or voting for either Democrats or Republicans.

She must improve her skills herself; it is her responsibility to be worth more and hers alone. It is kindness to tell her so in plain language; it is unkindness to continue the deception and call it progressive.

Only when she is worth more will she earn more. She must take courses, seek training, earn certificates and credentials, practice, and gain experience. And she must develop judgment, technical competence, trade mastery, interpersonal skills. She must not wait to be promoted; she must make herself promotable. And it will be very hard - no one is carried out of poverty; we all crawled.

In the process of increasing her worth, she will do something more important; she will liberate herself. She will declare her independence from government. She will own herself and she will have something of great value to pass on to her children – pride.

Statists will tell her she can't make it on her own, and they will smugly convince themselves they are right. But they will not convince those of us who have done it, because we know better. And they are no friends of the working poor, who will achieve no more than they believe.

Perpetual dependence on the state is not living, and no dependent wage is a living wage. The only way to be independent is to earn more, the only way to earn more is to be worth more, and being worth more is our own responsibility.

149

Looking Backwards

The Thursday headline read, "Survey: Obamacare Raised Costs". The byline was a head-cocker, "White House accuses survey of 'looking backwards'."

How else can we learn what actually happened besides looking backwards? Looking backwards is the only way to test theory with fact, to verify assumptions, and...never mind, I forgot the central tenet of liberalism: if it was supposed to, it did, and you are a hater if you dare to question it.

Obamacare was supposed to improve health care and lower cost, so we are supposed to simply accept that it did. Just like all those other programs were supposed to end poverty, improve education, extinguish racism, heal the sick, eradicate drug use, cleanse the environment, feed the hungry, house the homeless, reduce crime, make industry competitive, give the disadvantaged a leg up, create a safety net, give everybody a leg up into the safety net.

The Kaiser Family Foundation study found health care costs increased by 9% in the year after President Obama's signature reform legislation went into effect. This is nearly 3 times the rate of increase (3.1%) recorded in the year before the legislation kicked in.

Is anyone surprised? The Bill added 2.3 million 18-26 year-olds to employer plans, forced pre-existing condition coverage, and mandated so many other additional costs that waivers had to be handed out faster than Kleenex at a funeral. Do you think all those unions and businesses and charities were rushing to get those waivers in order to avoid cost savings?

The White House did not dispute the Kaiser findings; rather, it "accused" the researchers of looking backwards, as if that were a treasonous act. Mr. Obama's Deputy Chief of Staff's rebuke said, "When we look to the future we know that The Affordable Care Act will help make insurance more affordable for families and businesses across the country."

Oh, well, that settles it, then. Because it was supposed to, it will, or did, or does, or something. The sand would be an upgrade from the hiding place of the head naïve enough to believe that.

I can see why looking backwards would be uncomfortable for the Obama administration. When we look backwards, we discover that the stimulus did not create jobs, that the earth did not warm, that health care costs went up, that GDP has yet to recover, that home prices are still falling, that Solyndra went belly up, that ATF sold guns to Mexican drug cartels, and that boots are on the ground in Libya.

It is much more pleasant to talk about things that will never happen as if they already did. That's how he won the Nobel Peace Prize, after all, and the best jobs bill is always the next one. With real unemployment hovering around 20% and GDP growth within rounding error of zero, it is no surprise this White House prefers daydreaming to data.

To be fair, not all of the increase in health care costs was due to Mr. Obama's PACA; each year America gets older and fatter and new and better treatments hit the market which cost more than the ones they replace. No one likes it, but it is better to be alive and bitching about the price than to be affordably gone.

I don't work in the White House, so I am not required to see sunshine and kittens when I look into the future. That affordable health care for families and businesses they keep telling us about does not jump out at me when I peer into the dismal next they have created for us.

No, I see every single penny of the President's rich-bastard tax that will be levied on doctors, dentists, anesthesiologists, radiologists, surgeons, and high-end nurses being tacked onto our medical bills. I see nothing but new mandates, fines, and administrative red tape for every employer in the country; increasing the cost of doing business, forcing layoffs and depressing wages.

I see billions of dollars going to consultants to tell us what we have to do to be in compliance with a steady stream of new regulations from a dozen agencies that don't talk to each other. I see a string of court cases a mile long to sort out all of the conflicting mandates that those federal agencies and their counterparts in the states will impose.

I see millions of working Americans scurrying to enroll in state exchanges when their employers drop coverage. I see every liberal in the nation blaming the employers when this happens, not the Party that wrote the provisions of the law which incent employers to opt out. For the record, that was not the Libertarian Party.

Want to find a politician who actually did reduce health care costs? Try Wisconsin Governor Scott Walker. He exposed the WEA trust health insurance racket and busted it; in cities and towns all across the state, tens of millions – hundreds, ultimately – are being saved through choice and competition. The unions had to be broken for the cost curve to be bent. Our President doesn't have the stones.

There was never a health care problem in this country; we have a cost problem. President Obama and the Democrats imposed their big-government solution and premium costs went up by 9%. Governor Walker and the Republicans imposed their market-competition solution and premium costs have been reduced by tens of millions. The politics are debatable; the math is not.

The irony is that the same people who demanded the President's reforms are the ones screaming bloody murder about the cost of getting what they wanted. They also opposed the Governor's reforms with all their might and are hell-bent to recall him despite the daily flow of municipalities reporting lower health care premium costs, the very thing they coo and purr over Mr. Obama for merely promising. I suppose nothing is as affordable as forcing someone else to buy your care, but lowering its cost has to be the next best thing.

Mr. Obama went too far and Mr. Walker did not go far enough. Looking backward reveals trajectory, but not opportunity. The Libertarian solution is to withdraw government from the health care system entirely. Choice and competition will produce better care for more people at lower prices. Doctors and patients don't need any costly help from parasitic consultants, lawyers, lobbyists, bureaucrats, IRS agents, politicians, activists, advocates, pundits, think tanks, and social scientists.

It is neither the priest nor the policeman that keeps the auto mechanic honest in a small town; it is the second auto mechanic. Choice and competition, not government control, will make our health care system affordable and accessible. Real health care reform will come when Obamacare is repealed and the system is liberated from government interference.

That will be a good day to look backward. We will have accomplished something.

Loser

It started with Al Gore in 2000. He had every advantage possible; he was the incumbent Vice President, the economy was soaring, we were not at war, and the media was determined to discredit his less-than-stellar opponent at all costs. He felt *entitled* to be President, but he lost.

He lost the vote, the canvass, the recount, the legislative battles, and the court challenges. He cherry-picked his venues for appeal and still could not steal his victory. We watched his pathetic transition from a guy who lost, to a guy who lost it, to a loser. A man of character would have conceded defeat, congratulated his opponent and led the transition from partisan campaign to unified governance.

But Al Gore did not do the right thing. He held our nation captive to his petty self-indulgence for weeks, spending millions of other people's money in a futile attempt to take by force what he could not win by persuasion. His desperation was embarrassing; anything to stay in the limelight, to pretend for one more day to be important. Al Gore did not just lose an election, he legitimized losing.

In the process, he turned his Democrat party into the Party of Losers; and they made him a rock star for it. He went on to fail at teaching, to debase the Nobel Prize, to profit from a hoax, and to fail in his marriage. He perfected his craft.

Al Gore is the patron saint of losers, the inspiration to empty vessels like Al Franken and Wisconsin's Joanne Kloppenburg whose perverted idea of victory is to disenfranchise enough American citizens to cheat their way into an office they could not win by convincing voters they were worthy.

The more they pout, whine, stall, and connive, the more obvious it becomes that they possess no other marketable skills. Is it cruel to call Joanne Kloppenburg a loser? If the scarf fits...

Just as they say; this is what democracy looks like – unskilled leaders, mob rule, ends justifies means, win at any cost, class envy, disregard for rights, brute force, and self-enrichment shamelessly peddled as compassion.

Democracy looks like a big pile of other people's money to be pilfered and a free media spotlight for preeners and posers who have conned their faithful into the false belief that saying something is the same as doing it. A place for the losers to stick it to the winners – that is what democracy looks like...to losers.

Which is *exactly* why our founders established a Constitutional Republic instead of a Democracy. Our nation was founded by winners. Our forefathers did not sit in the capitals of Europe marinating in self-pity and bitching about the King; they got off their butts and came here to live in freedom and to reap the rewards of their own accomplishments. They came to own themselves. They came to serve their God, not their government. They came to win.

Wave after wave of immigrants from around the word did not risk their lives and their life savings hoping that someday they might see Joanne Kloppenburg trick her way onto the Wisconsin Supreme Court to restore state-union perks and privilege against the will of the people's elected representatives. That was not the dream.

They came here hoping to live in a society where it doesn't even matter who sits on the court, who is governor, and who holds legislative office majorities. That is the rule of law. They risked everything to live free and prosper in a country where government was too limited to covet its trappings. That is the American Dream.

We have dishonored their memories by allowing this nation to sink so low that losers are celebrated and a government office is a title of nobility; where connivance is lauded and competition is scorned; where this contested election for Wisconsin Supreme Court justice was even close.

The founding fathers knew all about losers. When the Constitution was written, there had already been over 200 years of American life; every manner of partisan slacker, weasel, and suck-up had wormed his way into a cushy government post and participated in the state-sanctioned looting of their fellow colonists. The loser's obsession with controlling other human beings is timeless; human nature does not change just because we type with our thumbs.

The framers created an ingenious system of governance where the losers who seek to rig the game for themselves and their cronies could not accumulate enough power to matter. They designed a framework where merit determined outcome, where prosperity was earned, where government was limited and freedom was not. They dispersed power to the states, separated power between branches, and expressly reserved unalienable rights for people.

We were the nation that celebrated winners – that's why we produced so many of them. The star athlete, the valedictorian, the virtuoso artist, the successful entrepreneur, the gifted student, the brilliant scientist, the military hero, the winning candidate, the hardest worker, the inventor, the brain surgeon, the rich merchant, the movie star, the most prosperous farmer, the self-made man or woman, the best you-name-it; these were the can-do people we praised, paid, and held up for our children to emulate.

In the real world, everyone does not get a hug, a sticker, or a seat on the Wisconsin Supreme Court. You get what you earn, not what you drum.

You win if you are better than the person you are competing against; one step faster, one stroke lower, one grade point higher, one price point better, one bouquet of flowers more thoughtful, one vote more. You do not win by earning 7,000 less votes than your opponent. That is losing.

Joanne Kloppenburg lost a race she could have won easily, given the momentum of the time and the money that poured in to purchase her victory. After an embarrassing premature victory claim, she spat on the public trust by making us endure a meaningless and costly recount whose only achievement was disenfranchising a few nuns. She must be so proud.

Ms. Kloppenburg has now decided to embarrass herself further and humiliate her Party yet again by taking their poor-pitiful-me act to the courts, hoping there to improve her odds of finding someone dumb enough to put her on the bench.

But this is not really about one woman's fight for justice and a seat on the Wisconsin Supreme Court. This is about the Democrat Party – a wholly owned subsidiary of the public-sector unions – refusing to honor the results of yet another election. It is obstruction of justice, by any reasonable definition of the two terms.

And by any reasonable definition, Joanne Kloppenburg is a Loser.

Mine

There are many economic arguments against the socialist demand for government to redistribute the wealth I have accumulated, but here is only one moral argument needed: because it's mine.

I don't owe you any further explanation. You aren't entitled to my money for the same reason you can't have my liberty – because it's mine. It's not yours, it's not ours, it does not belong to society – it's mine. If you can't understand that, then you have been brought up badly, and I feel sorry for you. But not enough to feel guilty.

Why should anyone feel guilty about what they earn or what they have accumulated? Because others have less? That is a reason for compassion, not guilt. There is only one person on the face of the earth who does not have someone poorer coveting what he has. You will not find that person anywhere in this country. Our poorest citizens live beyond the imaginations of a large segment of the world's population.

There is only one person who has a rightful claim to the money that I have earned, and that is the lovely and talented Mrs. Dr. Tim – and you can't have her either. We belong to each other because we took an oath before God to make it so. And we don't need government to redistribute our wealth; we are happy to do it ourselves.

If you ask nicely, we might just give you some of it; we do that all the time to worthwhile causes and worthy charities. If you offer us something in exchange, you can have even more of it; and if you happen to be offering shoes, bags, jewelry, furniture, kitchenware, hair products, or clothes in exchange, you will end up with a whole boatload of it, trust me. If you work for it, we will gladly part with our wealth in big gulps, especially if it is work we can't do for ourselves.

Ask, exchange, or work for it and we will live in peace; but if you try to take it, now that is a different story. About all I would be willing to share with you under that circumstance are several rounds of my ammo – at very high velocity.

And who would blame me? Is it selfish to defend what is mine from theft, to keep what I have earned, to protect myself and my family? No, it is selfish to take what someone else earned. There is no proper religion that I know of that does consider theft immoral. And there is no government that I know of that does not engage in it.

Government confiscates wealth by taxing it, inflating currency, regulating economic activity, or levying fines, fees, tariffs, and excises. The essential services that government provides to all of its citizens make up a small fraction of modern State's fiscal budget.

Government is largely a system of third-party forced wealth transfer, taking the earnings of some citizens to give to others. Those who advocate more government do not propose new programs to benefit all citizens; they insist on taking more from some of us to give more to some of us. Can you name an exception?

Socialism is not just selfish, it is foolish; wealth is never created by confiscation, it is only destroyed. Wealth is created through voluntary exchange. It is created most rapidly under free market capitalism; most widely dispersed through choice and competition. It is no accident that the most free nations are the most prosperous; it is it no coincidence that business thrive where they keep more of what they earn.

I, me, mine. These are the words that were banned by government in the Ayn Rand novella "Anthem". It is a morality play, contrasting of the opposing extremes of individual liberty and collectivist tyranny against each other in a future world that suddenly looks so not-so-distant.

I am somebody. I belong to me. What I have earned is mine.

Mommy Dearest

The libertarian argument for less government is made each and every day for us by the silly things that government does. The more distant the level of government, the dumber those things are. That is the founding principle behind the United Nations; some things are just too stupid for one country to do by itself.

This year's U.N. float in the Stupid Parade is a proposed treaty which would recognize the earth as a living thing with rights equal to humans – Mother Earth. This is the sort of notion that distinguishes blithering idiots from the non-blithering generic kind of idiots.

The language will be patterned after Bolivia's Law of The Rights Of Mother Earth, recently enacted by its socialist President Evo Morales. That Bolivian law establishes a Ministry of Mother Earth and provides an Ombudsman to listen to her complaints. No, seriously. I honestly can't decide which U.N. idea is goofier: ascribing human rights to a planet or emulating Bolivia.

For those unfamiliar, Bolivia is the poorest nation in the Western Hemisphere. Not coincidently, its President Morales has imposed the most anti-capitalist and anti-corporate policies in the Americas. While neighbors Peru, Colombia, and Brazil are prospering by developing their resources, embracing industry, and attracting foreign investment, Morales is digging himself a deeper hole with socialist insanity and superstitious hoodoo like his Mother Earth Law.

In the United States, the Mother Earth argument has already been used to block economic development, particularly in natural resource industries like mining, timber harvesting, water, and oil and gas exploration. The tortured reasoning goes that nature is a person, too, and every activity of man injures her. Get ready for a full dose of it as the mine project in northern Wisconsin moves forward towards permitting.

The word selection is important – she is always feminine, and always victimized by men. There is no movement for White Dude Earth, the uncaring rich old bastard that hoards his minerals and water underground where poor people can't get at them and rains on Gay Pride parades. No, the earth-person of the United Nations and communist environmental extremists has mommy bits, doesn't shave her legs, hates guns, and thinks teachers are underpaid.

The idea of inanimate object having human rights is proof that if you think long enough, you can make yourself believe anything. To state the obvious, human rights are – duh – the stuff of individual humans. Not collective humans, not their pets, not the Simpsons, farm animals, crops, trees, wind, planets, the universe, dead things, words, rocks, or cheese hats made of plastic.

Even if there were such a thing, Mother Earth would not be kindly June Cleaver, cleaning the oven in heels and pearls and offering up fresh cookies to Wally and Eddie Haskell after track practice. She would be Mommie Dearest, a raging Joan Crawford marinated in alcohol and stoked on amphetamines, cussing us out and beating the crap out of us with coat hangers. What comes to mind when you think back to that 24" inch blizzard this winter – "thanks, Mom"? Not.

Just to humor the UN whack jobs, let's say that Mother Earth does have rights; well then she has responsibilities, too. Hey Mommy - here's the $8 billion tab for Katrina; it's already a couple years past due and headed for collections. Tsunami, floods, blizzards, droughts, earthquakes, volcanoes – you went on quite a rampage recently, there, sister; hope you have paid up insurance and a good lawyer.

The Mother Earthers, I'm sure, would say that all those horrible natural disasters are the punishment we should expect for being loathsome humans. Oh, yeah? What did the dinosaurs do to deserve extinction, leave reptilian paw prints on the coffee table? Graze with their mouths open? And how do you know what she thinks - did she tell you? Do you two speak Earth when you chat? Ask her if this Global Warming thing was just a hot flash, now that it's over.

There is no arguing with the Mother Earth crowd – theirs is a religious conviction based on hatred of humans generally and human economic activity specifically. The only sure way to derail their Mother Earth movement is to tell them the Koch Brothers gave her a few bucks and watch them vibrate in place.

Earth Whore! Planet Bitch! Nature Slut! Misspelled signs calling her a K-word, Michael Moore cussing out vegans, Congresswoman Tammy Baldwin demanding Eric Holder's Justice Department put humanity in foster care until there is a recount – you get the picture. President Obama would appoint a commission to determine where her ass is so he could kick it. Sarah Palin would drop to #2 on the list of the left's most despised moms.

Clearly, the United Nations has too much time on its hands. Having secured world peace, eradicated hunger, lifted mankind out of poverty, vanquished disease, educated all the planet's children, and written thousands of sternly-worded letters to dictators, what is left to do?

Besides empower a new class of parasitic lawyers and a slew of mentally unbalanced Mother Earth activists to sue humanity on behalf of a plaintiff who can't file her own complaints because she is dumb as a stone. Not surprising, since she is a stone.

And speaking of lunatics, how in the world did we get to the brink of shutting down our own government without first defunding the United Nations? Democrats and Republicans agreed to cut $39 billion out of domestic spending but both thought it urgent that this bunch of foreign fruitloops maintain their lavish lifestyle on our dime? Is Rosetta Stone translation software co-owned by the teachers' union and the Ohio chamber of commerce or something?

Here is what we should do about the United Nations: cut them off, cut them loose, and when they throw a tantrum about it tell them to ask their Earth Mommy to increase their allowance and let them use her credit card.

My Business

Here is the difference: at a permit hearing for an open-carry pride parade, Democrats would be offended by the guns, Republicans would be offended by the gays, and Libertarians would be offended that you need a permit.

We libertarians get offended just like anyone else. But we are content to let others make their own offensive choices based upon their own conscience and beliefs. The default setting in the libertarian mind is "none of my business"; and besides, being offended reminds us we are still free.

The problem with socialists and statists is that they don't share this "live and let live" philosophy. They insist on making their choices my business. They tax, regulate, mandate, ban, license, permit, inspect, certify, confiscate, indoctrinate, conscript, fine, incarcerate, subsidize, and punish the choices of others in order to achieve their ends. Their idea of tolerance is for me to tolerate their tyranny because it is good for me; President Obama believes it is his job to make me eat my peas.

Libertarians and true conservatives have no such impulse to impose our choices onto others, and we are especially averse to employing the power of the state to do the dirty work. We share our Founders' view of government as a necessary evil, an unreliable and terrifying beast that must be bound, leashed, and caged.

Progressives could live according to their beliefs on their own; it is making the rest of us live according to their beliefs that requires government force. They are free to eschew energy, to share their wealth, to teach their children flavored history, to deny God, to avoid guns, to hire according to quotas, to marry whoever they wish in the church of their choice. No one is stopping them; certainly not me.

Join a union or don't. Buy a house or don't. Shop at Walmart or don't. Buy ethanol gas or don't. Be as gay as you want or as straight as you please. Drink Scotch or drink Coke (but don't you dare drink Scotch and Coke, even us libertarians have our limits). Pray all day or join a coven. Sleep around or sew your knees shut. Smoke, snort, shoot, or drink only distilled water and colon cleanse.

Drive a Prius, drive a Porsche, drive a tank, drive a Segway, or walk – I don't care; what you chose to do is none of my business. Until you make it my business.

You make it my business when you expect me to pay for your choices. You make it my business when you seek government sanction of your beliefs. You make it my business when you mandate what you can't afford, ban what you don't like, and tax what you don't do.

Those who don't drive want to tax gasoline. Those who don't smoke want to tax each pack. Those who rent want to tax property owners. Those who don't own guns want to tax gunners. Those who don't sin much want higher sin taxes. Those who don't work want to tax the work of those who do. Even liberal billionaires want their altruism merit badge on someone else's dime.

Bill Gates and Warren Buffet call for raising the top income tax rate to 39%. That would be laudable, except Gates and Buffet don't pay income tax; they derive their wealth from capital gains, which is taxed at 15%. Last year, Buffet paid 17% of his income in tax - not that there was anything to stop him from writing a check to the IRS for the other 22%. Check that - there was something that stopped him; his own hypocrisy.

It is taxes that turn our differences into divisions. We must not only tolerate things that offend us, but pay for them, and that makes us angry with one another. Imagine how much better we would all get along if government were confined to doing the things that are absolutely necessary to protect our rights and maintain physical infrastructure. If government was, dare I say it, limited.

Do you really care if the person plowing the Interstate is male or female, gay or straight, black or white, liberal or conservative, Christian or Muslim or Atheist, hunter or vegan? I don't. Would you care about indoctrination at one school if you had the choice to move your kids to another one? Would it matter what symbols adorn the courthouse grounds if you never had to go there to get permission slips to live?

Libertarians are often accused of being selfish. Au contraire – we care deeply about others. Our dream is for every single person to define happiness for themselves and seek it. To live as their own conscience dictates, not according the prejudices and preferences of someone else. To succeed or fail on their own terms, not simply to endure a lifetime of collateral damage inflicted by self-empowered fools. To bind government by its Constitution and take care of each other as we see fit.

When did those ideas become radical? This nation was founded upon them; the GOP that nominated Barry Goldwater fully embraced them; the civil rights movement of Martin Luther King embodied them. When Governor Chris Christie recently answered a constituent's question about his private life with "none of your business", even conservatives gasped. That is how far off our moorings we have drifted.

We will know when we have put our country back on the right track. It will be the day that we say "none of your business" and it is the question that is ridiculed, not the answer. That day cannot come soon enough.

My Occupation

The word "occupation" has another meaning. For those of us who have one, it refers to what we do to make a living. I am a businessman; that is my occupation.

Businessman was not always my occupation. My undergraduate majors were art and psychology, although I did not quite exactly graduate; it was more of a mutual agreement with the college administration that instead of coming back for my final year, I would benefit from matriculating at any other institution anywhere else on the planet. One suggested a facility with bars and guards would be a good choice.

In 1975 the economy was in the ditch, there was little demand for an art/psych dropout, the Marines wouldn't take me, and I as raised in the belief that it was a disgrace for an able-bodied person to accept welfare. My parents had made it clear their home would not be occupied by adult children, and the age of dependency had not yet been raised to 26. The party was over and it was time to grow up – kinda.

I cut my hair and shaved, ditched the jeans for chinos, put on a tie, and made up a resume that listed every job I ever held (12), all of my accomplishments and awards, my academic record and grade point, and all of my volunteer work – I didn't mention the rowdiness that got me expelled from my one-man Occupy Carthage College movement. No hard feelings, by the way; I had it coming.

And I hit the streets, stopping in every business and factory and asking to see the boss. Not the personnel department, the boss; the lines were too long at the personnel department and all the people there were just filling out forms. I didn't stop at night; I hit on every factory night shift foreman and restaurant manager and tavern owner right up until bar time.

It took a zillion rebuffs until one boss liked how I got around his personnel department firewall and gave me a job working in a warehouse for $1.15 an hour – minimum wage. I did not get that job because I could draw an apple or recognize obsessive compulsive traits in adolescents; I got it because I could lift 110 pound boxes over my head and that saved the company time waiting for a forklift driver.

That was my employable skill – lifting; that was how I could add value for the firm. It was my foot in the door, and I was grateful to be employed. And no, minimum wage was not a livable wage back then, either, so I added another job and then added a half-time job until I could learn enough and add enough value to cut back down to just one.

The rest is pretty boring everyday American Dream kind of stuff - small town boy makes good. I won't bore you with the details of how I went from human forklift to company President, and there are many more compelling stories then mine if you are looking for inspiration.

Over the past 37 years I have made it my business to learn new ways to add value for my employers and our customers – that is what the occupation of businessman is all about. Adding more value is how the ladder is climbed. I look now at the Occupy Wall Street protestors and wonder if they have any idea what it will take for them to swim with the big fish if and when they get around to the grown-up business of choosing and mastering a real occupation and providing for themselves and their families.

It is difficult for guys like me to sympathize with those protestors who expect high-paying jobs simply just because they have college degrees. In case any of you are reading this, I have to tell you that college isn't even that hard anymore, and your need to pay off your loan is not a reason why I should hire you to work for me. It is on you to show me what value you can add to my firm; it is not on me to provide you with income. And you must compete with others who want that job as much or more as you do. Hit the gym, vocationally speaking.

Do you have 12 jobs to put on your resume? Can you list the charity work, sports and club awards from your school days that demonstrate your commitment to excellence? Did you figure out how to get around the personnel department to get to me? Are you willing to start at the bottom and lift heavy things just to have the opportunity to show us what else you got?

If you are sincere about wanting a job, start with the basics. Pull your pants up; turn your hat around – better yet, take it off; and take that hockey puck thing out of your earlobe and all the staples out of your face – you look like a freakin' tackle box. Cover up your tats even if you have to wear a burqa to do it; either grow a beard or shave, knock off that indecisive stubble thing; comb your hair and wash those red and blue streaks out of it. And don't call me "dude".

But do tell me about the charity work you have done during your extended period of unemployment. Uh-oh...all that time on your

165

hands, such great needs, and you couldn't find a way to make a difference in some kid's life? Head Start, Big Brothers & Sisters, Junior Achievement, Boys and Girls Club, 4H, Scouts, any church, and you figure out how to do any of that giving back you keep talking about? That tells me a lot more about you than your misspelled resume does...dude.

You know who impresses me in an interview? Those who serve in the National Guard or Reserve and the veterans returning from their active duty service, especially those who served in combat. Many have left pieces of themselves in foreign lands, but few complain; in a job interview, the disabled veteran really stands out against the scores of inabled civilians whose first question is how much time off they will get.

These terrific young men and women who served gave up a life of privilege and denied themselves and their family in order to do defend our liberty. They understand sacrifice, discipline, teamwork, goal-setting, innovation, planning, strategy, and character. They know results matter, they have demonstrated an ability to overcome obstacles, and they possess instantly transferable skill sets and vocational training. Plus we owe them - to the serially ungrateful, this may seem like an obsolete sentiment; some would call it unfair. Tough Schlitz.

I don't need a law to tell me to give a hiring preference to veterans; it is good business as well as good citizenship. The Department of Defense has a program called Employer Support for the Guard and Reserves (ESGR) which helps employers reach out to current military and those leaving the service to return to civilian life. Check it out, employers.

The Occupier who took the dump on a cop car Wall Street is going to have a hard time finding and keeping a job – not because he took a dump on a cop car, but because he thinks taking a dump on a cop car with kids around is cool. That brain isn't a disability; it is a liability. We employers don't have the time or the inclination to fix him.

Occupied

The organizers of the Occupy Wall Street protest finally released their list of 13 demands, about two weeks into the protest. Better never than late.

First among them is a demand for a law that raises the minimum wage to $20 per hour. Leading with such a foolish idea makes it pretty hard to read the other 12 without thinking it is the first draft of a David Letterman Top Ten List written by someone who learned math in a government school.

Paying somebody $20 is easy, but it takes more than a law for someone's work to be worth more than $20. They have to possess employable skills that are in demand, exhibit a positive attitude, be accountable, and work well with others – and then actually do something that is worth at least $21 to someone else. Coming in two weeks late with a badly composed single page list is not the kind of performance that is worth $20/hour to anybody - I can see why they think a law is necessary.

But they are wrong; minimum wage laws are unnecessary. Median income in the private sector is just under $50,000 per year, or $25 per hour, which is roughly three times the minimum wage mandated by Congress.

What law makes a company pay an employee $25? Better yet, what law forced that employee to become worth more than $25? It is the Law of Supply and Demand; and it is apparently 3 times better, as laws go, than the one Congress passed to set a wage floor. It is useful to remind ourselves *why* more than half of the people working in this country are already paid $5 more per hour than what these Wall Street occupiers consider "justice". The answer, of course, is that their work adds more than $25 to the value of the company which employs them.

The story is the same for the $12 wage and the $12 million salary. Brett Favre used to be worth millions, and now he isn't; Aaron Rodgers wasn't worth millions watching Brett play; now he is worth every penny of the millions he makes playing, but in a few years he won't be worth millions again. It's what you do that pays, not what you know.

There is no government legislation that forces companies to pay more than the minimum wage, just as there is no law that forces companies to provide benefits, or schedule 40 hour weeks, or name holidays, or grant paid vacations. And yet most firms do.

Why? Because the law of supply and demand tells them to; and they must obey the laws of economics or perish. Unlike the perverted corporatism practiced in New York and Washington D.C., the free market has no mechanism to bail out fools, frauds, and failures.

In reality, there is no law that forces companies to actually pay that minimum wage either; most just eliminate the job that is only worth below-minimum. Setting the minimum wage to $20 would eliminate all the jobs worth $19.99 and under. This will add many tens of millions of Americans to the ranks of the unemployed and push us over 50% unemployment.

I don't think the occupiers understood how this economics stuff works, but as luck would have it they don't have to, since they included a separate demand that everyone who doesn't work receive a living wage. "Eaters", Henry Kissinger called them; who knew it would become a professional vocation one day.

Another occupation demand is a free college education for everyone. I'm all for that, but not for the reasons you might think. A no-cost education is only possible if there is no cost to it – no salaries, wages, pensions, maintenance, heat, light, books, etc. I think it is a terrific idea for University faculty and staff all across the nation to put their money where their mouth is and work for free in unheated classrooms to show their solidarity with the unionist occupation movement and stick it to us greedy, heartless, libertarian capitalists once and for all. Fists up, anyone?

The rest of the demand list is pretty lame and predictable economic suicide – cut off all the energy that is charging the iPhones, Droids, Bluetooth headsets, pads, and notebooks they use to spread the word about the occupation. And re-elect President Obama – appropriate, since their goal is to collapse the economic system.

But this one is bold: wipe out all debt all over the world. Private, public, corporate, sovereign – just forgive it all. Write off the tens of trillions owed to bond-holders and bank stockholders and start over; one giant global financial mulligan. I don't suppose it has occurred to them that the entire U.S. Social Security system and every other pension plan in the country would be immediately wiped out and nobody would ever loan a penny to anyone ever again. Dark Ages, Part Dieux, and not one of those fools could shoot his dinner once Taco Bell goes dark.

168

Maybe if the occupiers had another two weeks to think about it, they would demand we annul all the marriages in the world, too – as long as we are tossing aside solemn commitments. Just throw the whole world's car keys into one giant swingers' bowl to give everybody a fair chance at landing Miss Venezuela or George Clooney, as you prefer.

Why not – this is all about fairness and privilege, right? It is certainly not fair that the privileged 1% are so unnecessarily beautiful while us 99%ers have to struggle just to be presentable. That is the whole point of this occupation thing – forcing the privileged few to give it up. I bet most of those guys, and a bunch of the girls, would take Eva Mendes over Trump's money if you gave them the choice of which unjust deprivation they would cure first.

Don't get me wrong; the protestors have every right to protest, and watching them comforts me that we are still a free country, Hank Jr. notwithstanding. What they don't have a right to do is occupy; private property is private and public property belongs every bit as much to those Wall Street brokers as it does the dude in the dreads calling them names.

The occupiers should watch and learn from the Tea Party: get your permit, hold your rally, pick up your trash, and go back to work. Ask Nancy Pelosi if that was effective. And not to rub it in, but it is a safe bet that the Tea Party will send more of its own to Congress in 2012 again than will the Occupation Movement. Gingrich has a better shot of getting candidate pledges for his Contract Addendum with America than do the occupiers with their 13 points of light.

The good news, if you are an occupier, is that you got our attention and made your point; the bad news is that you got our attention and you have no point. You demand that we surrender our liberty to a mob that couldn't even get your list of demands typed up on time. Sorry, I'm taking "or else".

Want to do something useful to stand up to the Wall Street banksters? Why don't you take a break from your occupation to read Ron Paul's book "End The Fed" and then get back to us. Some of us have been rousing the rabble long before you occupiers were even born. Maybe we can do something useful together.

Occupy Fremont Street

It certainly is not fair here in Las Vegas. There are winners and losers; you can work at it all day and go home flat broke. The rich get the best of everything and much of it is free. Food is unaffordable and housing only barely so. The daily income gap is worse here than anywhere in the world.

The casino corporations' CEOs make hundreds of times more than the janitors, who appear to be all immigrants, probably illegal. Elton John makes tens of thousands a night while the Circus Soleil acrobats work their butts off for scale. The cocktail waitresses are made to wear revealing outfits and trade cleavage for tips; showgirls are fired when they get too old or too fat.

Not only do they have exploited consumers and oppressed workers, but the planet is taking a beating here as well. There are millions of too-bright lights, there are taxis and limos and busses everywhere, and air-conditioners blast while fountains pumping water into the dry desert air 24/7. God only knows how many salamanders were made extinct when they built the Hoover dam that helps power up this place.

Oh, the terrible exploitation, greed, harassment injustice, and abuse everywhere! No wonder tens of thousands of our fellow occupiers took to Freemont Street last night to rage against the...oh wait, that was not a protest; it was a Doors tribute and psychedelic light show up on the overhead canopy. And those weren't occupiers; they were just wasted.

Never mind.

No one forces anyone to come to Las Vegas, no one forces anyone to gamble, eat, drink, shop, shoot machine guns, ride helicopters, golf, hit the spa, see a show, tan, rent a Lamborghini, rent an Elvis minister, or rent an escort. Down on Fremont Street, you can get your picture taken with a midget dressed as Mr. T if you so desire; tip extra and he will say it: "I pity the fool." I'm quite certain that position was not advertised on the state job board; but it was probably counted twice in the Joe Biden "created or saved" sweepstakes.

Las Vegas teaches us the fundamental lesson of free market capitalism: choice and competition increases quality, reduces costs, and adds variety. You can get 4 Tees for $10 or you can get a Ferrari polo shirt for $165; $3 roulette at O'Shea or $100 blackjack at the Wynn; an evening with Elton John or your picture with a very small impersonator.

No government bureau mandated any of it; there is no Department of Impersonator Height to regulate the little Elvises. And here in Las Vegas, when Wall Street bankers lose their shirts, there is no Congressional bailout on the way – you are never too big to fail. And good luck to any 99%er who thinks us 53%ers will buy their buffet ticket at the MGM Grand.

Despite all this unregulated capitalist excess, unfairness, and exploitation, the place is packed. People actually pay to come here and then wait in lines to get ripped off by The Man. Of course, in Las Vegas you are The Man; you decide who gets rich and how rich you will make them. You pursue your own happiness; The Man can only offer it to you. Same as it ever was. That is what the occupiers, socialists, and leftists everywhere don't get, never have, and never will. There was no Las Vegas in East Germany; and there will be no Las Vegas in Occupied America.

We came to Las Vegas to see the GOP Presidential debates in person and hang out for a couple days spreadin' some wealth around the old-fashioned way. My objectives were modest; to catch up with my friend Herman Cain and give him his signed copy of my book, "Capitalista", and to meet my idol Ron Paul.

I am happy that both have made into the top-tier, even if the Demediocrats refuse to acknowledge them as serious candidates. The pundits at MSNBC have decided that Herman Cain is not black enough, and that Ron Paul is a tin-foil-hat crank. Herman is black enough for me, and since it apparently matters to somebody, Ron Paul is white enough for me, too. Dr. Paul has quite a bit going on under that tin-foil hat; he was right about just about everything the media and its leftist patrons have gotten wrong for a quarter century.

Herman Cain is my favorite conservative in this race and Ron Paul is my favorite libertarian. I didn't get to talk with Congressman Paul but I did get to watch them put on his TV makeup right before he announced his revolutionary economic plan – how many Americans can say that? And Mr. Cain was gracious as ever, his front-runner status not dissuading him from still associating with known libertarians like me. It would be a thrill to call him my President; it is an honor to call him my friend.

It is gratifying to see the nation discovering Herman, but now that he is in the lead, the powers that be will go all out to tear him down; they sure tried that again last night. I am pleased that he has decided to take his tormentors on head first; it is about time someone called out the press and paid campaign stalkers for their stupid questions and straw-man issues.

Here is the important question nobody has asked yet about Herman's tax plan: what is wrong with everyone paying taxes?

Why should any person – rich or poor – be exempt from paying a fair share of the cost of the government that benefits everyone? And who decided that zero is a fair share? Where else is that principle ever applied - when five friends go to lunch, is the lowest 20th percentile always entitled to eat free at the others' expense?

On Your Own

Speaking at a fundraiser this week, President Obama tried to frighten Americans with the grim warning that if he is not re-elected in 2012, "you will be on your own." Promises, promises.

Fear not, wards of the State; on January 21 of 2013, the only part of government that we will be rid of is the current occupant of the White House. There will be another President, and he or she will preside over the same unmanageable leviathan that Mr. Obama would like us to believe will simply vanish into thin air if he is not re-employed to run it for four additional years. If only it were that easy.

There is no question that this is now a nation divided, and the President's dire warning brings the line of separation into clear focus. To the dependent class, the idea of being left "on your own" is terrifying. To the producing class, it is liberating. Pick your side.

What is wrong with being on our own? That was our #1 priority growing up. As teenagers we could not wait to graduate from high school, to get our own car, to get the heck out of our boring little mining town, to get out from under our parent's stupid rules, and to go our and find our place in the world.

Some of us went into the service, some of us went to college, some of us went to work in the big cities, some of us went to California or Arizona or Las Vegas or Alaska, and some of us stayed home. We discovered that the world had not reserved a place for us to "find"; we discovered how to make our own way in the world. And we did - on our own.

We became doctors, lawyers, architects, executives, professional golfers, radio personalities, business owners, teachers, firemen, pastors, airline flight attendants, career military, casino dealers, accountants, public administrators, nurses, salespeople, artists, welders, loggers, firefighters, mechanics, beauticians, tavern owners, and every other profession and trade imaginable. We wanted to make our friends and family proud of us and we did - on our own.

We became parents, spouses, volunteers, advocates, investors, philanthropists, community leaders, chaperones, mentors, coaches, bloggers, advisors, board members, deacons, council members, scoutmasters, carolers, big brothers and sisters, fundraisers. We wanted to make a difference and we did - on our own.

We did not do all those things because government made us; we would not stop if there was no government to give us its permission. And "on our own" does not mean alone – we were taught by our mentors, encouraged by our friends, supported by our families, strengthened by our congregations, inspired by great leaders, challenged by our adversaries, and developed by our bosses, paid by our customers, made great by our competitors.

If President Obama is not re-elected, we will not be alone; we will still have our mentors, friends, families, congregations, leaders, adversaries, bosses, customers, and competitors. But according to him, we will be on our own; and thank God if he is right. Because that's what freedom is – being on your own.

The President encourages his constituency to think like children - afraid to be on their own, jealous of the other kids' toys, coveting the bigger allowances of the neighbor kids, angry at their own parents for not giving more, frustrated that life is unfair. They hate the rich for being rich, the pretty for being pretty, the happy for being happy, and the winners for winning. They demand a world of stickers and hugs and do-overs; they don't like bedtime and they don't like to get up and they don't mind pitching a fit in public so we can all be unhappy with them.

And Mr. Obama has also burdened his opponents - with the unwanted responsibility to be the parents of his beloved dependent class. We resent having to care for our shiftless and surly teenagers; we tire of their sass, their ingratitude, their eye-rolling certainty that we are stupid and uncool. We have tired of paying their way, fixing the car they crash over and over, apologizing for their rude behavior in public.

All of us have been teenagers, and many of us have now raised teenagers, so we can see a bit of ourselves in both caricatures. And we know what it took to put the rancor and resentments that builds between parents and children behind us and to start again to treat each other with respect. What it took was for the teenagers to move out and live on their own. That is when we got along.

When our son went out on his own, it was my proudest day as a parent. We knew he would struggle, as we did; we knew he would make bad choices and suffer painful consequences, as we did; we knew that he would become responsible when he had to;

as we did. And we trusted him that he would succeed on his own terms, taking care of himself and his family and helping others in their hour of need. The rebellious youth became a man - on his own. Same as it ever was.

Need is not an acceptable lifestyle choice; dependent is not a career. If we cannot live on our own, who are we supposed to live "on"? Who is it that owes us our existence at their expense? Why is it our neighbor's obligation to fend for us when we will not fend for ourselves? Who will keep us when all of our brothers are kept?

The President has done us the great service of presenting his vision for American with rare and remarkable clarity – a nation of stunted-development dependents incapable of living on their own. And he has revealed to us the full measure of his ego – the entire nation of wards could not possibly survive without him as our President.

Mr. Obama, you can spend the rest of your life dependent on the government and its pension – being President is a tough job and you have earned it. But the rest of us would be thrilled to live on our own, to make this the land of the free again. Thank you for telling us what we need to do to bring that dream to reality.

Opportunity and Outcome

This is a story about two nations with two very different ideas about equality. One nation is named Opportunity, and the other is called Outcome.

When they run a 100 yard dash in Opportunity, everyone starts at the same time and place and runs the same distance – they call that equality in the land of Opportunity. No two people finish exactly the same because some people run faster than others; that's how God made them.

When they run the 100 yard dash in Outcome, however, everyone finishes exactly the same. The only way to do this is to make the rules unequal, to let some people run a shorter distance and add burdens onto others to slow them down. Each runs according to his ability and starts according to his need – that's what they call equality in the land of Outcome.

In Opportunity, the winner of each 100 yard dash gets $100. Everyone else gets a dollar for each yard they have completed when the race is won. Some get $99, some get $80, and some only get $50. The slower runners who want to earn more train harder, run faster, and earn more. The faster runners who don't want to lose income also train harder, run faster, and earn more. So in the land of Opportunity, everyone runs faster and faster, earning more and more.

Some of the slowest runners in Opportunity decide they can't make very much money running, but think they could win the $200 singing contest. And some of the bad singers see that they can make a lot more money running than singing. So people find the work that is best suited for them, train hard, and compete against each other for rewards. Before long, Opportunity is a nation of very fast runners and exquisite singers and they are all earning more and more for their efforts.

In Outcome, however, everyone gets a sticker and a hug for trying, and keeping track of time is discouraged as it is believed to damage self-esteem. The fast runners see that they don't earn any more for all that hard work they put into to training, so they stop working so hard. The slow runners don't want to run faster because then they would be forced to run longer or start later. In Outcome, everyone runs slower and slower.

The people of Outcome think it isn't fair that the singers make more than the runners, so everyone gets the same income whether they sing or run, and whether they do either one well or poorly. Nobody in Outcome trains to get better at anything, and no one bothers to learn a new skill. Outcome quickly becomes a nation of slow runners and bad singers; they believe they are entitled to run or entitled to sing, no matter how badly they do it.

Meanwhile back in Opportunity, the fast races and beautiful singing make the contests very popular; people are willing to pay more to watch excellence, so the rewards paid to runners and singers increase. The runners and singers of Opportunity get rich, and everyone else works hard to afford the expensive tickets; there is abundance from all that hard work that everyone does in Opportunity.

In Outcome, however, no one is willing to pay their own money to watch slow running and bad singing. The only way for runners and singers to earn more money is to demand it from the government. The government in Outcome taxes everyone else to give money to the people who now feel entitled to high pay and lavish benefits for running slowly and singing poorly. Anyone who questions those high taxes is called greedy.

The fastest runners and best singers in Outcome begin to leave; they come to Opportunity where they are free to run or sing or do anything else they please. In Opportunity, they make more money and they keep more of what they make - no one covets the earnings of another. They are happy; that is the gift of liberty.

The leaders of Outcome assure their people that everything is fine; to prove it, they have their central banker print a bunch of fiat money so it looks to their grumbling singers and runners as if they are making more money, too. The whole world rejects Outcome's paper money as reserve currency and starts to buy gold instead.

The people of Outcome are angry that they are slow runners and bad singers with worthless currency. Their leaders blame Opportunity for all of their problems.

And then one day, there is an international competition; the slow runners and bad singers of Outcome must race the swift runners and face the glorious singers of Opportunity. Opportunity demolishes Outcome and wins all the prize money. It is clear to everyone in the world that the quality of Opportunity beats the quality of Outcome.

Everyone, that is, except the dull and unthinking people of Outcome. They were brainwashed in their government schools to believe Outcome is better than Opportunity, so they assume that Opportunity must have cheated in order to have won so much prize money. Some of them occupy spaces and poop on things. The President of Outcome cheers them on when he is not golfing or fundraising.

The slow runners and bad singers of Outcome send their union muscle and government agents to Opportunity to take away Opportunity's winnings by force. The fast runners and exquisite singers of Opportunity are not intimidated; they smile and calmly pull back their jackets to show their concealed-carry weapons. Outcome's thugs go lay by their dish, and the patriots of Opportunity live happily ever after.

Here is the moral of the story: don't mess with patriots in the land of Opportunity; we run faster, we sing better, and we are packing.

The End.

Own That

There could be no more perfect iconic image for the aimless socialist uprising spreading across this country than a skinny white kid with his pants around his ankles taking a dump.

They poop on burning flags, they poop on police cars, they poop on courthouses, and they poop on statues. When they are not pooping on things, they are smashing windows, stealing food, raping women, masturbating in public, using children to sell narcotics, sharing lice and syphilis, and beating up homeless people before refusing to share food with them, along with disrespecting civil rights leaders in sign language.

OWS is a franchise with stores in most major cities and college towns. As the weeks have passed, it has become clear that the "movement" is not a spontaneous and organic student protest, but an ordinary thugfest organized and funded by the latest incarnation of ACORN and a collection of leftist tyrant-wannabes which includes the usual suspects – unionists, communists, Nazis, and professional agitators for hire.

They hate capitalism but demand its abundance be allocated to them. They hate job creators but demand jobs. They hate the freedom of speech enjoyed by any who might disagree with them. They hate elections and representative government. They hate banks, corporations, profits, and anything that emits carbon dioxide, including everyone who disagrees that they are entitled to live free at our expense.

They hate America. And the leaders of the Democrat Party, including President Obama, embrace and applaud them. Own that, Democrats.

To a Libertarian like me, the difference between Republicans and Democrats is not always clear. But events like OWS remind us that while Republicans often lose sight of what liberty is, while Democrats know it perfectly well and hate it. From each according to his ability and to each according to his need; does this Marxist slogan not accurately encapsulate the Democrat platform planks on taxes and social welfare programs?

When someone booed a gay soldier's question at the Republican debates, every candidate quickly denounced it. Still, Democratic media pundits savaged the field for waiting even a few hours before issuing their rebukes. We have now had weeks of riots and over 3,000 arrests and I have yet to hear a single Democrat leader disown OWS. Just the opposite; President Obama, Nancy Pelosi, the head of their patron SEIU, and celebrity mouthpieces like Kanye West and Tim Robbins step forward to embrace and encourage the OWS protest.

When a fairly transparent smear campaign was launched against a black conservative front-runner for the GOP Presidential nomination, the liberal media obsessed for over a week about unsubstantiated allegations of indelicate words being spoken to anonymous women. At the same time, dozens of real women were raped in the OWS encampments; organizers of the anti-capitalist protests encouraged supporters to silence the victims and not report the crimes. Gossip for pay is more important to them than real crimes against real women.

That is all you have to know about the current sorry state of the Democrat Party and its liberal media propaganda arm. Own that, sock puppets.

I was appalled last month when the Tea Party humiliated civil rights icon John Lewis; the sight of a bunch of white guys shouting down a black Congressman who came to address them showed that racism still... Oh, wait, that wasn't the Tea Party, it was the OWS protestors, so never mind.

That video clip was very disturbing; the sight of all those young people repeating words mindlessly brought back haunting memories of the German masses "Sieg Heil" call and response. Mass hypnosis is the stuff of the Manson family or Jonestown; the only question is whether the least hinged among them will end up killing themselves or someone else when they lose their grip on that last marble. Thank you, thank you, Second Amendment.

Earlier this year, this same left-wing rent-a-mob distinguished themselves in Madison by booing the national anthem, drumming out the Pledge of Allegiance, screaming vulgarities at 14-year old girls, blowing the eardrums out of downs-syndrome kids, disrupting a Special Olympics ceremony, threatening to sodomize a reporter, issuing death threats against politicians and their families, extorting businesses, picketing a sheltered workshop, and committing mass insurance fraud.

Do you remember? Own It, Democrats. Now your boys are defecating in public, raping girls, assaulting policemen, killing small businesses, and lighting your cities on fire. Your poster boy in pink throws beer on people and harasses the children of the Governor and you cheer him on. Own that, too.

That's right – you own 'em all. You educated them, you encouraged them, you put them up to it, you paid them to turn out, you cheered them on as they did your dirty work – blaming others for your failed socialist policies. Knuckleheads led by knuckledraggers – that was Madison last winter, and it is OWS this fall. Did you think we wouldn't know?

The OWS protestors demand money from those who have earned it, health care from those who must provide it, education from those who can impart it, and housing from those who build it. In exchange, they offer nothing. Where did they learn this ethos? Not from reading Dr. Tim's Moment of Clarity. Someone needs to talk straight to these kids who are waiting for more government to solve their problems.

I hate to be the one to break it to you Jedi's, but drumming your demands for fairy dust is not a vocational skill that employers are looking for in a tight job market. Herman Cain is right – it is your own fault that you are unemployed. President Obama will not save you, your hinkey group talk thing will not save you, and your twinkling hands will not save you. Get a job - you won't find one here in the park you are squatting on.

But enjoy the sleeping bag sex with those idealist OWS girls while you can, gamers; because they will soon be grown up women with an appetite for Louis Vuitton and you will be back in your mom's basement dating your imaginations again. When it's time to pick the father of their children that prick from Citibank driving the BMW is going to start to look pretty good.

Amber and Chad won't be sharing that Condo in Boca with you, Poop Boy. So grow up, pull up your pants, go apologize to a Vet and learn a trade. You still have your whole life in front of you, and this is still a great country - don't mess it up for the rest of us.

Pensions For Dummies

The CATO Institute recently reported on the state of public employee pension solvency, summarizing the actuarial research of Andrew Biggs. The gist is that public pension funds are severely underfunded when the private sector regulatory standards are applied to them.

The State of Wisconsin's latest financial report states that its public sector pensions are 99% funded under the rules for public pension funds. But under the rules applied to private sector pensions, Wisconsin's pension reserves are 32% underfunded; so say Biggs and CATO, and I have no reason to doubt them.

No one knows for sure why actuaries disagree, as that would require us to actually listen to them speak. The amount of contributions made to date is pretty straightforward, but assumptions of future contributions and future returns can make funds look rock-solid to south-of-Enron or any point in between.

Biggs and others point out that in order to truly be "fully funded", most public pension plan returns would need compounding returns of 8.5% or better each year until hell freezes over. No dips, sags, crashes, doldrums, inflation, or hiccups of any kind between now and the day the last surviving spouse of the newest-hired state worker expires. The anti-capitalist wing of the public sector should stop and think about where those kinds of returns are possible.

There is no government-backed asset class that pays even half of that. Money markets pay zero; over 100 large municipalities are at risk of default, state bonds are wobbly, and U.S. treasuries run from .5% to 4.5%, and S&P just downgraded its rating outlook from "stable" to "negative". The University of Texas bought physical gold, but that is Texas - land of Ron Paul, gun racks, the 10th amendment, and the last laugh.

The only sources for 8.5% compounding returns are commodity futures or the stock market. In other words, public sector workers are completely dependent upon the capitalists they revile to fund the retirements they cherish from the profits they denounce. I wonder how many of them understand that.

While public servants fearing benefit cuts are leaping to take early retirements in droves, those who remain in government have gone hard after Boeing, oil companies, insurance

182

companies, pharmaceutical companies, the banks, the fast-food industry, tobacco companies, the automobile companies that compete with state-owned GM, utilities, Koch Industries, transportation companies, speculators, and basically anyone else that burns a gram of carbon, operates in a Right To Work state, builds or buys overseas, pays a bonus, or makes a buck.

Dummies is the kindest descriptor I can think of; depressing corporate profits lowers dividends and reduces capital gains – the only two means by which equities generate cash to fund public sector pensions payouts. Duh, winning.

Here is a suggestion to those statists and unionists who are hell-bent to hand us immoral capitalists our comeuppance: bet your retirement on your own team.

Sell off all of the company stocks in your pension fund portfolio and buy nothing but government debt (bonds) from now on. No, seriously - we liberty lovers would never think of forcing you to invest in something you don't believe in. Bet your own ranch on that government you love so dearly and trust so completely.

And let's say that by some miracle, the current government debt bubble does not burst like the housing bubble, the dot-com bubble, the defense bubble, or the savings and loan bubbles which preceded it like clockwork over the past 25 years.

And let's also assume that Bernanke and Geithner have figured out the secret to circumventing the laws of economics and can somehow keep their monetary policy plates spinning on their skinny spindles forever while "Sabre Dance" plays furiously in the background.

In that best case, you would get something like a 2% return on your invested funds. Not the 8.5% your "fully-funded" pension promise is currently based upon, but 2%. So take the amount you expect to receive as your annuity payment in retirement and reduce it by 76%. This is what idiocy looks like.

We capitalists don't mind carrying you on our backs, but you guys have to quit biting us in the ass and banging your stupid drums in our ears, ok? Those obscene and excessive profits we produce are your only hope of ever seeing your holy-grail pensions; and those demagogues encouraging you to keep going after us with gusto are not your friends.

Problem Solved

I asked a few of my fellow company Presidents how many rounds of golf they have played since our nation's President was inaugurated in 2009. I've only managed four myself, most others have squeezed in a couple dozen; nobody is within a 7 iron distance of President Obama's world record of 80-something and counting.

Apparently being President of whole nation with 310 million people is a lot easier than being President of a corporation with hundreds or thousands. By population extrapolation, China's President Hu must just be able to just phone it in from the 8th tee at the People's Pebble Beach.

A week or so ago, President Obama interrupted his 3-day vacation in Iowa to announce he would unveil a detailed plan for revitalizing the economy and creating jobs for Americans...right after his next vacation in Massachusetts. Let them eat lobster bisque, eh Michelle?

At first, that made even less sense than buying a Canadian bus to talk about boosting jobs in America. If he had a plan already, then why wait weeks to get it rolling; and if he had no plan, then why take a vacation – better to get to work on the plan since you just told the whole world you had one.

And then it hit me – the plan is to simply pass a law that says everyone is employed. Problem solved. No need to even call a meeting to explain it to his Cabinet. Fore!

That's how they roll at the White House these days. When some people couldn't afford health insurance, they just wrote a law that said everybody gets affordable health care. Problem solved. We still don't know what's in that law, but that's immaterial; the important thing is that they passed a law. That shows they care.

Economy needed recovering? Pass a law with "recovery" in the title and call it recovered. Problem solved. Worried about global warming and greenhouse gasses? Pass a law that says cars must get 100 miles per gallon or have a windmill on the hood. Problem solved. Too much deficit spending and debt? Pass a law that says we won't spend so much...someday...maybe. Problem solved. Banksters running wild? Call the take-out menu "financial reform", vote it, and send out the bonus checks. Problem solved.

They will name it something dopey like the "Every Person Who Ever Walks On American Soil Is Fully and Happily Employed For Life Because I Said So Act". Problem solved. Adjust unemployment to zero, schedule the Joe Biden victory lap, might as well pre-print the fourth quarter GDP growth at pick-'em - say, 8%. Tell Bernanke to fire up the printing presses and give the money to Goldman Sachs, we must be booming again because everybody is now back to work; we passed a law.

I can see the dramatic two-bar chart at Senator Kerry's Committee hearings – one bar that shows real unemployment in August at 17% labeled "hideous post-Bush transition era", then dropping instantly to 0% in September with a label "I – me, your President Obama - stopped waiting for Congress to care about you instead of the tea party era". The high-fivin' media will go so leg-tingling crazy that Rachael Maddow might even go straight. Headlines will shout: "President Obama Saves Humanity From Itself – Again!"

But wait a minute - what about all those millions of people who don't have any real job to go to? That's where his plan turns brilliant, with the addition of the "Unlimited Family Leave Extension For People Who Don't Have A Family Emergency Or Even A Family Amendment". Problem solved.

Nobody will ever be unemployed anymore, they just go on leave. The teacher's union told him you don't count as unemployed when you are on leave, and believe me, those public sector unions know a thing or two about time off. Family leave is genius; oppose the law and you are against families.

That explains why Maxine Waters told us to go to hell – we hate families. Busted. Ron Paul was just pretending to be libertarian to create millions – no, tens of millions - of families of prostitutes on heroin so that Michelle Bachman's husband could bill the state to counsel them in his Christian Cure camps. That's why they tied in Iowa; they were in kahoots. Oh yeah, it's a racket – Michael Moore is working with Oliver Stone on the documentary, working title "They Hate You And We Really, Really Care, Now Give Us The Rest Of Your Money". Oscar.

You have to hand it to 'em; their full employment law plan is pure genius. And how fitting that the least-working President in history delivers full employment to the fewest-working American public in history. How perfect that the teleprompter President fixes the job crisis by reading that it is over from his teleprompter. How appropriate that the guy who talks game but has none will simply declare it done.

In reality, of course, President Obama will have something else to say about jobs when he takes to the prime time airwaves in September. But we won't have any idea what it is, because we will be watching something more relevant, like "Hoarding Bridezillas Dancing With Swamp People". Or - thank you Jesus - football.

He does not have a plan; he does not even have a clue. Here is the only viable plan to put large numbers of Americans back to work: elect a new President in 2012. Problem solved.

Revolution

These are pretty good days to be a libertarian - all of a sudden, our ideas are popular again. They are not really our ideas, of course; we learned them in the Constitution and Declaration of Independence, and understood them through the works of Friedman, Hayak, Mises, Rand, and Paul.

For as long as I can remember, us libertarians have been dismissed by the political class as cranks and wing-nuts; the tin-foil hat guys on the margins who like guns, gold, gambling, pot, prostitutes, and pre-emptive surrender.

That is so unfair – I don't even know any prostitutes. The boring truth is that libertarians don't advocate any specific choice; we just object to throwing people in jail for making choices we don't like. As Milton Friedman said, the only real freedom is the freedom to choose. Those who read Moment Of Clarity regularly have heard me say this many times:

Liberty is the absence of government in choice. Government is the absence of liberty in choice. Tyranny is the absence of choice in government.

If you need help with the tyranny reference, just picture Nancy Pelosi and Newt Gingrich sitting on the couch together telling you why government should make your energy choices for you. The staunchest Democrat ever fabricated and the most partisan Republican ever hatched cooing and purring and smiling at each other like prom dates while they fit you for the yoke. Or RomneyCare; you pick 'em.

It is heartwarming to see so many Americans getting in touch with their inner crank and wing-nut. The libertarian belief that we can not just live with less government, but live *better* with less government has been rekindled by the grass-roots tea party movement and legitimized by the abject failure of the Obama presidency, the last great hope of socialists, Keynesians, and unionists.

My jaw dropped when New Jersey Governor Chris Christie recently responded to a reporters question about his belief in evolution with, "it's none of your business". Not so long ago, Republicans were laughing at us; now they are talking like us. Or if they prefer, talking like Barry Goldwater, who was one of us before it was necessary to give ourselves a name.

Freedom is popular, as our beloved Ron Paul says. Who would have thought we would ever see him breaking Ben Bernanke's stones from the Chairman's seat in committee? Or Congress locked in a showdown over how much to government to *cut*? Or the Wisconsin legislature haggling over whether carry should be permitted or constitutional?

Be honest - did you think the union stranglehold on government would ever be broken? That school choice would be expanded? That a public university endowment would buy over $1 billion in physical gold? That ObamaCare and McCain/Feingold would be found unconstitutional by a modern-day court? That someone would make a movie out of "Atlas Shrugged"? And that it would be good?

The revolution is on.

It is thankfully not being fought with bullets and blood; rather with ballots and blogs. Our liberty is being reclaimed, one battle at a time. There is much territory to recapture and the privileged are not giving up ground without a fight. But who can deny that liberty's opponents are everywhere in retreat? We must press on with diligence until our rights have been reclaimed, our liberty restored, our nation saved.

Libertarians are to conservatives what socialists are to liberals. We embody the extreme form of the principles that define a common worldview - free trade, limited government, individual liberty, private property. If conservatives are Dagny Taggert, then libertarians are John Galt.

And liberals will have no clue what that even means; the movie was not subtitled in drum.

Right To Work

With one bold stroke, Wisconsin Governor Scott Walker turned a decade of budget deficits into a projected surplus without raising taxes; all it took was to bust the public unions.

Most people run away from the term "union-busting" but the Wisconsin experience should make it clearer than ever that union-busting is a good thing. Union-busting is good thing, because compulsory unionization is vile. Take a pill, my dear union friends; I said *compulsory* unionism is vile.

It is vile because it denies a fundamental right – the right to work. We own ourselves and our labor; and we are free to set the terms of its exchange or we are not free. Forcing someone to join a union as a condition of employment is a denial of his/her self-ownership; it is as simple as that.

Key word: force. Unionists can talk in grand platitudes about worker rights, but when force is your first principle, the words used to justify it merely calibrate the depth of the lie. The rapist can quote the poet, but that does not make it an act of love.

As it turns out, public unions were THE fiscal problem in Wisconsin. The proof is in the thousands of municipalities and school districts throughout the state which have turned staggering deficits into to surpluses within days, once the Governor's Budget Repair Bill was liberated from the clutches of liberal courts which held it hostage for months. Now we know what they were so afraid of – it was this easy all along.

In city after city, and school district after school district, layoffs of public employees are being avoided, classroom sizes are being reduced, merit pay for good teachers is being funded, benefit plans are being improved at lower costs, and taxpayers are saving money. The winner in the "war on the middle class" is the middle class.

Teachers' jobs have been saved, despite their own unions best efforts to eliminate them. Except in the city of Milwaukee, where the unions and their rubber-stamp school board rushed to extend union contracts ahead of Walker's collective bargaining reforms. Hundreds of teachers lost their jobs, vital services have been cut, and class sizes will increase. Nice going, WEAC.

Milwaukee has been punched in the gut with the solidarity fist; or perhaps kicked slightly lower would be a more apt description.

Milwaukee parents and teachers can thank the public unions, the Democrats, Dane County judge Sumi, and Secretary of State La Follette for making the sorry state of their schools even sorrier.

Even with the political cover of "Walker made me", the unionist bullies could not bring themselves to do the right thing. When push came to shove, they couldn't stop pushing and shoving inner-city kids. That's what they do; it's who they are. MPS was the libertarians' best argument for school choice, and the argument got stronger.

Surprise, surprise - the world did not end with passage of budget reforms in Wisconsin; things got instantly better. This has come as a shock to liberals and unionists who have spent their lifetimes insulated from economic reality and marinating in their own propaganda. It should not have surprised anyone; instantly better is what happens when blight is removed.

If Governor Walker and the Republicans are serious about creating jobs in this state, they need to take the next step and pass Right to Work legislation now. Put the "free" back in free enterprise and then step out of the way; that's how you stimulate the economy.

Compulsory unionization destroys initiative, stifles innovation, increases costs, protects inefficiency and sloth, and its parasitic nature ultimately kills its host. The same union toxicity that cripples the effectiveness of government and education is even more deadly in the private sector, where firms compete to survive.

Wisconsin is littered with the carcasses of once-thriving businesses whose unions killed them. But it is also filled with private, non-union firms who compete around the world and against the world every day. We do not thrive in spite of our non-union status; we thrive because of it.

President Obama is doing everything in his power to stack the regulatory and legal deck in favor of the unions which fund his Democrat Party. Through executive order and NLRB actions, he seeks to impose by force what 93% of private sector workers have voluntarily rejected – union representation.

Given his administration's track record on economic matters, the President's unionist agenda should be opposed simply because he has proposed it. You do not need a Ph.D. in economics to know the path to American prosperity; you only need to learn the elements of President Obama's plan and choose their opposites. Wisconsin cannot wait for a national Right To Work law; we must act now.

Right To Work laws do not prohibit or even inhibit union representation; in fact, RTW preserves the right of every worker to join a union and collectively bargain. But Right To Work also preserves the equal right of every worker to represent themselves; it preserves the basic right of self-ownership. And there are no "kinda" rights; rights are digital, not analog.

Unions which add value in the workplace will have no problem in an environment of choice. Workers will gladly choose to join a union that benefits them, and employers will eagerly accept a union that improves the quality, safety, and morale of its workforce. Like everything else, choice and competition in labor representation improves quality and reduces cost.

Compulsory unionism is like forced marriage; the groom has a million reasons why it is good for the bride. Right To Work gives her choices and respect. Be a friend of the bride.

RINO

If you ask me, Ron Paul is the RINO – Republican In Name Only.

Don't get me wrong; that's a good thing. I have been a Ron Paul guy since I first heard of him in 1988 when he ran for President as a Libertarian Party candidate. I just think it amusing that the term RINO is the pejorative used by those on the fringes of the GOP to smear the Republicans they don't like – i.e. most of them.

Who is under the fat hump of the GOP bell curve? 47 Republican senators signed on to a non-binding balanced budget resolution which, if enacted, would require Congress to balance the budget within five years. But yesterday, 40 of those 47 Republicans voted *against* a real budget bill – Senator Rand Paul's - that does exactly that.

Those 85% whose gut-check bounced are not RINOs; they are R's. They are the mean plus one standard deviation, the center-cut, the sweet spot of the Republican Party. They talk like libertarians when they are running for office, talk like conservatives after they win, and then vote like schmucks. Heartbreakers.

Paul the Younger did himself doubly proud this week; he also filibustered the Patriot Act singlehandedly on the Senate floor this week. How pathetic is that? One lone defender of the 4th, 5th, and 2nd amendments out of that whole Republican Party that made such a grand show of reading the Constitution to start the session.

And while Dr. Rand Paul fought his own Republican Party to defend our 2nd Amendment rights in Washington, D.C., Dr. Pam Galloway fought her own Republican Party to defend them here in Madison, Wisconsin with her Constitutional Carry bill that the leaders of her own Party are trying desperately to water down.

The mind boggles; two doctors - rookies with no prior legislative experience – are our fragile grip on the Constitution. And thank God for both of them. What a perfect commentary on the absurdity of our times: our doctors are fixing government while our government is ruining health care.

Here is the list of Republicans who have won their Party's nomination for President since I have been old enough to vote: Nixon, Ford, Reagan, Bush, Dole, Bush Dance Remix, and McCain. Congressional leaders I remember include Bob

Michaels, Newt Gingrich, Bill Frist, Mitch McConnell, Denny Hastert.

There hasn't been a Goldwater Republican since...Goldwater.

So quit calling big-government Republicans RINO's; call them NADS, but not because theirs are particularly large. It stands for Not A Democrat, which most days seems to be the only principle they have left. If Obama is for it, they are against it and vice versa. I would not be surprised if they reverse themselves and vote to double the subsidy for wind energy after it mussed up Michelle Obama's hair in England.

Is there even such a thing as a DINO? Do the anti-war lesbian unionists reef on the foodstamp PETA greenies for not being Hispanic enough? I don't know that much about Democrats - just that they want to take all my money and tell me what to do. I've never gotten past those two things to discover goal #3.

And I've never heard a Libertarian called a LINO, either, although I did recently learn that we have been further subdivided into *Cosmotarians* and *Paleotarians*. I think the difference is whether you base your Presidential campaign on legalizing drugs or ending the Fed. It sounds a lot better than wing-nut A and wing-nut B.

Paleotarians, I am told, hold conservative personal values but oppose the imposition of values by the state. Works for me. And if we strip away all of the Party labels, I think that thumbnail sketch describes a majority of Americans. We don't want Democrat government or Republican government; we want *less* government.

What we want most from government is to be left alone. We don't want someone else's values written into law. We don't want someone else's choices to be our mandates and prohibitions. We don't want to tell others how to live their lives and we don't want to be told how to live ours. We want to pay our own way and choose for ourselves the means to help others less fortunate.

Is there a label for that? Yes, it is called *American*. The idea that government is limited and liberty is not; the belief that free people and free markets improve the human condition. It's not a Democrat thing, or a Republican thing, or a Libertarian thing; it is an American thing – or used to be. This weekend we honor those who have given their lives for that American thing.

193

How many of our politicians in either party vote as if they truly believe in free people and free markets? How many of them vote as if the United States Constitution they swore an oath to protect and defend is the law of the land?

How many are Americans In Name Only? Too many.

Roll Your Own

The Cowboy was once a symbol of freedom, a uniquely American icon. He wore his guns with pride, he said "thank you, ma'am", he prayed before supper, he rolled his own smokes, and if anyone would dare tell him he couldn't, well, "them's fightin' words!"

When we were kids, we all wanted to be one. We wore little cowboy outfits, we said "howdy, pardner", we rode the pony machine outside the A&P store, we went to the Saturday matinees and we cheered when the good guys in the white hats shot the bad guys in the black hats - saving the town and winning the gal.

What the hell happened to us? When did we start hating the good guys? When did we become the nation that cheers for that fat guy in the paisley vest, the slimy lawyer that forged the deed, the crooked judge who ignored the law, and the sneering tax man who foreclosed on the orphanage?

Wisconsin's Department of Revenue apparently has enough excess cube monkeys on its payroll to waste our money closing down stores that sell loose tobacco and provide the machines for people to roll their own cigarettes. I don't smoke myself, but I understand these Roll Your Own (RYO) stores have become pretty popular since the government taxed the bejesus out of manufactured cigarettes. To quote that great economist Gomer Pyle, "surprise, surprise, surprise!"

The owners of these small businesses earn their own way, employ other people, pay a boatload of taxes, and sell a legal product to adults who want to buy it with money they earned themselves. That is called liberty; it drives some people nuts.

One such driven group calls itself Smoke Free Wisconsin, who has nothing but praise for Governor Scott Walker's ham-fisted RYO crackdown. These are the same folks who led the drive to ban smoking on private property. There should be an injunction against them using the word "free"; real liberty lovers would insert one more little word to get our priorities straight: Smoke [in] Free Wisconsin.

Where is the outrage from the left over the RYO beat-down? Rich people can afford to buy manufactured cigarettes and pay all that tax; it is the poor and middle class who roll their own at these locally-owned stores. Why aren't you Madison moonbats

195

drumming on Walker about taxing the poor and hammering small businesses? And aren't you guys supposed to be pro-choice, or does a woman only own her body while a second life shares it?

I have no idea what the Governor was thinking, but it's stupid crap like this that turns Republicans into Libertarians. He may want to take a mulligan with another recall season just around the corner, but hey - I'm not the coach of their team.

Look, if someone wants to smoke that is their business; I am not threatened by their choice. The real danger to the public is not smokers or RYO stores, it is allowing ourselves to be ruled by self-righteous prigs with so many sticks up their butts they fart sawdust.

We are not safe from the Sawdust People when they are awake, so I say coffee is a public health hazard, too. Let's tax the snot out of it; make it a dollar for each word it takes to order a cup of the stuff at Snob-bucks. Extra grande fair-trade iced minty whipped mocha mocha latte? Ten bucks tax - welcome to Marlboro country, Tiffany.

That's it - tax Big Coffee and then send out the goons from DOR to start shutting down all those brew-your-own, tax-evading sons of bitches with their subversive don't-tread-on-me Mr. Coffee machines. Make them pay fines and permit fees and buy licenses and keep bleeding them until they die. Start with the quickie oil change joints; theirs are the most disgusting, anyway. Then roust the mom-and-pop motels, the real estate agencies, the hair salons, the bridal shops and work your way up to the Indian casinos.

On second thought, why not start with the Indian casinos, and why not start tomorrow? Forget the free coffee - why do those rich guys get to smoke, give away tax-free drinks, gamble, and sell untaxed cigarettes in their businesses while the State is stomping down the tiny RYO stores for doing none of the above? And don't say respect for their traditional way of life unless you think "ding-ding-ding-ding-ding" is some kind of sacred rain chant that makes prairie grass grow to fatten the buffalo. They bought their privilege with campaign cash and it was the last Governor, not this one, who sold us out to get re-elected.

Here's a radical idea - how about our government respect *everyone's* way of life, including the poor working stiffs who feel like rolling a smoke after putting in a double shift? And how about we let the Constitution tell the government what to do

196

instead of letting the Sawdust People tell the government what to do to *us*?

And before you uber-caring heart-bleeders start thumb-typing your anonymous comments wishing me a fatal disease because I dared to defend smokers' rights, don't waste your time. I've lost as many family members to cancer as anyone, but I won't force everyone else to suffer for my loss, ok? I cry on my own time.

The phrase "roll your own" is a slang expression meaning to do something your own way; and doing things your own way is what liberty is all about. It is not about forcing someone else to conform to your idea of a proper lifestyle - that is called tyranny. Crushing those little RYO entrepreneurs is a fitting symbol of government over-reach; it is do-gooder tyranny, the most insidious kind, the easiest to ignore.

So go ahead and look the other way while the brutes shake down the RYO industry and throw even more people out of work. But when you brew that next cup of java at home on your own subversive Mr. Coffee, just remember that someone somewhere in the Department of Revenue is reading this post and thinking, "hmmmmm...coffee tax...now there's an interesting idea."

Maybe then you will understand why we libertarians keep fussing over silly things like the Fourth amendment...and why we thank our Founding Fathers for the Second. If you do too, support your RYO entrepreneurs and share this post with your friends.

Safety Net

Libertarians are often asked how we would provide a social safety net with the Constitutionally-limited government we advocate. My answer is that there is only one reliable social safety net – a job.

Our first obligation to each other is to be economically autonomous, to produce more than we consume. We cannot be our brother's keeper if we can't even keep ourselves, and there is no reason to believe that only some of us are capable of carrying our own weight. Libertarians believe that *every* able-bodied person is capable of self-reliance and independent living – we don't consider ourselves to be gifted or special.

To be economically autonomous we must become employable; that is our own responsibility. We are not born that way; we are born helpless and dependent, our only native skill is annoying someone more capable until they give us what we want. Some people spend a lifetime perfecting that craft.

Last month, Wisconsin's employment fell by 4,000 jobs. And yet, 20,000 job openings were added to the state's job bank website. Job boards overflow with open positions that require vocational training, certificates, credentials, and professional expertise. A company seeking a certified lab tech to test for hydraulic fluid contamination will not hire a public high school graduate with 39% math proficiency, a union foundry worker with 30 years experience, or a person with a masters' degree in 19th century Lithuanian atheist literature.

Liberals' pro-job rhetoric never turns into reality because they defend the policies that produce mediocre public school graduates, protect union privilege and subsidize occupational obsolescence, and have raised academic irrelevance in post-secondary education to an art form. Employment starts with being employable.

Employers complain of shortages of skilled trade workers, and also report candidates who decline employment offers in order to take advantage of extended unemployment benefits. We have been conditioned to think that everyone wants to work, and that unemployment is a misfortune visited upon a person by luck. But for many, if not most, extended unemployment is a choice - a very bad choice.

Because a job does not merely provide income; a job also delivers self-esteem, pride, respect, confidence, and responsibility. It is the uninterrupted aggregation of job experience over a long career that prepares one for the highest-paying positions. Over time, a job instills discipline, imparts wisdom, teaches teamwork and compromise, and gives a sense of community.

The great fallacy of the progressive movement is the notion that government could deliver any those things. Government can only take money from one person and give it to another; it cannot transfer pride, or responsibility, or confidence. It cannot turn boys into men, girls into women, apprentices into masters, existence into prosperity. The value of a dollar given evaporates when it is spent, while the value of a dollar earned compounds forever.

It is the job that turned us boys into men; that prepared us for fatherhood, marriage, community service. It is where we learn accountability, consequence, the pride of achievement, the confidence that we can grow and learn and teach. It is how we learned to control our tempers, to self-regulate, to self-motivate, to leave the party early, and to get up before the alarm goes off. It is the place we discovered our parents were right all along. It is where we started to take things seriously.

It was the truly disgusting, awful jobs we did that motivated us to gain the skills that make us employable in more comfortable surroundings. It was the realization that we had nothing to offer worth even minimum wage that pushed us to learn how to become more valuable. It was the long-ago discovery of the pride of pulling ourselves up by our bootstraps that keeps us yanking on our wingtips today.

It is a job that sparks the entrepreneurial spirit that drives people to self-employ, to invent, to change the world. Jobs teach valuable life skills: courtesy, problem-solving, persuasion, negotiation, judgment, decision-making, urgency, time management, prioritization, handling disappointment. Is there a course in the public schools that can teach even a fraction of that?

In reality, the so-called safety net of the modern welfare state is a snare that captures and binds the spirit. It is no coincidence that communities most highly dependent on the "safety net" are afflicted with all manner of social pathologies and dysfunctions. It is the workplace, not the welfare office, which stabilizes families and builds vibrant communities; in no sense is perpetuating dependence on government welfare charitable.

199

To think that compassion can only be measured by the amounts spent on government programs ignores thousands of years of history and denies the role that families, churches, fraternal orders, clubs, and communities play in the development of whole persons. A whole person needs to work, or support the spouse who does.

Employers are the *most* charitable of citizens; we not only provide income, we provide the opportunity for people to discover how high is up for them. We provide a place for them to develop their character, to become skilled, to produce in surplus, to be part of something bigger than themselves, to create, to add value.

A handout won't do that; a government check won't do that; a temporary make-work job funded by a government agency won't do that. Do you want to help your fellow man? Then lift the burdens that government has imposed on employers in this country – excessive taxation, regulation, and permission - and let more of our neighbors and friends become whole persons again.

Separation Anxiety

While expressing his solidarity with the Occupy Wall Street movement this week, President Obama said something very weird - that OWS and Tea Party protestors share the frustration of feeling separated from our government.

No we don't. I desperately want to be separated from my government again; separation from government is the whole purpose of the Constitution and the Bill of Rights. It draws the lines between us and our government; it is our national restraining order against a stalking pervert who climbs through our windows every chance he gets to steal our stuff and cop a feel while we are sleeping.

I doubt if separation from government is what makes the employees of Gibson Guitars frustrated these days. My guess is that the feds busting down their doors and shutting them down indefinitely for no reason whatsoever is probably more of a concern. They are probably a more than a little frustrated that the guy who keeps yammering on about his jobs bill is the reason they lost theirs.

And it is a safe bet that the small regional banks that are being choked to death by regulators under the Dodd-Frank bank "reform" bill don't see separation from government as a major problem. Congressman Frank sees no conflict between his taking heaps of cash from the giant Wall Street banks and writing the new rules that effectively take out their smaller competitors while guaranteeing their profits. He supports OWS, too, providing a role model for schizophrenics with political ambitions.

And weren't you happy to learn that First Lady Michelle Obama wants to "shape" your children for you? Personally, I would like to establish some considerable distance between me and someone who thinks children should be shaped, like little pieces of clay. Does she want to dress them up and take pictures, too? We like our kids to be separated from strangers like that...and we like our First Ladies to be a little less creepy. I'm not sure how the OWS crowd feels about it.

By linking the Tea Party and OWS, President Obama once again shows us he doesn't know his country very well. Most of us do not want government to sit in our lap; we want it to go lay by its dish. Americans are united in the things we are against; what divide us are the things we are for.

No one wants more crime, poverty, injustice, racism, drug abuse, inflation, illiteracy, pollution, unemployment, bankruptcy, fraud, illness, and premature death; we only disagree about how to combat them. And everyone sees war as the last resort; we just disagree on what comes second to last.

President Obama and his ideologically aligned liberals, Democrats, progressives, and socialists are for more government and less liberty. Like helicopter moms, they see separation from government as way too risky for their citizen/children; they demand a government that protects us from ourselves at our grandchildren's expense.

Conservatives, libertarians, constitutionalists, principled Republicans, and political agnostics are for less government and more liberty. We do not want to be mothered by government; we want to live free of government supervision and approval. Separation from government does not cause us fear and anxiety; we crave it.

When asked if we want more government or less of it, Americans consistently choose "less" by 2:1 margins. That has been one of the most consistent polling questions over the past three decades. OWS is not the 99%; it is some tiny fraction of the 33% who say "more".

When I went off to college, my mom and dad did not cry and neither did I; after 18 years of dependence on them, we were both happy to empty the nest. I was grateful to them for preparing me for that day, and they were even more grateful that it finally came.

There were other kids who spent that whole day bawling with their parents; I didn't understand why back then, but a little wisdom has stuck to me over the decades that have passed since. We all grew older but we didn't change much.

Some Americans see every new day as an opportunity to learn and grow, to overcome new challenges, to succeed and prosper, to be responsible, to discover how high is up for ourselves and to help others do the same. The happy kids.

Others wake to dread the dawn; seeing only hurdles that can't be overcome, barriers that can't be breached, disadvantage and unfairness, and a world so difficult to manage that only government can protect us from it. The bawling kids.

The painful truth is that we choose which of those two worlds we will live in. The happy kids and the bawling kids all went to the same campus. And the awful truth is that politics is the imposition of one viewpoint upon the believers of the other. The genius of democracy is that is allows us to change who wins without killing each other.

In the natural order of things, the mighty fall. The prodigal squanders, the haughty are brought low, nations decline, empires implode. This creates space at the top for the lowly to rise. Our iconic national story is one of humble beginnings which end in glory.

The problem with government is that it disturbs that natural order; it props up the mighty and crushes the meek. In a free market, privilege cannot be defended, it must be re-earned. Enron's separation from government allowed it to rightfully perish alone; Fannie Mae's incestuous relationship took us all down with it.

Maybe the bawling kids are still fooled by the teleprompter President, but the happy kids aren't buying it. We are not still mired in recession almost four years later because government can't clutch us tight enough to its bosom; we are stuck in the ditch because it won't get off our backs.

Mr. President, with all due respect, we are not frustrated over our separation from government; it is that your separation from government can't come fast enough.

Smarter Than a 10th Grader

Gaius Sallustius Crispus, generally known simply as Sallust, was a Roman historian, moralist, and politician who lived more than 2,000 years ago.

Back in those days, the Roman Senate consisted of two factions – the elitist Optimates, who favored the entrenched aristocracy against the people, and the Populares, whose name literally means "favoring the people". While Cicero was the most notable spokesman for the Optimates, his rival Sallust was the voice of the Populares. Sallust was a keen observer of the politics of the day.

"To someone seeking power, the poorest man is the most useful."

Once a powerful political force in Roman politics, the Populares had declined by the time Sallust came onto the scene. The faction, including Sallust himself, had turned cynical about the people it claimed to represent, choosing political victories over principle.

"Few men desire liberty: the majority are satisfied with a just master."

When Sallust retired from public service, he wrote important histories of Roman wars and political life. His later writings took on a moral tone, and his outlook became more of what might be described today as libertarian.

"They envy the distinction I have won; let them therefore envy my toils, my honesty, and the methods by which I gained it."

His writing style was unique for its time; compact, severe, absent the customary descriptive prose, even sarcastic at times. It inspired many later philosophers, Nietzche among them, who admired his ability to make a profound point efficiently and his habit of using epigrams liberally to make his points.

"Every man is the architect of his own fortune."

I first learned of Sallust in the 10th grade, when Latin was taught in the Ironwood, Michigan public schools and a foreign language was a requirement for admission into college. The short, crisp style of Sallust made for easier translations that the works of his contemporaries, so we liked the guy. I had forgotten all about him until recently.

I hated Latin. I did not like our teacher, Mr. Pinski. I thought it was a stupid language whose extinction was deserved. I barely passed; I cheated and got caught, punished, and docked grades. I was angry that my GPA was affected and afraid that I might get kicked out of football over it; I was ashamed that I let my parents down.   I didn't see what I could possibly learn from some old Roman geezer ruminating about politics back in the day. Turns out, I learned a lot.

"Ambition drove many men to become false; to have one thought locked in the breast and another ready on the tongue."

More than 40 years later, I realize that I owe a great debt to Mr. Pinski, Principal Sheridan, Vice-principal Ostrom (disciplinarian) and the Ironwood school board. I learned a language of root words that expanded my vocabulary tremendously and helped me to learn rudimentary Spanish when our business demanded it. I learned to write concise, meaningful sentences. I learned to create and imbed epigrams in my own writing and speeches.

More importantly, I learned about liberty, tyranny, governance, human nature, leadership, and the wisdom of the ancients. I learned ethics, fair play, and accountability - the hard way. All of that reinforced what I learned from my parents and in Sunday School. And I gained confidence that I could tackle a difficult subject, that I could understand adult concepts, and that I could recover from a mistake. I learned to value people who were not like me, who thought differently than I did.

"To like and dislike the same things; that is indeed true friendship."

And perhaps most important of all, I learned that there are many different ways to look at the world and interpret its lessons; that it has been that way since the dawn of time. These are the things we were taught before we learned to drive. I wonder what is taught and what is learned in 10th grade at the public schools today – probably not Sallust and Cicero.

Each generation must discover anew what was known 2,000 years ago to Cicero and Sallust. And each individual person must decide for themselves what is true and what is right: a*gere sequitur credere* – action follows belief.

It was always difficult for me to understand how the knowledge of the Romans, Egyptians, Chinese, and other ancient civilizations could have been discarded and the world plunged into the Dark Ages. I often wonder where we would be today had not a whole millennium been lost in the advancement of knowledge and culture. As I watch our nation decline, the idea of falling backwards no longer seems impossible.

Our founding fathers did not invent the liberty principle 230 years ago; they institutionalized it. It was known to the Romans 2,000 years ago; the Greeks centuries earlier. The gift of free will was what distinguished man from the rest of creation in the Biblical teaching of the origins of life - a gift so precious it was withheld from the angels.

We cannot be the generation who extinguishes liberty. We must be the generation who restores liberty to the generations to come. That is why this all matters.

Special Needs

In recent weeks, opponents of reform in Wisconsin have done themselves proud – going after the civil rights of small businesspeople, 14-year old girls, nuns, the entire city of Brookfield, gifted children, and opening-day fishermen. Now add parents of special needs children to the hit list from the most misguided campaign to win over hearts and minds ever conceived.

Governor Walker proposed to give parents of special needs children a voucher to enroll their child in the school of their choice – public, charter, or private. Naturally, the liberal defenders of the government/union public school monopoly are outraged at the prospect; outrage is their reflexive response to any idea younger than the age of their pension eligibility.

A lawyer for Disability Rights Wisconsin went a little overboard, promising that the bill would cause parents to send their special needs children to private schools which do not "even have a single special needs teacher or therapist on staff". Back before it was a Class A felony to use the word "retarded", that is exactly what we would have called such a stupid thing to say. Get the cuffs – it is retarded.

Does anyone really believe that a parent would choose to remove their disabled child from a public school providing adequate special education and move him/her to a private school with no services whatsoever?   Then why would the advocacy industry stoop so low except to defend their market share in the highly lucrative victimhood sector of the public trough?

And a spokesperson for the State Department of Public Instruction got her undies all in a bunch because private schools would not be accountable – to the state.   She frets that her department would receive "no tests, no attendance reporting, no graduation rates, no drop out reporting, and no other measure" to satisfy them that the children's needs are being served. Oh, dear.

Here is your "other measure", dipppies: parents are sending their kids there.

What a convenient time for DPI to suddenly discover the virtue of accountability. Yet even in their epiphany they get it all wrong - parents are not accountable to the state; the state is accountable to parents. Besides, in every one of those metrics she listed off, what the public schools are reporting on those precious little forms is that they suck. Recently, it was reported that the administrators in Madison high schools are no longer able to identify gifted children; that's how bad it has gotten. $50 says the janitors can still tell.

If the headlines are any indication, our public schools' specialty these days seems to be cranking out fat kids that can't read. Only the government could screw up feeding children. Even the Neanderthals got the hang of it, and thankfully the wheel and fire occurred to them before they got sidetracked with liberal visions of hot lunch and hairnets and k3 and forced bussing and school administrators fixated on banning chocolate milk. We would be the feline descendants of the saber-tooth tigers that ate them while they banged on their drums.

My sister-in-law is a licensed behavior analyst for a school district in Florida, where McKay Scholarships have provided school choice for parents of special needs children for many years. One private school in her district does such a great job with Autistic children that they have filled their 80 student program to capacity, each child bringing their state funding to the school along with them.

Tomorrow she will present her plan for her public school district to improve their programs in response, hoping to attract students and funding back to the district schools. The school board will listen to her (if they are smart) and they will get better, causing the private schools to lose students and make new improvements to their programs. Lather, Rinse, Repeat – it is not difficult to see why markets work.

And that, my friends, is why the public education elites in Wisconsin and all across the country oppose school choice – because it works *and they know it works*. When it works, it exposes their union/government monopoly model for the failure that it is.

What is not to like about school choice? More options for parents, better outcomes for students, lower costs for everyone; the private schools get better, the charter schools get better, and the public schools get better.

Here's the thing about school choice: you cannot be for children and against the thing that improves their education. Pick your side.

We all know parents of special needs children. They are the experts when it comes to their own children and the most tenacious advocates for their care. They alone know what is best for their kids and their decisions are guided by a capacity for love that the rest of us will never fully appreciate.

I trust them completely to do the right thing for their children; the state cannot be trusted do the right thing nor the thing right. School choice is an easy choice.

Stimulated?

When he took the job in 2009, President Obama told us the cure for our economic problems was more government; he and his economic team spent over a trillion dollars of borrowed money on a series of bills to stimulate the economy.

They told us their plan would kick start GDP growth, keep unemployment below 8%, stave off bankruptcy for GM and Chrysler, prop up home prices, stem the tide of rising foreclosures, and boost incomes.

They told us we would be all stimulated by June of 2011, remember? Well, it's now June of 2011; the trillion is gone, and we are still waiting to be stimulated.

Incomes have declined, foreclosures have increased, home prices continue to fall, GM and Chrysler both went bankrupt anyway, the number of people on food stamps has doubled, and unemployment is somewhere between 9-17% depending on whether you count all the people out of work or only those collecting unemployment benefits. Yes, the stock market has recovered, and why not; operating in other countries is quite profitable.

And economic growth, the very thing that all that stimulus spending was supposed to stimulate, has remained below 3%, the tread-water mark. That is, if you believe the government's numbers, which I no longer do.

Just how bad do you have to suck to get less then 3% GDP growth out of a trillion dollar stimulus? 1 trillion is 7.6% of 13 trillion, the approximate size of the U.S. economy as the President took office.

We could have grown the economy by 7.6% if we had simply given $1 trillion in cash to monkeys and pointed them towards the banana bin at the Pick N Save. But we did not wisely give cash to monkeys; we foolishly gave appropriations to politicians.

Guided by government economists and social scientists, they figured out how to fritter away that 7.6% monkey-dunk into a lousy 2.5% belly-flop. Those 5 evaporated GDP points translate into millions of jobs uncreated, billions in home equity lost, and many more billions lost to the inflation of our currency - inevitable when you shove trillions of new dollars into the system with no noticeable change in output.

We made our debt problem a trillion dollars worse and we will never recover the two years we wasted proving – yet again - that Keynesian economic theories do not work. And still they teach that crap on campus as if it was Biblical truth.

The only two things President Obama did that might actually stimulate the economy was send Larry Summers back to Harvard and Christina Romer back to Berkley. Now if we could just send Timothy Geithner back to the IMF...

The problem with the U.S. economy is simple: too much jockey and not enough horse. Our government is too big; it does too much, spends too much, and borrows too much. Doing more, spending more, and borrowing more makes things worse, not better.

For the first 130 years of American History, all government combined – local, state, and federal - consumed less than 9% of GDP; and we prospered like no nation before or since. That is what happens when you leave over 90% of what is earned in the hands of those who earned it. Write that down, Mr. President.

Today, our government consumes over 60% of GDP when mandated private spending is included. In thoroughbred terms, our government jockey now weighs a crushing 800 lbs., eating all the oats and drinking all the water while whipping the ribs of our starving private sector that can barely move under all that weight. And we wonder why China is about to go zipping right on by.

The socialists' argument for more government rests on the bizarre assumption that people working for government make better economic decisions than people working for themselves. They are wrong; here is the correct order: 1) people spending their own money, 2) monkeys, and 3) government.

The government's quota system does not reserve jobs for angels and geniuses. As a general rule, government makes hideous decisions with our money. It props up companies that fail; it pays people not to work; it subsidizes products people do not want; it promotes unions, it loans money to people who can't pay it back; it pays people to write rules so stupid it must pay other people to grant waivers; it borrows money from one country to give to another; it sues itself; it gives money to people with Ph.D.s to study really complicated and mysterious things like why kindergartners won't sit still.

Because they are five years old; where is my $650,000?

Truth is, there is very little the government can do to stimulate the economy, but there is a lot it could *not* do that would work wonders. Not tax so much, not spend so much, not borrow so much, not regulate so much, not mandate so much, not promote unions so much, not jack up energy costs so much, not devalue the currency so much, not join in international treaties so much, not try to pick winners and losers so much, and not reward donors and appease lobbyists so much.

And not blame us for their mistakes so much. Just leave us alone – that would be the best stimulus of all.

Cato Institute estimates that it would cost only $450 billion for the federal government to perform the enumerated powers authorized to it by the Constitution. That other $3.1 trillion it will spend this year could be returned to those who earned it or pay down our debt if we had a Congress who took its oath seriously.

Noted Keynesian economist and Obama cheerleader Paul Krugman says the President's plan failed to improve the economy because $1 trillion of stimulus wasn't enough. I agree with him completely; $3.1 trillion would be much better.

Constitutional government – there's your stimulus.

Tax the Terps

Liberals view income disparity as social injustice, proposing to remedy the income gap by taxing higher income people and giving the money to lower income people. The premise for such action is that rich people have more money than they need and poor people are entitled to that surplus.

The state of Maryland has the nation's highest median family income of $69,202. It is nearly twice the state of Mississippi's median family income of $36,646. Using the logic of the redistributionists, that income gap is unfair and unjust and the only way to lift Mississippi out of poverty is to tax the Terps.

Now, I'm sure that once the Terp Tax is enacted those Marylanders will work a lot harder knowing that the money they no longer keep for themselves will go to someone who needs it, don't you? And Mississippians will work harder too, just to show their appreciation to those Terps who leveled their playing field, don't you think?

Not to mention that famous 1.6 Keynesian multiplier that kicks in anytime you take money away from one person and give it to someone else. No, no – it really works. I took a dollar from my wife's purse and told the guy at the Kwik Trip it was worth a buck sixty. The only thing was, I couldn't prove it was her dollar, so next time I have to get it notarized by a mental health professional, he said. That's cool; I didn't know I had to do that.

Yes, taxing the Terps would solve everything. You don't suppose anyone would move out of Maryland once the Terp Tax kicks in, do you? If we equilibrate all the states, then the Terp gets to write a check for $18,991 while his cousin right across the border in West Virginia deposits a $12,786 transfer payment. Can't imagine that would cause any family stress, would it?

Well, you see where this all is going. If you think taking the wealth of one state to give to another by force is a dumb idea, you are right. It does not get any smarter if it is county to county, city to city, or house to house. Taxing the rich, whoever that even means nowadays, will not make the poor richer. It will only incent the rich to avoid, evade, move, or to simply quit producing.

And subsidizing the poor does not change the factors that caused their poverty – it would be nice if it were that simple. The people of Mississippi are not poor because the people of Maryland are rich.

The only people who prosper when forced wealth transfers occur are the people doing the transferring. It is no accident that the top two ranks in median income are now locked down by the company town of Washington, D.C. and its suburb-state, Maryland. The redistribution industry – the U.S. Government – is thriving.

Karl Marx described the essence of his socialist philosophy, "From each according to his abilities, to each according to his needs." Can you think of a more concise description of our nation's tax and welfare framework? Can you find justification for either progressive taxation or entitlement transfer payments in our Constitution?

In the months to come, Republicans and Democrats will once again posture and preen over tax policy, and journalists will read partisan sound bites with no earthly clue what they mean and call it news. Pick you victim and your villain – billionaires and paupers will work fine in either role – and you will have no problem finding "proof" on the internet that some other guy is not pulling his weight. About all you will really prove is that data is not information.

Over the past decade, our government has nearly doubled while our median income has remained flat. The former explains the latter; in fact, there is not a lot more we need to know to judge the wisdom of the Keynesian prescriptions that President Obama and Chairman Bernanke continue to promise will restore our prosperity. They haven't and they won't because they are wrong.

Our prosperity will only be restored when we produce more. Our median income will rise when our work adds more value. We earn more when we are worth more, not the other way around. You will make more if you can weld a pressure vessel than if you can weld a bike frame; more still if you can weld a leaking gas pipeline; even more if you can weld it underwater.

And taking more money from the folks who own the underwater welding firm will not increase their welders' incomes. Giving it to Pakistan will not trigger some fictitious magic multiplier effect here in this country. Printing fiat money at the Fed that is given to Goldman Sachs to lend to the U.S. Treasury who bails out Citibank so they can pay billionaires' bonuses that are taxed to fund government is not the way to fund government, even if Krugman says different..

Our real billionaires – Buffet, Gates, Zuckerman, Whitman, Jobs, Turner – did not start out that way; and Government did not select them. We bought their products; they are rich because we decided to make them so. I gave Steve Jobs a few hundred dollars for an iPad; if I wanted that money to go to ACORN, I would have given it to them myself. I don't need President Obama to do it for me; more importantly I don't *want* President Obama to do it for me.

Why not take the billionaires money? For the same reason we should not take it from all the Terps of Maryland - because it is their money. There is a commandment against such things. We should not kill them, either, or commit adultery with them, or covet their house, or covet their things, or bear false witness against them, or worship them.

We should buy their stuff, or not, as we see fit. As *we* see fit.

We're Number Ten!

Each year, Forbes magazine publishes a ranking of the best countries in which to do business. The United States has fallen to tenth place.

Canada, our good neighbor to the North (and the home of Athabasca University, my grad school alma mater I may add) has moved up from number four to number one. Sandwiched in between are Hong Kong and Singapore, some of the smaller European countries, and New Zealand. Not a sweatshop nation in the bunch – toldya.

This is not your father's America. Once the undisputed economic champion of the world, we have let ourselves go to seed. Overtaxed, overregulated, over-entitled, over-governed, we have taken our prosperity for granted and deluded ourselves into thinking that printing money is the same as creating wealth.

Tenth place is disgusting, and yet only a small fraction of Americans will be disgusted. An even smaller fraction will feel any responsibility for our decline in the rankings. Fewer still will feel any personal obligation to turn things around and only a tiny minority of those will actually do anything about it. A few will even cheer that we have received our comeuppance.

And that is why we are number ten.

A generation of stickers and hugs for trying hard has made us a nation complacent and confused about actual achievement. Many can no longer distinguish between demanding a reward and earning it. We have not lost our ability to compete, we have lost our will. Those of us who are still driven to succeed in the world economy are vilified for our success. Perhaps the call will come to occupy Canada, now that winning itself deserves punishment in the eyes of the class-obsessed.

The governments of the countries who are climbing in the world rankings have reduced taxes on businesses, eased regulatory burdens, avoided deficit spending, pursued sound money policies, and maintained competition (and sanity) in their banking industries. Capital loves predictability and a balance of both risk and reward. Capitalists do not choose to dine with cannibals when there is a choice.

The best thing about Canada is that it is full of Canadians. While it is tempting to paint the country with a broad leftist brush because of its public health care system, there are many elements of the Canadian system that libertarians and conservatives admire and all Americans can learn from.

It is ironic that while the United States central government has usurped authorities guaranteed to the states by our Constitution, Canada maintains a relatively weak central government deferential to Provincial authority - Newfies don't get to tell Albertans what to do. And their governmental units are, by and large, competent.

Although I am fond of teasing my Canadian friends about needing a law for everything, they take their law-making seriously in the legislatures and abide by what their elected representatives have enacted. Not like America where Presidents and governors circumvent laws by executive order and judges just make it up as they go from the bench.

Canadians develop their natural resources. They mine, they drill, they extract oil, they harvest timber, they make wise and responsible use of all of nature's abundance, unlike Americans who have banned drilling, outlawed mining, and limited logging. Canadians are happy to sell us the stuff that we sue ourselves over and leave in the ground.

The United States of America has been blessed with abundant natural resources, strategic geography, a heritage of enterprise and innovation, cultural diversity and a tradition of liberty. There is no reason on earth why we should not be the number one place to do business; free market capitalism is largely an American invention.

We are number ten because we have chosen to be number ten; or rather number ten has been chosen for us by foolish leaders whose understanding of economics and commerce is only slightly less developed than their common sense.

Congressman Jesse Jackson, Jr. has proposed that President Obama declare a national emergency and take "extra-constitutional" measures to create jobs. Note to Rep. Jackson: President Obama IS a national emergency. Every time he talks, his mine-mine-mine tax plan drives businesses to more hospitable places. The nine of them ahead of us are not low-wage countries; they are low-hassle countries.

As my friend Herman Cain says, "we don't do two". We are Americans; we are a nation founded on an economic foundation of free market capitalism. We are wired to prosper, to win, to reach beyond our place and dream beyond our reach; failure is not in our DNA. We can beat the industrialists and workers in the factories of China, Mexico, Vietnam, and South Korea; we do it every day. But we can't beat the bureaucrats in the cubicles of Washington, D.C. and statehouses around the country.

Those consumed with directing the allocation of a shrinking pie should get out of the way of the pie makers. Those content to be number ten should get out of the way of those of us who know how to erase the zero behind the one.

And those who think going around the Constitution is the sure path to prosperity should read it first.

Thank You, One Percenters

I wonder how many of those we-are-the-99% OWS protestors know what household income it takes to join the evil 1% they seek to destroy: the answer according to the IRS is $384,000.

Not exactly the millions and billions President Obama keeps talking about, but why let numbers get in the way of a good demonizing? Did you ever think about who makes that kind of money? Well, doctors and lawyers for sure, dentists, optometrists, small business owners, architects, builders, lobbyists, chiropractors, motivational speakers, popular authors, professional athletes, pension managers, car dealers, couples who teach in Universities (or high schools in Wisconsin if both pull that double-dip retire and come back to work maneuver), retired Democrat congressmen, union bosses – folks like that.

And of course, those devil-dog bastard CEOs. The AFL-CIO tells us that CEO's average income is $11.4 million, calling it immoral that our top executives earn 642 times the median secretary salary of $29,980. Not to diminish the profession, but I am pretty sure that a committee of 642 secretaries at Caterpillar could not run the company. The unionists demand is a return to the pre-Reagan 1980 ratio of CEO pay, when top executives made 29 times the median wage of all workers. Give me a button; I'm in.

In fact, I would bet that a majority of CEO's would take that deal, since the real median CEO pay, according to Salary.com, is $706,000 while 29 times the national median wage of $49,000 would be $1.4 million. Who knew the AFL-CIO would be the ones to make the case for doubling the pay of CEOs? Not even them, apparently; and I bet the guys taking dumps on police cars and sniffing feet at OWS New York didn't see that one coming either. Some minds are a terrible thing to waste; others are just terribly wasted.

Maybe CEOs should form a union, because the average income of the ten highest-paid CEOs is only $27 million, while the average income of the top ten celebrities is nearly double that - $43 million - and they are all union. Clearly, celebrity greed is the cause of CEO suffering; let's all go occupy Rodeo Drive.

Packer linebacker Clay Matthews is another evil one-percenter. You want to talk injustice - how is it fair that one guy gets to be so handsome, rich, athletic, smart, and cool while the rest of us can't see our shoes anymore and have to ask what fork to use?

219

And what is Clay Mathews supposed to do about our man-crush envy - cut off a bicep so we can have one, too? Spread the hair around? Share some of his snaps with the unemployed and uncoordinated?

Clay Mathews is in the top one percent of income earners because he is exceptionally good at doing something only a few other people on the planet can do; he got that way by working harder and longer at it than the millions of other kids who dreamed about being an NFL player but didn't put in the work. He earned it; just like the surgeon, singer, business owner, CEO, and derivatives trader who made it into the top 1% of income earners in this nation did. They get paid a lot because they are worth even more. Even Lady Gaga.

Drumming all day long won't change a thing; it is the purchase of the drum that picks winners and losers. That transaction decides which manufacturer, distributor, and retailer will take one step towards membership in the 1% club, the bane of the coveting class. The market decides who will be a one-percenter, and free market capitalism is the purist of all democracies; each dollar has one equal vote.

$384,000 isn't an excessive amount of money to pay for exceptionalism when you think how many civil service and political patronage jobs pay six figures for mediocrity these days. Don't you think the guy who repairs your baby daughter's heart valve is worth four times more than the fellow who will teach her to read poorly when she reaches school age? If she ends up on food stamps, it will not be the fault of that one-percenter surgeon; it is the slack-o-crat teacher and his union protectors who will condemn her to the impoverished life of the opinionated illiterate.

There are 1.4 million Americans who make up the top one percent. They earn 16.9% of the nation's income and they pay 37% of all the taxes. If the eat-the-rich crowd got their way literally, our nation's GDP would drop by 17% and taxes on the rest of us would go up 58% to make up for what we just devoured. And we would still have a 1%, but it would be today's second stringers. Great idea, lefties – pure genius.

Is killing the one-percenters a little too extreme for you? Ok, how about we just round up all 1.4 million of them and exile them to an island. And then let's round up the bottom 1% and send them off to their own island, too. The socialists' playbook says that the rich 1% are parasites who would die without the 99% to oppress. They would also tell you the poorest 1% only find themselves in that predicament because their opportunities have been denied by the richest 1%.

If the socialists have it right, then the citizens of Poor Island would prosper while Rich Island would perish. What do you think - who would prosper and who would perish? Which island would you choose to live and raise your family? Where do you think your children would have more opportunity? Which would you throw in with if your life depended on it?

And now quit kidding yourself that it doesn't.

The fools who are trying to destroy our nation's one-percenters don't understand that it takes wealth-builders to build wealth. Ask the folks in Venezuela or Cuba or North Korea how much fun it is when The Occupation works. President Obama and his OWS mobs have sent a clear message that one-percenters are no longer welcome here. Well, I have a different message for them: thank you.

Thank you for employing us, feeding us, housing us, clothing us, curing our illnesses, giving us sight, bringing abundance to market, financing our startups, inventing new technology, buying our insurance, contributing to our 401k, teaching us employable skills, heating our homes, sponsoring our educations, entertaining us, paying more than your share of taxes so we can pay less than ours, funding our charities, endowing our universities, and sacking opposing quarterbacks so the Packers go back to the Superbowl, as God intended.

Thank you very much.

Thank You, Veterans

Tomorrow is Veterans' Day, and I would like to take this opportunity on behalf of all of my Moment Of Clarity readers to thank our nation's veterans and their families for your service.

Those of us who have not worn the uniform will never fully comprehend the range of emotions that you veterans will feel tomorrow on the day that the whole nation pauses to honor you. We can only pray that your pride will match our gratitude.

You are our sons and daughters, mothers and fathers, family members, school mates, friends and neighbors, employers and employees. You may sit next to us in church or attend a different church, you may belong to our clubs or belong to clubs we would not choose to be associated with, you may share our political party affiliation or a wear a different button, you may stand with us at Tea Party rallies or attend OWS protests instead, you may cheer for the Packers or perhaps the Bears. We will even forgive you for that - but only tomorrow.

Most of you chose to give up your liberty to serve your country; you volunteered to join the military. You sacrificed years of your lives, time with your loved ones, your own safety, and in many cases your health, so that we could live free. You answered the call; you did not leave it to someone else to defend the freedoms that we all hold dear. No one hates war as much as a warfighter, yet many of you volunteered to return to combat on multiple tours.

I have no idea how many Americans will read this post, or how many of you are veterans. But I know that every single one of the former wants to say this to every single one of the latter:

Thank you. Thank you for your service.

We remember with respect the soldiers, sailors, marines, and airmen who were denied by death the opportunity to return to civilian life, as well as those who returned broken, either in body, mind or spirit. The honor of military service does not end with discharge and neither do our obligations to veterans and their families.

And what too many veterans need now from us is a job. I urge my fellow employers to seek out veterans, as well as current members of Guards and Reserves, for openings we have in our companies. It is not charity; these are men and women of character and commitment with a demonstrated ability to work and lead in teams to achieve goals. You want these folks on your side.

They have given it all up for us, and now it is our turn to repay the favor. On this Veterans Day, I would like every Chief Executive to walk down to his/her HR department and ask them what they have done this past year to hire veterans. And if they give you that 2nd Lieutenant salute, then go all CEO on them – you will feel good about it, trust me. And you will upgrade the talent in your organization.

"Thank you" is nice, and we should all say that to every veteran we meet tomorrow; but what many would rather hear is "you're hired." Let's see if we can do both. Happy Veterans Day to all my veteran friends – you are too many to list, but you know who you are, and you know how we all feel about you. God Bless You.

Thank You, Scott Walker

The past few weeks debt-ceiling jabberwocky in Washington D.C. has produced only one clear winner – Wisconsin Governor Scott Walker.

Watching our nations' leaders flop around like carp in a bucket trying to concoct some incomprehensible mix of bullsnot and pixie dust that will make doing nothing look like doing something has become even more boring than it is pathetic, and that is no mean feat. Markets have not lost confidence in America; they have lost faith in America's President and our Congressional leaders. We all have.

Governor Walker is looking like Winston Churchill next to these cobs. Residents of the Badger state are lucky to have a Governor and legislature who did their jobs and passed responsible budget reform as their first order of business. The results have been immediate, remarkable, and indisputable. Washington could learn something from Wisconsin, and here it is: you balance a budget by balancing a budget.

Walker inherited a $3.3 billion deficit mess from his predecessor, including a cynical $144 million turd dropped in the punchbowl on his way out the door. Unlike some U.S. President who shall remain nameless, Governor Walker did not make blaming the last guy his re-election strategy on day one of his first term. He went to work; he did his job; he fixed the budget. It was not easy; doing the right thing rarely is.

The socialists' unleashed a torrent of hate at Walker more furious than anyone ever dreamed might be directed at our first black President, but the Governor did not sulk or pout or pitch a fit in prime time. He did not berate his adversaries. He did not say an unkind word about the public employees whose unions vilified him and his supporters. While the opposition party abandoned their posts and fled to another state, the Governor quietly went to work each day and moved his plan through the legislature.

Walker's budget fix liberated the state from the fiscal death grip of its public sector unions. He saved taxpayers hundreds of millions, and he saved the jobs of tens of thousands of state workers, municipal employees, and teachers who would otherwise have been laid off, as was the case in Milwaukee and Madison where teachers' unions shot themselves in the foot by

extending contracts before the Walker budget reforms took effect. Those workers whose jobs were saved won't say it, but I will:

Thank you, Scott Walker.

All over the state, local government and school districts are saving money, instituting merit pay for teachers, reducing class sizes, improving services, and reducing tax burdens on the real working class. The rank-and-file teachers in Milwaukee have now mutinied, forcing their own union leaders to re-open contract negotiations to bring back teachers laid off by their union's intransigence. Whose plan do they demand their unions adopt? Governor Scott Walker's plan – imagine that.

Wisconsin has already paid back its long-overdue debt to the state of Minnesota, and it is paying back its debts to trust funds raided over the past decade. Walker's fiscal responsibility led to favorable borrowing terms, saving millions each month in lower interest and fees. Paying down debt improves credit ratings – did you catch that, junk-bond U.S. President who shall remain nameless?

Governor Walker began his term by announcing, "Wisconsin is Open For Business". With changes both overt and subtle, he has turned a hostile business climate into a far more favorable place for businesses to operate. While a certain anti-business President's state-suckling show ponies used their subsidies to move overseas – GM to Mexico and GE to China – Walker's Wisconsin companies stayed here and led the nation in job creation in June, creating over half of all net jobs in the country. 40,000 jobs have been created since he took office in January – that is how you raise revenue without increasing tax rates on anybody.

Employers across Wisconsin have thousands more job openings we can't fill for the lack of qualified, educated workers. The Governor has announced an initiative to reform our education system to improve the relevance and effectiveness of our schools, once the best in the nation. The state teachers' union, still seething that Walker's budget fix did not cause the sky to fall, refuses to participate. Thank God for that, and now Governor Walker is going ahead without them.

It is ridiculous that Wisconsin taxpayers must indulge the vengeful unionists who are trying to recall Walkers' legislative allies out of pure spite. Those legislators did nothing wrong; they did their jobs - unlike a certain U.S. President who shall remain nameless, or a certain U.S. Senate who has not passed a budget in two years, or a certain Wisconsin former Governor and his legislatures who spent eight years digging the hole Scott Walker filled in only six months on the job.

Recall? Here's what I recall: I recall that the Democrats who preceded Walker raised billions in taxes and still left the state billions in the red. I recall they looted state trust funds earmarked for transportation and malpractice insurance to feather their union nests and then pleaded for federal rail and health care. I recall that the eighth graders who spent all eight grades under a liberal Democrat governor and legislature tested out at 39% proficient in math. I recall an attorney general's DUI, springing a legislator out of jail to vote a bill, a prosecutor hitting on rape victims, and bonuses paid to Capitol staffers while 300,000 Wisconsinites lost their jobs. And I recall a few million dollar pile of useless train cars the former Governor bought in secret on a junket to Spain. Drum on that.

All those millions being spent this summer by the unions to recall a handful of State Senators could have been used to help their members meet those new contributions to their own health premiums and pensions that caused them to come unglued. That is, if the unions gave a spit about their members. But they don't; this week's union priority is harassing a charity for the developmentally disabled that the Governor supports. You can't wash off that kind of scum with a chemical peel.

Libertarians like me can find plenty to criticize in Governor Walker's first six months. He killed Constitutional Carry, supports the smoking ban on private property, is dragging his feet on raw milk, sold out micro-breweries, extended unemployment benefits, is on the wrong side of medical marijuana, and should have passed school choice and Right To Work while the AWOL Democrats were channeling their inner Jay Cutler down in Illinois, moping on the sidelines with their hoodies pulled up tight.

But for the life of me, I cannot understand why Republicans in this state have not turned this recall nonsense into a victory dance. Walker took on the unions and he won. He had a plan and it worked. The left revealed its vile and corrupted true self for the whole nation to see. Each day's new clown act in D.C. reminds us of how much chaos the voters of Wisconsin avoided by having that little recall of our own last November that gave the GOP a shot at governing in Wisconsin.

If they don't have the nards for it, let me say it for them and every other fiscally responsible citizen of this state: Thank you, Scott Walker.

Gone

Once again, the June employment data confirms the obvious: the Obama economy still sucks. And once again, his administration economists are mystified, confounded by the contradiction they describe as a jobless recovery.

Let me help you with that, Timmy. There is no recovery. And there is no contradiction; what you have there in D.C. is a bunch of fools doing bad arithmetic while out here in the real world people make, move, and sell things. Big difference.

Government economists' forecasts don't drive the economy any more than the weatherman makes the corn grow. That takes sun and rain and a farmer who works his butt off instead of waiting for some theoretical Keynesian multiplier to kick in.

President Obama is getting testy about the private sector not hiring enough people to get him re-elected, as if that is what should motivate us. He would dearly love for the 15 million Americans who don't have a job to be working come November of 2012.

But they won't. Because this one-term President and his economic team still don't get it: the jobs those people had once are not coming back. They are not coming back because the businesses that employed them are gone. Gone – just like this President will be in January of 2013. There are 1.2 million fewer small businesses than when President Obama took office. 1.2 million businesses – gone.

The workers waiting to be called back to work at those firms will wait until the rapture, because there is no one to call them back. This is not a jobless recovery; it is a business-less recovery, which is to say no recovery at all.

Existing U.S. businesses already employ everybody they need to do the work that they need done. UPS is not going to run out and buy 15 million trucks and hire 15 million people to get some bogus tax credit, or add to Joe Biden's fantasy stimulus job count, or to get some politician re-elected.

They are only going to buy more trucks and hire more drivers when there are new businesses to deliver to and pick up from. And those new businesses are where the jobs are going to come from, not from the econometric forecasting models at the Department of Labor.

Before we can have new jobs, we need new businesses to create them. Is the Obama administration focused on that? Hint: his SBA does not even count small businesses in real time; their most recent data is from 2009.

To hire 15 million Americans we need to create about 1 million new businesses. And to do that, we will need a million American entrepreneurs who are willing to risk their life savings and safe jobs for the opportunity to become rich. That's right, lefties – rich. Not green, not fair, not diverse, not progressive – rich. Entrepreneurs don't risk everything they own for the chance to be modestly comfortable.

And tell us again why anyone should risk it all, Mr. President. You are the one who told those college graduates not to waste their lives in the private sector, remember? You are the one who reminds us constantly that rich people are greedy, unpatriotic, and immoral. You have made it more difficult than ever to succeed. You punish people for even trying.

You force unions down their throats. You ration the energy they need and raise its cost. You force them to provide health insurance to your specs or pay a fine. You tell them what wages to pay. You dictate the performance of their products.

You tax their profits, their gains, the income they draw, the income they pay their employees, the dividends they pay, the earnings they retain, and the estate they leave to their children. You license and permit their ideas back to them.

If they price too high, you call it a windfall and tax it; if they price too low you call it predatory and fine it. You will sue them if they don't hire to your quotas, you will cite them if they don't please your inspectors, and you will shut down their processes if they don't fit your preferences.

And you wonder why the economy is just not that into you?

Maybe a million new entrepreneurs will want to get rich bad enough to overcome all the obstacles our government has put in front of them. But why should they have to? Why not just remove all those obstacles and let the free enterprisers restore our prosperity?

I'll tell you why. Because liberals would rather see 15 million unemployed people suffer than watch a few hundred thousand get rich. There's your moment of clarity.

229

They care more about gay marriage than gay prosperity; they care more about teachers' unions than the future of the children they teach; they care more about a puff of carbon dioxide in the air than freedom for people who exhale the stuff. They are too busy coveting to create; they chose envy over enterprise every time.

You can't be for jobs and against the businesses that create them. You can't erect obstacles to business formation and expect new businesses to form. You can't subsidize your donor buddies at GE without making it harder for the next GE to get off the ground.

And it is that next GE, and the millions of other firms not yet formed, that will create the new jobs that will lift us out of recession and put people back to work. All government can do to help them is to get out of their way; the genius of free enterprise is the "free" part.

Our economy can't be stimulated by government, but it can be liberated; hopefully the next President will make that his/her first priority.

The Next Kid

It is a rare day when the radical left does not give us at least one or two more good reasons NOT to let them run the country. Yesterday was a triple play day.

It started at the local level with the discovery of Milwaukee's outrageous $150,000 license fee for taxicabs, imposed because too much choice and competition was driving down fares. God forbid there would be a choice of affordable taxis when you need one.

Moving to the state level, the Governor of North Carolina proposed doing away with representative democracy for a while so President Obama could implement the rest of his jobs agenda unimpeded by such trivial distractions as Congress or elections. As if the Constitution was written only to cover those times when we don't need jobs.

And then there is the wisdom of Elizabeth Warren, candidate for United States Senate from Massachusetts, the state whose idea of conservative is Mitt Romney. Ms. Warren believes rich people who own factories do not deserve to keep the money they have earned because there are roads and schools. It is unclear what she thinks about Michael Moore, George Soros, or Oprah Winfrey's money.

Her arguments deserve to be answered one at a time. She begins by saying, "You built a factory out there? Good for you. But I want to be clear: you moved your goods to market on the roads the rest of us paid for..."

Where is "out there", Elizabeth? Do you mean on our own private property that we bought, improved, and pay taxes on? Do you mean the formerly empty urban lots inhabited by rats, garbage, and dregs where people are now employed? Do you mean the small towns where a factory is the prime employer, the engine of economic life? I lived in a township once where there were no property taxes for homeowners because the industrial base paid for all local services and schools – is that the kind of place you mean by "out there", Elizabeth?

And is "Good for you", the best you can do? How about "thank God for you". When a young child is gravely ill, the doctors and nurses do not hold hands and chant; they use devices and machines to bring her back to life. Every one of those devices was made in one of those factories out there, Elizabeth. Every

231

one of those machines consumes energy, Elizabeth - energy you want to cut off. Somebody got rich, and someone's child lived; ask the parents who got the best of that deal.

Just who are "the rest of us" that paid for those roads, Elizabeth? The people pedaling in the bike lanes? People who travel on subsidized urban mass transit? People who demand high-speed trains for free? Do you even understand gas tax and highway trust funds? Who pays more highway taxes, the guy driving the Ford F-250 or the guy driving the Volt with the Recall Walker sticker? Or how about the guys and gals who drive those big rigs that move all those goods from where they are made to where they are needed? Are they the rest of us?

And who benefits by having roads to get goods to market? Do you prefer that you take your donkey and cart along trails to the factory and haul your refrigerator home from Ohio, Elizabeth? Are you running your Senate campaign hiking from Quincy to Hyannis, or are you using the roads the rest of us paid for? You should be giving money to gas-tax-paying Teamsters instead of the other way around.

"...you hired workers the rest of us paid to educate..."

You had me at "you hired workers". Should have stopped there. Since public education is funded primarily by property taxes, it is those awful, terrible, capitalists in their big fancy houses who pay most dearly to educate those workers. And to be honest with you, Elizabeth, your team is doing a pretty lousy job of educating tomorrow's workers. We have to do a lot of warranty work on the functional illiterates and clueless dependents you guys crank out of your union-government monopoly schools; where do we send the claim forms?

"...you were safe in your factory because of police forces and fire forces that the rest of us paid for. You didn't have to worry that marauding bands would come and seize everything at your factory, and hire someone to protect against this, because of the work the rest of us did."

Actually, none of us would have to worry about marauding bands if you would read the Constitution all the way to the second amendment, Elizabeth. Do you even read the news? The roving bands doing the factory marauding these days work for the Government – ATF, DOJ, EPA. Ask the folks at Gibson guitars who did them more harm this year, the Visigoths or the Feds? It is precisely that work the rest of you did that has left our liberty is in tatters.

"Now look, you built a factory and it turned into something terrific, or a great idea? God bless. Keep a big hunk of it. But part of the underlying social contract is you take a hunk of that and pay forward for the next kid who comes along."

You will let us keep a hunk of what we earned? How big of you. Rich people take big hunks of their wealth and give it to charities all the time; they don't have any problem paying forward. They have a problem paying the government, since it screws up just about everything it tries to do. Roads, education, and domestic security make up about 4% of the federal budget. Why don't you explain to that next kid what you want to do to him with that other 96%? And how, exactly, does giving his money to Pakistan help him succeed in Poughkeepsie?

You want to do something to help that next kid, Elizabeth? Teach him about liberty, capitalism, competition, self-reliance, patriotism, ingenuity, individual rights, American history. Give her parents the choice of where to educate her, let her compete for rewards, and give her faith its rightful due. And quit trying to turn this country into Greece.

You had one thing right, Elizabeth: no one can get rich on their own. They need customers to buy products, employees to join in producing them, bankers to finance operations, investors to provide capital, suppliers to provide material and technology, distributors, transporters, exporters, and firms to assist in marketing, legal, accounting, and other necessary administrative services. Voluntary exchange between all those free people is what creates the wealth you seem to think is yours. Its not.

They need limited government – my kind of government. They need their property rights secured, their contracts to be enforced, the roads to be plowed, their currency sound, and their patents to be respected. They do not need a government that will punish their success, unionize their workforce without a vote, or subsidize competitors who bankrolled an incumbent's campaign – your kind of government.

And they do not need another socialist Harvard law professor in the Senate, especially one whose last gig was handing out TARP bailout money to the world's most despicable banksters. Why don't you explain to that next kid how paying bonuses to Swiss derivatives traders enriched anyone but the Swiss derivatives traders, Elizabeth?

Unacceptable

This seems to be the consensus policy on Iran's nuclear weapons program - Republicans say it, Democrats say it, Europeans say it, their neighbors in the Middle East all say it. The word "unacceptable" has been said so many times it means nothing.

To state the obvious, it is not for us to accept or not accept the decisions of another sovereign nation. If the government of the United States decides we need to build a weapons system, we do not ask Iran for permission, and that knife cuts both ways. If we believe that the development of a nuclear arsenal is an act of war against the United States, then the proper Constitutional remedy is for Congress to declare one. Our track record in that regard is a little spotty.

We have chosen not to declare war against any of the states who have developed nuclear weapons - Russia, France, England, China, North Korea, Pakistan, India, Israel or South Africa. But we did take military action against two states after they abandoned their nuclear programs – Iraq and Libya – that deposed their leaders by force.

While there is nothing defensible about the theocratic dictatorship in power in Iran, it is not difficult to understand their calculus. North Korea developed a nuclear bomb and Kim Jung Il is living large; Libya gave theirs up and Gaddafi is dead. Israel went nuclear and it gets billions from us every year; Iraq gave up the chase and got itself invaded. Pakistan went nuke and can now engage in openly hostile actions against the United States while still receiving massive amounts of U.S. aid.

When the U.S. government gives ultimatums to other nations, "or-else" has worked out pretty well.

As frustrating as it is, there is virtually nothing the United States can do to deter Iran if it is determined to develop a nuclear weapon. But we can make it very painful to do so, we can defend ourselves from attack, and we can make it suicidal for Iran to ever use one.

If we would deregulate our domestic energy industry and develop our own sources of oil and gas, the price of crude would tumble on world markets, and Iran's nuclear weapons programs would become unaffordable. Chances are quite good that the unpopular regime would be toppled without oil revenues to keep in power. Not to mention that lower energy prices would trigger an economic boom here at home.

Liberty is good economic policy, good domestic policy, and good foreign policy.

We can also develop and deploy missile defenses that protect ourselves and our allies against ballistic missile attack. Opponents of ballistic missile defense leave us vulnerable, with preemptive strike as our only means of protecting ourselves from a strike. It is naïve and foolish to think we will never be attacked, and preemption is not a viable defensive strategy.

The doctrine of mutually assured destruction (MAD), as distasteful as it may be, has kept the nuclear powers from using their weapons against each other for 65 years. Instead of going to the United Nations for another useless resolution, our President could make it crystal clear to the Iranians that if they use a nuclear weapon, we will annihilate them with ours. No winks, no nods, no obtuse send of messages; speak plainly and say it only once.

The most recent GOP debate reminds us why the framers of the Constitution denied the federal government a standing army, a central bank, and the authority to tax income. All of those candidates so quick to use force to deny Iran its nuclear weapons should have been asked how much they would be willing to spend in dollars and American lives to put their rhetoric into practice. Talk is cheap in 60 second bursts; action is not. How much and how many – those are reasonable questions to ask before we launch into another war.

The Constitution directs that war is to be carefully considered and declared by the people's elected representatives; the army is to be drawn up from the citizenry, and the war is to be funded by increased tax levies or bonds drawn up only for that purpose. These mechanisms were put in place to insure the nation was committed before a single drop of blood was shed.

How about you? How much would you be willing to pay to keep Iran from having a nuclear weapon? Which of your own sons or daughters could you look in the eye and say it would be worth the sacrifice of their life or their limb? It is a much more difficult question when the real costs are considered and the sacrifices are personalized.

Our founding fathers warned against entangling military alliances so that Americans would not be drawn into the disputes of other nations. While they were focused on Europe in their time, their admonitions are just as valid in any place and any time. The deeper the U.S. has become involved in the problems of the Middle East, the more intractable they have become.

Each of our last five Presidents – two Democrats and three Republicans – have committed our nation to wars in the Middle East region without Congressional declaration. None resulted in an armistice; each was concluded with a murky de facto cease fire that has required a continuing U.S. military presence and a perpetual commitment of foreign aid to enforce.

There is no one who thinks it is a good idea for Iran to have a nuclear weapon; it is a waste of time to engage in an unacceptability contest. The parties in the region really don't care what we will or won't accept - only what we will pay for. And the peace has not been purchased with our blood and treasure, only rented.

It is time for the United States to realize that our only vital interest in that region of the world is oil, and we have made it so by blocking development of our own energy resources here at home. Our unilateral economic disarmament has forced us to engage militarily.

Bumper sticker sympathies notwithstanding, there are times when war is indeed the answer; Iran is not one of them.

Un-American

Many Americans have forgotten who we are, and many more were never properly taught. This nation was founded with liberty as its first principle; it is liberty that made us exceptional, and exceptionalism that made us great. Simple formula, really.

Citizens of the United States are independent and separate from our government. Our government exists only to protect our rights; rights that are endowed to us by our Creator. This is the distinctive American understanding of the relationships between our God, His people, and their government.

We are a nation of limited, defined government powers, distributed across several authorities and jurisdictions to preserve the sovereignty of the individual. We are nation of law, not of laws, where the Constitution prevails over the ambitions of partisans. We are a Constitutional republic, not a democracy.

We trust our prosperity to free market capitalism, the only economic system that respects the principle of self-ownership. We own our individual economic capacity, and we are free to trade or retain our labor and our property as we see fit. We are not victims of economic exchange; we are empowered actors who secure our own prosperity through innovation, industriousness, and trade.

Free to choose; that is the American idea condensed to its essence. Equal at the starting line; free to determine our finish line for ourselves. All of our freedoms are freedom *from* government. The Bill of Rights does not list grants from government; it is a recounting of specific prohibitions and limits put upon government as a condition of its employment.

If there were no government whatsoever we would be free to speak, associate, worship, bear arms, publish, secure our homes, defend our honor, and reserve testimony. Creating a government to protect those rights does not diminish them. The mansion owner does not turn the deed over when he hires the lawn boy.

Individual rights, self-ownership, free trade, private property, and limited government are the original American ideals we revere. Their opposite numbers are by definition un-American - group rights, collective claims, trade-by-permission, public property, and unlimited government. They may be what we have become, but they are not who we are. I pray.

Those are the un-American ideals that guide the liberal/progressive movement; a movement which has dominated our politics and government for a century now. Creeping socialism is not progress; it has brought our nation to the brink of ruin.

It is un-American to require citizens to purchase their rights from government. It is un-American to force individuals to join unions. It is un-American to dictate wages, prices, working conditions, and benefits. It is un-American to legislate from the bench. It is un-American to rule by decree using executive orders to circumvent the legislative process. Forced equality of outcome is a fundamentally un-American goal.

It is un-American to grant special government privileges to one group at the expense of others. It is un-American to subsidize industries, corporations, and technologies. It is un-American to tax some citizens and not others. It is un-American to invade other nations without a declaration of war. It is un-American to take from those who earned and give to those who did not. Redistribution of wealth is the primary objective of socialism; it is a particularly un-American goal.

The Democratic Party has sold out entirely; the Republicans only somewhat less so. Socialist government is like a grizzly bear mauling and devouring everything it encounters. Democrats want to rile it up and point it towards their successful neighbors, while Republicans think they can potty train it to keep its crap out of their family rooms. Libertarians want to kill it, or at least send it back to Canada.

Restoring American to greatness will happen in spite of, not because of, the establishment political parties. There are only two paths forward: more liberty or more government. One leads to prosperity, the other, Greece. One guides the tea party movement, the other, the public sector union protests.

We will not fix the problem of too much government by choosing a new management team every four years. We must hire a demolition crew to dismantle the apparatus of the state and pare the beast back to its only purpose – to protect our rights and our property. That is the job the 2012 Presidential hopefuls should be applying for.

The way forward is to go back - back to the founding principles that made America great in the first place. America will be great again as soon as we quit being un-American. Let's start now.

Ungovernable

The basic problem with government is that people are ungovernable. The bigger government becomes and the more it tries to do, the stronger the resistance to its commands and mandates. History's tyrannies have all collapsed of their own weight.

We gave rebellion our first test drive at age two – our tantrums drove our parents nuts and that pleased us greatly. When it was time to go off to kindergarten, we discovered that we could refuse to move and negotiate a sugary cease-fire breakfast. When the training wheels came off the bike, so did the boundaries of our travel and our regard for curfew. Our first declaration of independence: "bye, Mom!"

As teenagers, we turned pro. Hair, clothes, music, friends, recreational chemicals, dating explorations – anything our parents told us not to do was instantly our #1 obsession. Better still if parents and teachers both told us to not to AND it was illegal. We couldn't wait to leave home, to get out of town, to be free, to make our own rules, and to find our own way.

In college, we discovered rationalization and convinced ourselves our rebellions were important and relevant. We were not skipping class and getting loaded; we were sticking it to the man. We weren't sluts and hounds; that was peace and love in the Age of Aquarius. We weren't mooching off our parents and society, we were fighting income inequality and seeking justice. Some of us admitted we were full of it at the time; others have made peace with themselves over the years; still others still cling to the delusion that it mattered.

And we are still rebellious, just lame: we drive over the speed limit, fudge our taxes, call in sick when we aren't, fill out our brackets on company time, tell the pastor that we gave in cash, keep buying jeans the size we used to be, count half the cigarettes and only the winning nights at the Casino, and light a Styrofoam cup on fire just to stick it to the planet. Ok, that cup thing was a little over the top, but so was spamming me a video of some leaf-eater crying an apology to a tree. I thought the planet should know that Bark Girl did not speak for me.

Punks right to the end; we will fight the move to the nursing home as hard as we did going off to kindergarten; even when the

239

hour comes for us to join in the full glory of God, we will pitch a fit that would make our inner two-year-old proud.

Our founding fathers recognized the concept of Natural Law; a set of universal rights and responsibilities endowed to us by our Creator that precedes any governments we might form for the purposes of protecting and enforcing them. Numbers 5-10 of the Ten Commandments are sufficient for us to live in peace with each other, and most of us instinctively follow them, whether or not we believe in the God of the first four.

When six is the upper limit of our tolerance of things we will be told we can't do, 2,000 pages of "shall" and "shall not" don't stand a chance. We are Americans; we don't do shall. That seems so obvious.

Americans are the perfected DNA strand of rebelliousness. Each of us is the descendant of the brother who left the farm in the old country when his mom and dad and wimpy brother told him not to; the sister who ran away rather than marry the guy her parents had arranged for her; the freethinker who decided his fate would be his own, not decided by a distant power he could not name. How did you think we would turn out?

Those other brothers and sisters, the tame and the fearful, the obedient and the docile; they all stayed home. Their timid DNA was passed down to the generations who have endured warfare and poverty and hopelessness and the dull, boring sameness that is the price of subjugation.

They watch from the old countries with envy as their rebellious American cousins run with scissors. They covet our prosperity and our might and our unbridled celebration of our liberty; but try as they might they have not been able to replicate our success in their own countries.

Why? Because they are governable and we are not. The framers of the Constitution were smart enough not to try to limit our liberty; they limited government instead.

Liberty still works. In the late 1970's, our government decided to achieve energy independence through the creation of the government Department of Energy. At the same time, it decided to liberate a network of government computers from government control.

In the thirty year aftermath of those two decisions, Liberty's argument has made itself. Government control has *increased* our dependence on foreign oil, while the ungovernable Internet has led to unimaginable prosperity, abundance, and freedom. Who is so blind they cannot see which direction we must turn?

Those who cling to the promise of government ignore its reality. Which side of liberty are you on - the Department of Energy side, or the Internet side? Which do you trust to deliver your prosperity – yourself or the government? Who owns you?

That is the question for our time. A self-owned person is ungovernable; and ungovernable is our natural state. Liberty is our birthright, and prosperity is its reward.

Weak Dollar

The theory goes that a weaker U.S. dollar helps the economy by making American-made products cheaper for people in other countries to buy.

See if you can figure out how that actually works: the iron comes from Argentina, copper from Chile, castings from Poland, rare earth magnets manufactured in Japan from Chinese raw materials, all shipped to a factory in Brazil which assembles the electric motor that will come to a U.S. plant to be installed on a crane that will be exported to Canada. And the oil that transported all that stuff around the world comes from the Middle East.

When the dollar is weakened, that $100 of American installation labor is "cheaper", but that $15,000 imported motor is more expensive – the net effect of weakening the currency is an export disincentive. To make matters worse for consumers, everything we buy from other countries - which is to say nearly everything we buy - is more expensive as it takes more and more of those weakened dollars to buy things in our stores.

100 years ago, the Keynesian monetarists' idea of weakening currency to boost exports may have made some theoretical sense – to the Keynesians, anyway. American-made goods were actually made and consumed in America back then. The iron came from the Gogebic range, the copper from White Pine, the castings from Gary, and the motors assembled in Milwaukee, and the trains which hauled it all ran on oil from Oklahoma refined in South Chicago.

Today, you would be hard pressed to find any product that was produced in any single country using a single currency. Even China, which seemingly makes everything, imports raw materials, technology, and energy from many other countries. And you only drive up export jobs if you make things that can be exported; Wisconsin's top ten employers now are six governmental agencies, two hospital networks, and two retail giants. The South Koreans will not rent our prison guards no matter what Bernanke does with the money supply.

In reality, the Federal Reserve's weakening of the dollar (quantitative easing) has little to do with jobs and exports and everything to do with debts and deficits. Flooding the market with new money turns dollars into dimes, reducing the debt in real terms and funding our massive federal deficits so politicians don't have to bother with fiscal restraint. The collateral damage is higher prices at the pumps and in the Walmarts.

Unfortunately, it is also theft. The value of your savings is depleted when the dollar is weakened, just a surely as if a man in a mask stole it from your account at gunpoint. When the Fed fixes interest rates at near-zero, it is screwing investors out of several percentage points of market rate interest; the effect compounded over several years can add up to a major confiscation of wealth that rightfully belongs to the saver. If you don't think market-rate interest compounding adds up, don't pay your taxes for a few years and see how much the IRS tacks on to your original bill.

The world's true reserve currency is gold. We leave it to markets and private producers to regulate the supply, demand, and price of gold, so why is it so difficult for us to believe that markets can regulate the supply, demand, and price of dollars? Why do we delude ourselves that the handful of Federal Reserve member banks can do anything better than thousands of independent banks? When did a cartel ever work for the benefit of anyone but its members?

We can't have an economy where everyone cuts each other's hair. We must export goods and services and trade with the world. But the way to lower the cost of American products abroad is not by the Federal Reserve weakening the dollar; it is by government at all levels reducing the tax and regulatory costs that are tacked on to everything we make, and to reduce tariffs and duties added in both directions on goods traded with other nations.

That would lower both the $100 price of American labor and the $15,000 for the Brazilian motor, making our crane more attractive around the world. We would hire and train more workers to keep up with demand, and the capital invested in expanded domestic production would set off an upward spiral of prosperity, reversing the downward spiral we have been on for some time now.

Weird Science

Recently, another Nobel-winning scientist has come out publicly against the claim of climate alarmists that the science of global warming is "incontrovertible".

Norway's Dr. Ivar Giaever has joined over 1,000 other notable scientists now on record as skeptical of the theory that human activity endangers life by raising global temperatures.

Politicians and eco-priests firmly wedded to their belief in environmental apocalypse have perverted the meaning of two terms – consensus and skeptic – in their zeal to control other humans under the guise of saving the planet.

Science is skepticism. It is the testing of theories, the search for alternative hypotheses, the corroboration and refuting of the existing literature. Expanding our understanding only occurs when we are skeptical. Blind acceptance rots the mind.

And consensus is a universal agreement to adopt a course of action; it is not universal belief. I've served on many boards; we first debate alternate courses of action and ultimately arrive at a consensus for single course to be followed. It doesn't mean that single mind has been changed or opinion reversed; it simply means that we all agree to move in one direction.

There is no consensus on the theory of man-made global warming, let alone the course of action to be taken in response; Americans are perhaps more divided now than we were ten years ago. Even world leaders sympathetic to the cause have been unable to agree on any particular course of action; not even the wording of meaningless proclamations from their last two international conferences.

To use the term "climate skeptic" as a pejorative, as do the climate change zealots, is to applaud ignorance. To simply declare "consensus" on global warming in order to avoid debate is to engage in intellectual tyranny.

Most people still do not understand that the vaunted "science" of global warming is only computer modeling of the effects that increased carbon emissions might have on the earth's temperature in the future. It is your weatherman giving you his 5-day forecast day after day, and never telling you the temperature.

These models were developed over 20 years ago; they assumed carbon emissions growing at roughly half the rate that which has actually happened, and they forecasted a temperature rise more than six times that which has actually occurred. In other words, they whiffed it by a factor of 12. I hope that is not what passes for incontrovertible across the board in the sciences these days.

When I first read about global warming, advocates warned that if global greenhouse gas emissions were not rapidly cut in half from then-current levels (this was 1990), the polar ice caps would be melted in 20 years, Manhattan would be under water from the ocean rise, and U.S. agricultural output would be halved. Who would not have been concerned?

But those 20 years have now passed; carbon emissions have gone up, not down, the poles remain ice covered, Manhattan is dry, and agricultural output has increased dramatically. Temperatures have not risen at all for the past decade, even though Chinese and Indian industrialization has increased carbon emissions enough it should have caused our hair to spontaneously combust.

The real inconvenient truth is that the models of the global warming theorists were wrong; that is what the science tells us today.

In recent months, we have discovered the earth's ability to both absorb heat in the oceans and throw off heat from the atmosphere is vastly more robust than the climate modelers – those incontrovertible guys – knew. Recent research strongly suggests that solar flares – not SUV's – most likely cause temperature variations on earth.

If anything, these recent discoveries of the earth's adaptability support the theory of intelligent design, an idea mocked by elitists as ignorant religious superstition. I would suggest that ignorant religious superstition is clinging to 20 year MS-DOS floppy disks whose temperature predictions have been proven false by actual temperature readings.

Dr. Giaever called the earth's temperature "amazingly stable' in his resignation letter from the politicized American Physical Society. He cited the society's own published data that concluded the earth's temperature has changed from ~288.0 to ~288.8 Kelvin during the past 150 years of global industrialization.

Less than 3/10 of one percent - that's what this has all been about.

We have wasted two decades, trillions of dollars, billions of man-hours, and a generation of research combating the stuff we exhale. Those resources could have been put towards reducing real pollution, a far more serious threat to our environment, property, health, and safety.

Misappropriation of resources on such a grand scale is inevitable when government controls choice; science and research are not immune from the corrupting ineptitude of State control. Government has shielded corporations (and itself) from liability for pollution of the commons, sacrificed our industrial base to appease advocates of a theory (global warming) now largely discredited, subsidized colossal failures of favored firms, and distorted the operation of markets in order to advance an unsustainable "green" agenda.

Every thoughtful person supports conservation, environmental protection, and responsible resource development. The libertarian reverence for property rights and individual liberty demands strict accountability for damage done to the persons and property of others. Private ownership improves the environmental quality - no one dumps toxins in their own garden.

The lesson to be learned from the global warming episode is that when it comes to environmental stewardship, the only thing more dangerous than government is world government. Collective ownership and collective response produces collective failure.

What's In A Name?

Whoever named it MF Global Holdings sure had some foresight.

Today's business headline: Securities firm fails by loaning money to people who can't pay it back. By-line: Duh.

Only this time, the deadbeats are the governments of Europe. And the CEO of MF Global is a government guy too - Jon Corzine, Democrat ex-governor of New Jersey, ex-Senator, and former head of Goldman Sachs, the AAA farm club for U.S. Treasury Secretaries.

Corzine's bankrupt MF was one of just 22 institutions offered direct trading privileges with the Federal Reserve, our shadow government.

So with the bankruptcy of MF Global, can we now please stop pretending more government is the answer? Oh by the way, $700 million is missing from that lousy MF, and that MF CEO Corzine will receive a $12 million bonus as his lovely partying gift for running his giant MF right into the ground. So can we also stop pretending Democrats aren't greedy, too?

This spectacular Wall Street crash-and-burn comes after the implementation of Dodd-Frank, mind you. Corzine is the guy the unions supported, mind you. Corzine is the guy who said we should be happy to pay more taxes, mind you.

Mr. More Government bet the ranch on government and sunk a $40 billion firm that had survived in the private equities markets for over a century. It is the eighth largest bankruptcy in history. He took down all the stockholders and a bunch of pension funds with him – funds invested in government bonds to avoid the risk of the stock market.

Now what? Our President told us he fixed the problems of Wall Street – all that unregulated greed and betting of house money on leveraged deals...gone with the stroke of a pen, remember? And the leaders of the EU were high-fiving last week when they fixed the sovereign debt problems on the continent by another stroke of a pen, remember? Their stupid deal – default on 50% of the Greek debt held by private institutions – didn't even last a week. MF Global is just the first casualty.

Betting on government is a bad wager.

Solyndra, Evergreen Solar, Beacon Power, and now MF Global – the list of firms whose business models rely on either government subsidy or simply government competence grows by the month. If the smartest of the Keynesians – Bernanke, Geithner, Summers, Romer, Corzine – can't make that dog hunt, it is time to quit hoping something might change.

The United States debt just went over 100% of GDP a few days ago, and the media is consumed with whether or not Herman Cain made a gesture 15 years ago. Romney actually touched Perry – that must count as sodomy. There isn't much to cover anyway; no politician in either party that has a plan to pay it off. Gary Johnson is the closest thing; he promises to balance the budget, which would merely freeze the debt where it is.

We can't just hold down government spending and grow the economy; it is too late for that. We need to cut government spending and cut it dramatically. Those same Keynesians who don't know how to fix the economy today will warn us that cutting government spending will hurt the economy tomorrow. Yeah, whatever.

I received a research report form the Mercatus Center at George Mason University last week that recounted the 75% cut in spending that occurred in the United States after WWII. The economy boomed. In the 1990's, New Zealand faced up to its debt crisis by cutting government by 75% also – and the economy boomed. Canada has cut its national debt in half in recent years – and has shot up to #1 on the Forbes list of best countries in which to do business.

Do we see a pattern here? Cut government spending and reduce debt and the economy booms. Let's try that again...cut government spending and reduce debt and the economy booms. Krugman, are you listening? Reich? How about Cain, Romney, Perry, Gingrich, Bachman, Huntsman, Santorum? I know Ron Paul gets it.

The argument for free enterprise is won at "free". The un-free kind has shown itself to be unsustainable even with massive infusions of capital borrowed from future generations. If anyone could thrive in the debt economy, it would be MF Global, wedged between the "free" money of the Fed and the "guaranteed" returns of sovereign debt. It could not make it sitting in the catbird seat.

Nothing is free. Nothing is guaranteed. Let's all quit pretending.

Who Owns You?

It is a serious question: who owns you?

Libertarians believe that you own yourself; that you and you alone have sole dominion over your person and the fruits of your labor. No one else has a claim to that which is yours, and you have no claim to that which is not yours.

Self-ownership is a point of reference we share with principled conservatives and many, if not most, political agnostics. While liberals, progressives, socialists, and most Democrats believe that an individual exists to benefit society, we libertarians believe the opposite - that society's purpose is to benefit its individual members.

We believe that each of us has the exclusive right to be who we are, to own what we earn, and to exchange voluntarily with whomever we choose under any terms that are mutually satisfactory to us. And along with this freedom to choose the terms of exchange comes the responsibility for the consequences of our choices; we alone are accountable for our actions.

Democrats and liberals seem capable of embracing self-ownership in matters of personal liberty, but reject the notion in matters of economic liberty. Modern-day Republicans mostly do the opposite – demanding economic liberty for themselves but withholding personal liberty from others.

Economic liberty and personal liberty are two sides of the same coin; you cannot pretend to keep heads when you throw tails away. What good is money if you are told what you must spend it on, and what good is the freedom to choose your purchase if all of your money is taken from you?

Virtually no one would defend slavery – the owning of one person by another. Slaves are compelled to work for the benefit of their masters, to surrender 100% of the value of their labor. Is 90% morally tolerable? 80%? 50%?

Milton Friedman pointed out that the effective tax rate is the rate of government spending. Total government spending, including mandates on the private sector, now exceed 60% of GDP. We are 60% free and 40% slaves to the state.

Does it make a difference whether the beneficiary of slave labor is a single person or a group of people? If the plantation owner takes the slave's work product and gives it to others, keeping only a small portion for himself, is slavery then tolerable?

The socialist says yes - not only is it tolerable, but it is admirable. That is, as long as the socialist is the one deciding how much to take, who to take it from, and who to give it to. The socialist sees this as the primary purpose of government – to take income away from those who earned it and give it to those who did not, according to his own sense of justice and fairness.

It does not have to be a transfer from rich to poor. The subsidies for "green" energy projects transfer money from the poor consumers of electricity to the rich owners of companies that live off government subsidies. Affirmative action programs benefit rich minority businessmen at the expense of poor taxpayers.

When someone says they have a "right" to a product or service that must be produced by another person, they are asserting a right to own that person's labor, and therefore to own that person. Those who demand free health care, or housing, or education, or food, or any other thing, are demanding that someone else be enslaved for their benefit, and slavery is immoral.

There are only three ways to get what you want: you can trade for it, you can beg for it, and you can steal it. Stealing the property of others is always wrong, and begging for it is dehumanizing. The only moral economic transaction is voluntary exchange, and voluntary exchange is the brick upon which free market capitalism is built.

It is said that Democrats are the party of government, and Republicans are the party of markets. I disagree; Republicans talk a better game, but rarely walk the talk. Libertarians are the party of markets.

Government is the sanctioned use of collective force. Government is organized stealing and begging. Private property is confiscated through taxation, mandates, and monetary inflation, and then lobbyists beg for allocations of the booty through entitlement transfer payments, subsidies, grants, monopoly privilege, tax preferences, and regulatory exemption.

Self-ownership is the foundation upon which all libertarian political principles are based. It is simple, pure, and without contradiction.

It demands a system of limited and separated government, as government is the existential threat to self-ownership. The amount of it required is just enough to maintain civil order, no more. The term "necessary evil" perfectly describes the libertarian view of government.

Libertarians are not anarchists; we simply recognize the lesson of history that too much government is the greater danger than too little. The only just purpose of federal government is to protect the rights endowed to us as individuals by our Creator; to perform the few and rare tasks that citizens cannot do for ourselves – national defense, diplomatic exchange, things like that.

Those over a certain age will find this understanding of Liberty familiar; the themes libertarians repeat today are enshrined in the foundation documents of this nation – the Declaration of Independence, the Constitution, its Bill of Rights, as well as the letters, essays, and pamphlets of our founding fathers. The basic tenets of libertarianism were once universally accepted by all Americans. It is a measure of how far we have strayed that they now seem radical and extreme.

We once found certain truths to be self-evident, requiring no further explanation than to be spoken. That all persons are created equal; we are a nation of 300 million kings and queens, each of us self-sovereign over our persons and our property. That our rights are endowed to us by God; our rights precede government and cannot derive from it. That our lives, our liberty, and the pursuit of our happiness belong exclusively to us.

Our sovereignty is not be relinquished to our servant government, not to a majority of voters, not to the whim of a judge.

Who would deny these truths? Who does not believe that all persons are created equal? Or that individual rights supersede government rule-making? Or that we exclusively own ourselves, our lives, our liberty, and our right to pursue happiness as we see fit? Liberals, Progressives, Socialists, Democrats, Occupiers, Republicans, Neo-conservatives, Fascists, Unionists, Communists – that's who.

The sudden and spectacular rise of the Tea Party in the United States shows that Americans have not lost their instinct for liberty. It is a movement that defies conventional definition. A broad spectrum of political philosophies and party affiliations have come together organically for the sole purpose of limiting government power over our lives. We stand united on Constitutional principles and a commitment to free market capitalism.

Capitalism is the only economic system compatible with the notion of self-ownership. The argument for free enterprise is won at "free". There can be no form of un-free enterprise that does not rest on the immoral proposition that one person is superior to another - entitled to dispose of the latter's rightful property in addition to his own.

There was a time when these understandings of Liberty were taught in public schools. We pledged our allegiance to them every day with our hand over our heart. Many of us have sworn an oath to uphold, protect, and defend the Constitution we studied. Millions of Americans have died in that endeavor.

"...with Liberty and Justice for all." We have said those words so many times we overlook their profound meaning. There is not an "or" between the words liberty and justice; there is an "and". There can be no justice without liberty.

This divorcing of liberty from justice is the central difficulty with the progressive/socialist philosophy of government that has come to dominate our politics over the past century: its notion of justice comes only at the expense of liberty.

Justice and Liberty are mutually exclusive to the modern liberal, who believes that justice can only be delivered by government. Government meets out the liberal sense of justice by advantaging one set of wards at the expense of the liberty of others. After decades of trading our liberty for the promise of justice, we find ourselves with neither. This is the "progress" that the Progressives have delivered.

Liberty is the absence of Government in choice; Government is the absence of Liberty in choice, and Tyranny is the absence of choice in Government. That is how I have explained it for years to young people who are no longer taught the proper meaning of these terms in their government-union schools.

Humans have existed for tens of thousands of years. Our recorded history spans over 70 centuries. Over that time, nearly every conceivable type of social arrangement has been tried, tested, modified, and rejected - tribalism, feudalism, monarchy, theocracies, fanaticism, cultism, militarism, democracy, representative democracy, utopianism, fascism, corporatism, socialism, communism, anarchism, and nomadic cliques, many others.

Near the end of the 18th century A.D., an experimental nation was formed with liberty, not government, as its first principle. Self-ownership, individual liberty, private property, rights endowed directly to persons, unlimited freedom and limited government, the rule of law, and equality of opportunity were guaranteed to each citizen by a new form of government, a Constitutional Republic. It was as radical an idea then as it is now - imagine a federal government which spends only 2.9% of GDP.

With our government properly shackled, our national commitment to Liberty turned a backwater colony into the most powerful and prosperous nation on earth in just one century. This was no accident; happiness is the inevitable result of a nation dedicated to its individualized pursuit. When people keep what they earn; they produce in surplus. When people own themselves, they share and exchange willingly.

It was the preservation of individual rights that advanced the public good in that first American century. Slavery was abolished, life expectancies grew, the middle class was established, literacy became the norm, charity was institutionalized, industrialization created leisure time, inventions and innovations exploded onto the scene like no other century in history, and human productivity accelerated at a rate not seen before or since. For the better part of a century we lived in peace with the community of nations.

When government was constitutionally limited, Capitalism delivered abundance, and Liberty distributed prosperity more widely than any civilization which had some before. In terms of real progress, the 19th century – before the progressive movement came to be – was the most progressive period in the history of world.

In the 20th century that followed we gradually abandoned our national commitment to Liberty. The notion of individual rights gave way to group privileges; equality of opportunity gave way to forced equality of outcome; equal protection under the law gave way to government-sanctioned looting; private property gave way to vague notions of national resources; freedom to choose gave way to public good; we engaged in six major wars overseas. Our government grew to where is now consumes 24% of GDP; its debt is nearly six times its income.

America's abandonment of the Liberty principle has been an unmitigated disaster.

Government control of schools has ruined education; government control of energy has cut us off from it; government allocation of wealth has diminished it; government assignment of race and gender class privileges has produced a permanent underclass; government regulation of economic activity has ruined our economy, legislating morality has broken down our moral fabric. Judicial advocacy has corrupted the law. Socially engineered "equality" has left us a fractured society.

We have known the answer to the problems that face our nation for over 200 years; the manual for happiness and prosperity is so thin I carry one in my jacket pocket most of the time – it is the Constitution.

Libertarians believe that the enumerated powers delegated to government in Article I, Section 8 represent the proper role of government. We believe the Bill of Rights properly delineates the State from the People and sets the correct boundaries for the limits of State power against its citizens. Liberty is good foreign policy; Liberty is good domestic policy; Liberty is good economic policy.

The less your government takes from you, the more of yourself you own. Self-ownership is the path to economic recovery, a path that requires the obstacle of government to be *removed*, not improved.

And self-ownership is also the path to pride and self-respect. No one wants to grow up to be a ward of the state. No one aspires to be dependent upon someone else for sustenance. Dependency must be learned; the spirit must be broken before subservience can be achieved. Is that really our dream for America – a nation of broken spirits dependent on government for sustenance? I think not. I pray not.

Perhaps you do not believe in this principle of self-ownership; perhaps you are skeptical of an idea that runs counter to the preaching of the socialist progressives over the past century. Perhaps this is not what you have been taught in your government-union school. What, then, is your alternative?

If you do not fully own yourself, than who owns you? Society? And who is that but your neighbors? Why do they own you? In the economy of two, the rest of society is me. What is the basis of my claim on you, and why is mine superior to your own?

254

Which will be the more peaceful coexistence between you and I – voluntary exchange, or surrender by force?

The operational theory of the progressive welfare state is that my need represents a superior claim against your property. The socialists' purpose for government is to re-allocate wealth that a handful of people determine to be surplus in order to achieve their notion of justice – a notion that forced upon both the self-owner and the recipient of the taken property. Your obligation as a citizen is to surrender yourself to them for the good of society – good as they define it.

This is also the operational theory of piracy.

The underlying moral premise of the socialist – my need trumps your right of self-possession - is no different than that of the pirate, the looter, the rapist, the con-man, the gold-digger, the extortionist, or the thief. The socialist wraps the taking in high-minded words of compassion; so does the pimp. The socialist excuses his brutality on the basis of superior moral intentions; so does every fallen evangelist.

Who owns you? That is the first question to be answered. It is the only tough one; the rest are easy.

Who is selfish - the person who asserts his right to self-ownership or the person who demands the taking of that which he has not earned?

Who is compassionate – the person who gives his own money quietly to the charity of his choosing, or the person who loudly redistributes the money of others?

Who is just – the person who respects the rights of others equally or the person who forces his beliefs onto others and takes it upon himself to allocate rights and privileges?

Who is moral – the person who takes instruction from God with humility or the person who imposes his personal beliefs on others through the force of legislation?

Who is the patriot – the person who advocates adherence to the Constitution or the or the person who wraps the flag around any proposal which benefits himself at the expense of another?

Compassion, justice, morality, patriotism – the collectivists and statists do not own the franchise on the attributes of civil society. In fact, they have demeaned them and perverted their meanings in order to facilitate the subjugation of a nation founded on the principle of self-sovereignty.

The Libertarian engages his fellow man as an equal self-sovereign. It is the only moral basis upon which citizenship can be enjoined in a nation that calls itself the land of the free. We do not wish to own you, and we do not permit ourselves to be owned.

Wood Ticks

Last week, a liberal columnist dismissed the libertarian philosophy as "survival of the fittest". No dear, our philosophy is simply survival.

The social welfare state that the progressives have constructed is a suicide pact between the parasite and the host, and the pace of our self-destruction is accelerating now that we have the Jack Kevorkian of Presidents assisting us.

There is nothing compassionate or caring about destroying the greatest nation in the history of the world. Survival is a good thing when freedom is on the line. And fitness is a good thing, especially the fitness of a people to self-govern.

My use of the term "parasite" will no doubt cause welfare state apologists to vibrate in place, but it is kinder than the alternatives returned by the Thesaurus – slacker, scrounger, sponge, moocher. The American Heritage Dictionary defines parasite as "an organism that grows, feeds, and is sheltered on or in a different organism while contributing nothing to the survival of the host". The origin of the word is the Greek *parasitos* - a person who eats off another's table. Any takers?

The thing about parasites is that they cannot live without the host, while the host thrives in their absence. There is no doubt that if the wood tick could speak, it would list all the laudable reasons why it needs our blood worse then we do. The Wood Tick Party would call us greedy and heartless for keeping it all for ourselves when there are so many ticks in need. They would annoy us daily with their pathetic displays of buffoonery so we might learn what tick-ocracy looks like to them.

You need not be poor to be a parasite; the wood ticks come in all shapes and colors, and belong to both establishment parties. There are plenty of millionaires and billionaires with their snouts in the public trough – profiting from unproductive subsidies, preferences, grants, credits, bailouts, government-sheltered monopolies, and near-perpetual warfare. They are sucking us dry just as surely as the little drummer boys.

At least in nature, ticks can't recruit hosts over to their side. The only thing progressive about socialism is the progressive elevation of dependency; it has risen from something scorned to something avoided then tolerated then excused then enabled then encouraged and finally entitled. Throw in a dozen foreign wars and you have the progressive century distilled to its essence.

Dependency has risen from a temporary condition brought about by external misfortune to a revered lifestyle choice. Victimhood is now a career; activist is a job description; advocate is a profession; collective grievance is how we now define community. It is our modern day caste system - just ask Sarah Palin or Herman Cain or Juan Williams or Ron Paul or Clarence Thomas what the wood tick media do to you when you don't know your place.

The progressive's bedrock belief that you are entitled to the benefits of someone else's labor is toxic; their entitlement culture is the poison that is killing our nation, organ by organ. You are entitled to only this: the respect of your individual rights as befitting a co-equal child of God. Not one more thing. Not one.

The idea that the State's rightful purpose is to confiscate the property of its citizens is what has set this country on its downward path. We were founded on the exactly opposite belief - the State's only just purpose is to protect the rights and property of every citizen from confiscation.

That is what America means; and allegiance to the liberty principle is what it means to be an American. We are not an accident of geography, a pile of dirt that keeps the two oceans from co-mingling their sea water. We are a people; a nation borne of liberty and sustained by its enduring blessings. Our rights are not of our own making; they are the endowment from our Creator. We squander free will at our peril, and it is peril of our making that now surrounds us.

State-ownership of our work product is the immoral foundation upon which socialism, or progressivism if you prefer, is built. Libertarianism is the polar opposite of socialism; it is the philosophy of self-ownership. Socialism and Libertarianism are two different utopian destinations, and utopian destinations can only be approached, never reached. At one extreme is complete slavery to the State; at the other complete freedom from the State. Choose your course; with each step you either face liberty or turn your back on her.

Self-ownership relies on voluntary exchange between equal sovereigns to create and distribute wealth. State-ownership relies on forcible seizure and authoritarian allocation to redistribute the wealth created by others; it creates no wealth of its own. That is the simple reason why totalitarianism always impoverishes; it is why turning to government for prosperity never works. Never.

"Survival of the fittest" may sound cold and heartless to those not accustomed to thinking for themselves, but it certainly more humane than the socialist alternative, "certain demise of the universally unfit". The rising tide lifts all boats unequally, that is true; but the slack tide leaves all boats stranded on the mud flats, equally useless and completely dependent.

We can see the finished product of socialist progressivism everywhere – flashmobs, unionist vandals, legions of permanently unemployable, crony corporatists, petty bureaucrats, elected degenerates, race pimps. Unfit, useless, dependent – parasites in the truest sense of the word.

The worst of the unionist haters were out in force last week protesting an inner-city choice school in Milwaukee that works miracles with the same kids that the government's union-monopoly schools – 2nd worst in the nation - have given up on. Thank God those beautiful children inside were saved from the angry selfish bastards carrying signs and carrying on outside - what a waste of liberty they are.

And what a blessing that those kids inside will have a fighting chance because enough of us are still brave enough to stick the match-head to the wood ticks' ass and leave it there until they drop off and go away, not matter how loud they squeal or how long they kick their tiny little legs.

And one more thing...I'm going to go out and buy another Gibson guitar to say go-strum-yourself to President Obama for his brutish shake-down of that great American company. Been more of a Fender guy lately, but from now on I'm going to play Gibsons until this guy is done playing President.

Your Money's Worth

One good thing that has come from the OWS protests is the light that has been shed upon the economics of college degrees.

In 2009, the year before local banks were cut out of the action by Team Obamalosi in their eleventh hour amendment to the health care reform bill, outstanding student loan debt was $114 billion, a staggering figure. It is now $392 billion, an incomprehensible one. Those numbers come from the Federal Reserve so they must be right – they know a thing or two about staggering, incomprehensible debt.

It didn't even take two years for the government to turn a routine family financing decision into an unsustainable collective entitlement that has triggered riots in several American cities. This may be a new land speed record for socialist rot.

The first thing to know about post-secondary education is that over the past 30 years, its costs have risen at more than three times the rate of inflation. Yes, those same academics and government employees who lecture us incessantly about greed, oppression, and profiteering in the private sector are three times as greedy and oppressing when it comes to pricing their own products.

Recall that it is the iconic capitalist pigs at Walmart – not the University of Wisconsin - who give us rollback pricing with a smiley face. Occupy Regent Street! And like most other things in the real world, individual choices greatly determine how badly a student will get mauled by the debt he/she takes on to purchase a college degree.

According the College Board, the average annual tuition paid by full-time students at four-year institutions last year was $21,198. Average does not mean everyone; on average, humans have one breast and one testicle. 44% of students attend colleges with published tuition under $9,000 per year, and 28% attend colleges with tuition and fees higher than $36,000 per year. By way of comparison, the average cost of tuition and fees at two-year colleges is only $2,963 - and Econ 101 is the same at any price.

The average dorm fee for four-year institutions was $4,785 last year, and the average boarding rate (food) was $3,937. The average full time student also spent $1,082 on transportation, $2,066 on personal expenses, $1,168 on books and supplies.

That puts the average total cost of full-time resident attendance in four-year institutions at $34,236 per year.

The College Board advises prospective students and parents not to be overly concerned about those high published costs, however, since student loans and other forms of financial aid make college "affordable". Of course, "affordable" just means someone else pays, mostly that is someone is the student himself after graduation. The average amount of aid per student last year was $12,455; about half of that is loans and the other half grants and scholarships.

So roll up all the data together and the average college graduate will have spent $136,944 of somebody's money and owe $25,250 in student loans if they finish their degrees in eight semesters. And what is the return on that $136,944 investment? Just like the cost of education, the value of a degree in economic terms varies greatly.

The website www.payscale.com lists the median starting pay and median mid-career pay for 125 common bachelor degrees. Petroleum engineers start at $97,000 while elementary education majors start at $29,000. No wonder the world's social scientists hate big oil.

High school seniors, pay attention here - the top-paying bachelor degrees in order are: petroleum engineering, chemical engineering, electrical engineering, materials science, aerospace engineering, computer engineering, physics, applied mathematics, computer science, and nuclear engineering.

And the worst-paying degrees in order are: child and family studies, social work, elementary education, culinary arts, special education, recreation and leisure studies, physical education, public health, theology, and art. The various ethnic and gender studies majors are not even listed separately as there is no market for them.

Going on to graduate school will not fix a low-paying degree choice, either. According to Forbes Magazine, the worst master's degrees for employment (job availability and pay) in order are: music, history, divinity, English, psychology, social work, library science, counseling, education, and chemistry.

So if your goal is to get the best return on your investment in post-secondary education, then start out taking your math and science foundations at a two-year college and then transfer to the cheapest four-year college that offers a degree in Petroleum

Engineering. You will spend less than $30,000 for a credential that carries a $97,000 median starting pay. Ask a business major (#58) to explain ROI to you.

But the College Board offers much different advice to prospective students: "Your goal is to choose a college that's a good fit for you; think about whether you like the campus culture and if there is enough academic support to help you do well in your classes."

Well, if "a good fit for you" is the object and you really like the campus culture at one of those $36,000 yacht club schools (who wouldn't?) with enough tutors to help you get through your degree in child and family studies, you will spend north of $200,000 to earn a credential that pays $28,500 per year. Should you find yourself in such a predicament, my advice is to marry a Petroleum Engineer – with the new relaxed admission standards to marriage, you no longer have to settle for one of the opposite gender.

Some pandering Democrats trolling for votes among OWS protesters have proposed forgiving all student loan debt. But bailing out the children of bankers in 2012 is just as wrong as bailing out their dads was in 2008. Is it fair to ask engineers and scientists who worked their way through school to pay off the debts that the leisure studies majors racked up while protesting at the Capitol and hitting the bong? Can we ask veterans who earned their tuition benefits the hard way to pay off the debts of those who chose not to serve? I think not.

Millions of people have managed their student loan debt responsibly; millions more chose vocational training and work over university studies. Those who did should not have to pay the obligations of those who didn't. Living large on borrowed money is always fun; it's paying it back that's the bitch. That may be the most valuable thing many graduates will take away from their college experience.

If it makes you twenty-somethings feel any better, most of us old guys would trade places with you in a heartbeat, debt or no debt. You can change poor; old is forever.

Bring It

They are at it again on Wisconsin. The perpetual hissy fit that is the Union Democrat Party in this state has launched its campaign to recall Governor Scott Walker. The rallying cry of Walker's Republican supporters is "I stand with Scott Walker".

Well, not me. I don't stand with Scott Walker.

Nope. I stand for the right to work. I stand against compulsory unionization. I stand for the right of every employee to join a union, and for the equal right of every employee to work free of union impairment. I stand for the right of every union to collect its own dues directly from its members.

I stand for the right of every business owner to deal directly with his/her employees or to work through an intermediary as he or she sees fit. I stand for the right of any business to refrain from political activity altogether without being targeted for boycotts by extortionists.

I don't stand with Scott Walker. Scott walker stands with me.

I stand for fiscal responsibility. I stand for balancing the state budget. I stand for making government services both accessible and affordable. I stand for repaying our old debts and not taking on any new ones. I stand against raiding trust funds set up for one purpose to pay for another. I stand against increasing taxes on the overtaxed to fund lavish new benefits for the over-lavished.

I don't stand with Scott Walker. Scott Walker stands with me.

I stand for choice and competition that will improve the quality and reduce the cost of our schools. I stand for letting local school boards, teachers, parents, and taxpayers decide how best to educate their kids. I stand for rewarding the great teachers and I stand against letting the bad ones waste one more hour of our children's precious learning time. I stand against spineless administrators, conniving pension-grubbers, placeholders counting down their days to retirement and serial indoctrinators who see 4th graders as political props.

I don't stand with Scott walker. Scott Walker stands with me.

I stand for representative Democracy where a majority of citizens elect a government which serves its full term and then stands for re-election. I wish they would vote for Libertarians but I accept it when they don't. I stand against voter fraud. I stand against rigged elections. I stand against one political party spending millions of taxpayer dollars to overturn an election they lost they lost fair and square.

I don't stand with Scott Walker. Scott Walker stands with me.

I stand against death threats. I stand against tormenting the families of public officials at their private residences. I stand against the profanity, vulgarity, and brutishness of the weak-minded who can only find courage in the anonymity of the mob or an alias on Facebook. I stand against the seizure of our public places, the occupation of our streets. I stand against those whose twisted moral compass equates breaking a monopoly with killing millions of Jews.

I don't stand with Scott Walker. Scott Walker stands with me.

I stand for the right to bear arms. I stand for the right to defend myself, my family, and my property. I stand against those who would leave me defenseless simply because they do not value their own life enough to defend it. I stand for Senator Pam Galloway, who stood up for me and my right to carry.

I don't stand with Scott Walker. Scott Walker stands with me.

I stand for jobs. I stand for job-creators. I stand for free markets, lower taxes, and sensible regulation. I stand for a business climate that attracts employers, not one that drives them away. I stand for private property rights for every citizen. I stand for developing our natural resources, for encouraging entrepreneurs, for rewarding hard work and for celebrating those who succeed in global competition.

I don't stand with Scott Walker. Scott Walker stands with me.

I stand for less government and more liberty. I stand with the overwhelming majority of Wisconsinites who had the opportunity to vote for Democrats in 2010 and chose not to. I stand against shipping in busloads of paid operatives from out of state to nullify that choice. I stand against those who believe pro-choice means the right to inflict yours by force.

I don't stand with Scott Walker. Scott Walker stands with me.

I am a Libertarian, not a Republican. I don't let the Koch brothers or Fox News or Rush Limbaugh or Vicki McKenna to tell me what to think. I am a grown man, a self-sovereign with my own conscience and beliefs.

Those beliefs do not include overturning election results because my side didn't win. We have learned that the effort to recall Governor Scott Walker was initiated before he even took office; this has nothing to do with policy and everything to do with privilege.

The Democrat Party in the state of Wisconsin believes they have a Divine right to rule; perhaps it explains why so many are hostile to real Divinity. It is inconceivable to them that the citizens of this state would have decided to give the Republicans an opportunity to fix what the Democrats could not or would not. It is humiliating to them that their coarse and unrefined rivals achieved in just a few months what they could not do in a decade.

265

Their panic is understandable, but that does not make it actionable for the rest of us.

I can't say whether or not I would vote to re-elect Scott Walker. If he is to win over libertarians, he has a lot of ground to cover between now and the next election for Governor, which is not until 2014. This recall process is not an election; it is a subversion of an election, and I will not vote to subvert elections. The reasons for or against this recall are irrelevant; every assassin has reasons. This is a contract hit; the motivation is money, and it is the taxpayer who will pay the contract.

So no, my dear Democrat friends, I will not be signing your recall petitions. When you come to my door I will not be ungracious; I will not be unkind. I will not tell you "I stand with Scott Walker" and slam the door in your face.

I will tell you instead that I stand for Liberty, and then I will ask you why you will not stand with me. It is a reasonable question, and I expect you to answer it. It is the least you can do if you want me to help you turn the whole state upside down to rehash your grievance over again for the umpteenth time.

And don't send the junior varsity, either. I don't speak drum, I don't cuss in mixed company, I am not going to learn those twinkly-thing hand signals, and "shame-shame-shame" just reminds me of a lame disco tune. When I point to New Berlin on a map, if that poor rent-a-mob kid in a Bucky tee-shirt with the tags still hanging on it says it like they do in Germany, I'm going to boot his bony ass all the way back to Ohio. Figuratively speaking, of course.

I'm ready. Bring it.

BRING IT!

Meet Dr. Tim

Tim Nerenz is the President of a global manufacturing company, a blogger, a published academic, a libertarian activist and speaker, a volunteer, and a one-time Congressional candidate in Wisconsin's 2nd District.

Dr. Nerenz holds three graduate degrees in business and commerce – an AGDM and MBA from Athabasca University and a Ph.D. from Northcentral University.

Tim was inducted into the Order of Athabasca University in 2011 for his many years of board service and commitment to removing barriers to post secondary education around the world through distance learning.

His popular libertarian blog *"Dr. Tim's Moment of Clarity"* is published on his website www.timnerenz.com and reposted on many liberty and patriot sites, newspapers, and radio links.

Tim is a popular speaker and a regular guest on Vicki McKenna's Wisconsin radio program and on Brian Wilson's radio program in Toledo, Ohio. Tim's posts have also been read on the air by radio personalities Neal Boortz, Jay Weber, and Charlie Sykes.

His first two books, "Tooth Fairy Government", and "Capitalista!", are both available on his website, or at Amazon.com in either hardcopy or Kindle format.

The son of a Lutheran minister, Tim grew up with two brothers in Ironwood, Michigan. He and his wife Joanne have a grown son, Erik, and they split their time between homes in Wisconsin and Florida.

Made in the USA
Lexington, KY
29 November 2012